Landscape as Urbanism

Landscape as Urbanism

A General Theory

Charles Waldheim

Princeton University Press

Princeton and Oxford

Published by Princeton University Press, 41 William Street, Princeton, New Jersey 08540

In the United Kingdom: Princeton University Press, 6 Oxford Street, Woodstock, Oxfordshire OX20 1TW

press.princeton.edu

Cover illustration: Ludwig Hilberseimer, planner, with Alfred Caldwell, delineator, the city in the landscape, aerial view, 1942. Canadian Centre for Architecture, Montreal, gift of Alfred Caldwell.

Library of Congress Cataloging-in-Publication Data

Names: Waldheim, Charles, author.

Title: Landscape as urbanism : a general theory / Charles Waldheim.

Description: Princeton, New Jersey : Princeton University Press, 2016. |

Includes bibliographical references and index.

Identifiers: LCCN 2015022445 | ISBN 9780691167909 (hardback)

Subjects: LCSH: Urban landscape architecture. | City planning. | BISAC:

ARCHITECTURE / Landscape. | ARCHITECTURE / Urban & Land Use Planning. |

ARCHITECTURE / General.

Classification: LCC SB472.7 .W33 2016 | DDC 712/.5—dc23 LC record available at

http://lccn.loc.gov/2015022445

British Library Cataloging-in-Publication Data is available

Design: Thumb/Luke Bulman with Camille Sacha Salvador

This book has been composed in Executive

Printed on acid-free paper. ∞

Printed in China

10 9 8 7 6 5 4 3 2 1

Contents

Preface

Landscape has emerged as model and medium for the contemporary city. This claim has been available since the turn of the twenty-first century in the discourse and practices of "landscape urbanism." This volume offers the first monographic account of the subject, locating the impulse behind landscape urbanism in a broader set of historical, theoretical, and cultural conditions. *Landscape as Urbanism* proposes a general theory for thinking the city through the medium of landscape. It rehearses recent claims for the landscape architect as the urbanist of our age and describes landscape as a medium of design from a variety of disciplinary formations and professional identities. The volume surveys the emergence of various professions responsible for the shape of the city across the nineteenth and twentieth centuries, including landscape architecture, urban planning, and urban design. It describes the origin of the profession of landscape architecture in the nineteenth century as a "new art" charged with reconciling the design of the industrial city with its ecological and social functions. *Landscape as Urbanism* locates the origins of landscape urbanist discourse in the intersection of progressive architectural culture and populist environmentalism in the context of neoliberal economies. In this context, landscape practices accelerated ecological thinking across the urban arts, and landscape urbanism emerged to occupy a void created by urban planning's shift away from design culture in favor of social science, as urban design committed to neotraditional models of town planning.

Acknowledgments

This book would not have been possible without the contributions and support of many individuals and institutions over many years. First, thanks to the editorial team at Princeton University Press for their commitment to the project and careful attention to detail through every phase of the process. I am particularly indebted to Michelle Komie for her enthusiasm for the project from the very first, and to Mark Bellis and the team at PUP for adeptly moving it from a manuscript into a book.

The Graham Foundation for Advanced Studies in the Fine Arts provided early legitimacy and crucial institutional and financial support for my work through a number of research and publication grants over the past two decades. I was fortunate to befriend the late Rick Solomon during his tenure as director of the Graham Foundation. Rick's generosity of spirit and commitment to the topic remained an undiminished source of motivation throughout the life of this project.

The research and writing of the book was made possible by a variety of institutions over the past dozen years, most notably through the support afforded by academic appointments at the University of Illinois at Chicago, the University of Toronto, and the Harvard Graduate School of Design. I remain indebted to those institutions and to their leadership, who have supported my work on this topic over many years. This work has also been enabled by a number of visiting academic appointments in design schools, most notably my experiences as design critic at the University of Pennsylvania, Sanders Fellow at the University of Michigan, Driehaus Visiting Professor at the Illinois Institute of Technology, and Cullinan Chair at Rice University.

In each of those academic contexts, I have benefited from the presence, participation, and polite pushback of graduate students subjected to this material in formation. I remain indebted to them for their patience with my recurring obsessions in various seminar and lecture formats, as well as for their eyes and ears on this work over many years. I have also enjoyed the opportunity to present portions of the book as public lectures in a variety of contexts internationally. The immediate feedback and stimulation of a live audience has focused and improved this project immeasurably.

The primary research and space for developing the arguments for many chapters was made possible by residential fellowships at the American Academy in Rome; the Study Centre of the Canadian Centre for Architecture, Montreal; and the Bauhaus Foundation, Dessau. This work was also enabled through exhibitions and public discussions hosted by the Graham Foundation for Advanced Studies in the Fine Arts, Chicago, and the Storefront for Art and Architecture, New York.

Initial drafts for portions of the book first appeared in essay or chapter form in a range of venues over the past several years. These include the journals *Bracket*, *Harvard Design Magazine*, *Landscape Journal*, *Log*, *Praxis*, and *Topos*, as well as edited anthologies published by Actar, Prestel, and Princeton Architectural Press. I am grateful to the editors of those publications for their cultivation and support for this work. I am equally grateful to James Corner, Cynthia Davidson, Julia Czerniak, Ashley Schafer, Rodolphe el-Khoury, Hashim Sarkis, Ed Eigen, and Emily Waugh who included earlier versions of some of this work in journal or anthology form.

I have benefited from conversations with a number of people who have shared their enthusiasms and advice on these topics. I am particularly grateful for the ongoing conversations with Mohsen Mostafavi, James Corner, and Christophe Girot. The book has also been informed by the public and private response to my work from a number of individuals, including David Leatherbarrow, Kenneth Frampton, Marcel Smets, Paola Viganò, Alex Wall, Stan Allen, Jean Luis Cohen, Pierre Belanger, Julia Czerniak, Clare Lyster, Mason White, Alan Berger, Christopher Hight, Chris Reed, Gareth Doherty, Hashim Sarkis, Richard Sommer, Robert Levit, Rodolphe el-Khoury, and George Baird, among many others.

Over the life of this project, I have enjoyed the advice and consent of several talented editors. Nancy Levinson was among the first editors to see the potential of the topic. I am particularly indebted to Melissa Vaughn for her gentle improvements to my draft prose. I am also grateful to several graduate research assistants who have contributed to this and related projects over the past several years, including Diana Cheng, Fadi Masoud, Conor O'Shea, Ryan Shubin, and Azzurra Cox. Thanks also to my patient and proficient administrative assistants Ana da Silva Borges, Nicole Sander, and Sara Gothard who enabled the work by keeping so much off my desk over the past many years.

I am pleased to dedicate this book to Siena and Cale who have remained unending sources of true inspiration and quiet comfort over the life of the project, and without whom, nothing would be possible.

Introduction: From Figure to Field

There are, in fact, no cities anymore. It goes on like a forest.
—Ludwig Mies van der Rohe, 1955

Landscape has recently emerged as model and medium for the contemporary city. This claim has been available since the turn of the twenty-first century in the discourse and practices the term "landscape urbanism" describes. This volume offers the first monograph account of the subject and locates the impulse behind landscape urbanism in a broader set of historical, theoretical, and cultural formations. Moving beyond the original assertions and ideological charge of landscape urbanism, the book aspires to provide a general theory for thinking the urban through landscape. This begins most productively through the definition of terms.

This is a book first and foremost about urbanism, albeit an adjectivally modified urbanism. The term *urbanism* in this context refers reflexively to both the empirical description and study of the conditions and characteristics of urbanization, as well as to the disciplinary and professional capacity for intervention within those conditions. The term appears in English near the end of the nineteenth century adopted from the French *urbanisme*. As adopted from the French, and in present usage, the term refers to cultural, representational, and projective dimensions of urban work specific to the design disciplines that the social science term *urbanization* lacks. Urbanism has been found particularly useful as a single term, in English, to reconcile the academic and professional split between the social sciences and planning on the one hand, with the disciplinary and professional formulations of the design disciplines on the other. As the foundational term for this study, urbanism is understood to signify at once the city as an object of study, its lived experience, and its inflection through design and planning. In this sense, we would define urbanism as the experience of, study of, and intervention upon processes and products of urbanization. To problematize urbanism with landscape is, in the first instance, to simply add an adjective. In this formulation, the compound neologism *landscape urbanism* qualifies the subject *urbanism* with the adjective *landscape*. As such, the term signifies an understanding of urbanism read through the lens of landscape. More than a book about landscape per se, this is a book about the potential for thinking urbanism through the lens, or lenses, of landscape.

. . . . .

Landscape is used in this volume in several of its standard English-language meanings. Building on the term's irreducible plurality of meanings, the book argues that the promiscuity of the term is central to its conceptual and theoretical utility. Over the course of several chapters, various definitions of landscape are unpacked, each offering a distinctly revised reading of the urban sites and subjects in question. The etymology of the English-language term *landscape* has been the subject of significant scholarship over the past several decades. Seminal essays on the subject by Ernst Gombrich, J. B. Jackson, and Denis Cosgrove, among others, point to the origins of landscape as a genre of painting as early as the sixteenth century. By the seventeenth century, landscape had migrated to form a way of seeing or experiencing the world. By the eighteenth century, landscape as a mode of subjectivity had slipped into a description of the land viewed in such a way, and ultimately to those practices to modify that land to such effect. This volume describes the very origins of landscape in English emerging from the representation of the formerly urban. This corroborates recent scholarship on the origins of landscape painting as fundamentally bound up in questions of urbanity. As such, the volume reflects on the various readings of landscape itself, understood *as a form of urbanism*. In so doing, the argument examines the plural and promiscuous meanings of landscape in order to excavate their potential for revising our received understandings of the urban.

Various meanings of landscape are situated throughout the argument, as appropriate to the site or subject in question. Each of these various uses suggests a shading of the subject matter, while retaining a precision about its meaning. Landscape is used here to mean a genre of cultural production, as in landscape painting, or landscape photography. Equally, landscape is used as a model or analogue for human perception, subjective experience, or biological function. Alternatively, landscape is used as a medium of design, through which gardeners, artists, architects, and engineers intervene in the city. Multiple chapters refer to the development of landscape as academic discipline and design profession. Given the significance of these varied and multiform meanings, these distinctions are often developed as microhistories within the larger arc of the argument in question.

.....

This account situates the emergence of landscape as a medium of urbanism in a variety of sites. Most often the sites associated with rethinking the urban through landscape are found at the limits to a more strictly architectonic order for the shape of the city. Most often these are sites where a traditional understanding of the city as an extrapolation of architectural models and metaphors is no longer viable given the prevalence of larger forces or flows. These include ruptures or breaks in the architectonic logic of traditional urban form as compelled by ecological, infrastructural, or economic change.

Landscape has been found relevant for sites in which a strictly architectural order of the city has been rendered obsolete or inadequate through social, technological, or environmental change. The discourse and practices of landscape urbanism have been found particularly useful for thinking through large infrastructural arrays such as ports and transportation corridors. Airports, in particular, have been central to the discourse and practices of landscape urbanism as sites whose scale, infrastructural connectivity, and environmental impacts outstrip a strictly architectonic model of city making.

Landscape has also been found useful as a way of thinking through urban form in the wake of macroeconomic transformations. This includes so-called shrinking cities as well as the countless individual sites of brownfield abandonment left in the wake of economic transformations. Thus landscape as a medium of urbanism has often been invoked to absorb and in some ways mitigate various impacts associated with social, environmental, and economic crises. It has equally been found relevant for thinking through sites at the intersection of large, complex ecological and infrastructural systems. Most recently, landscape has been found relevant to questions of green infrastructure in the informal city, and in response to questions of risk and resilience, adaptation and change. The cumulative effect of these sites and subjects has been to foreground the potential for landscape as a medium and model for the city as a collective spatial project. In its most ambitious formulation, this suggests the potentials for the landscape architect as urbanist of our age. In this role, the landscape architect assumes responsibility for the shape of the city, its built form, and not simply ecological and infrastructural exceptions to its architectonic structure. Rather, landscape thinking enables a more synthetic understanding of the shape of the city, understood in relation to its performance in social, ecological, and economic terms.

.....

The landscape urbanist discourse emerged at the close of the twentieth century in the ascendency of design culture and populist environmentalism and in relation to progressive architectural culture and post-Fordist economic conditions. These confluences prompted an acceleration of ecological thinking across the urban arts. Landscape urbanist practices evolved to occupy a void created by urban planning's shift toward a social-science model and away from physical design over the past half century, as urban design committed to neotraditional models of town planning. Landscape urbanist practices flourished through an unlikely combination of progressive design culture, environmental advocacy, increased cultural capital for designers, and in the context of laissez-faire development conditions. They were further fueled by new forms of public agency and donor culture in relation to planning, at the moment that both urban design and planning were described in their respective literatures as confronting crisis.

This book describes landscape as a medium of design from a variety of disciplinary formations and professional identities concerned with the contemporary city, including landscape architecture, urban design, and planning. Taking up the emergence of landscape as a form of urbanism from the nineteenth to the twenty-first century, it relates the origins and historical evolution of various professions responsible for the shape of the city. Stepping back from partisan and ideological construction of disciplinary identity allows for the development of a more historically informed and synthetic argument for the relations between landscape and the urban. Recently renewed interest in landscape as a medium of urbanism is the third such historical moment in the past two centuries, the first being the nineteenth-century invention of the profession of landscape architecture as responsible for the shape of the industrial city, and the second the development of twentieth-century landscape planning practices.

In the dense industrial city of the nineteenth century, landscape architecture was conceived as an exception to the traditional order of the city, capable of compensating for the unhealthful social and spatial dynamics. In the decentralizing city associated with a mature Fordist industrial economy, landscape was reconceived as a medium of ecological planning, lending spatial coherence and occasionally social justice to the otherwise centrifugal sprawl of urbanization. In the contemporary post-Fordist industrial economy, landscape has been reconceived again, this time in the guise of landscape urbanism. Here landscape is invoked as a performative medium associated with the remediation of formerly industrial sites left in the wake of the Fordist economy's collapse. In this third era, landscape is also called on to structure the redevelopment of those sites for new forms of urban living, through a unique combination of ecological performance and design culture. This most recent formulation, rather than offering an exception to the structure of the city or planning for its dissolution, aligns with the return to the project of city making associated with contemporary service, creative, and culture economies. In this context, landscape urbanism promises to clean the sites of the formerly industrial economy while integrating ecological function into the spatial and social order of the contemporary city.

Landscape urbanist practices have found traction on either end of the uneven development spectrum—equally relevant for cities that continue to shrink as capital recedes from the previous spatial order and for those awash with capital in the new urban configuration. In some senses, landscape has been called on to absorb the shocks the changing industrial economies of the twentieth century generated, as the landscape medium has been found responsive and flexible in relation to the more durable yet brittle urban orders founded principally on architectonic models and metaphors. Landscape has been increasingly deployed to insulate urban populations from the worst social and environmental impacts of these economic transformations. Rather than a stylistic or scenographic deployment, this book argues that landscape has been invoked over the last two centuries in a structural relationship to urban industrial economy. As macroeconomic and industrial transformations have left the previous urban form redundant in its wake, landscape has been found relevant to remediate, redeem, and reintegrate the subsequent form of urbanization. Economic geography and critical urban theory have recently articulated specific spatial orders associated with the economic transformations associated with various eras of industrial economy. Rather than posing a simply stylistic or cultural question, this volume describes a structural relationship between landscape as a way of thinking through urbanism and transformations in the industrial economies that underpin processes of urbanization.

·····

This book offers a general theory for thinking about the city through landscape. In so doing, the origins of urban design and planning are placed in relation to the formation of landscape as architecture, making an argument for the landscape architect as the urbanist of our age, and for landscape urbanism as a new set of practices. It also reminds us of the central role for landscape found in the most environmentally informed planning practices of the twentieth century. The book locates the origins of landscape urbanist discourse in a particular strand of postmodern architectural thinking and its critiques of modern planning. For those architects and urbanists committed to the city as an object of study, yet wary of the style wars associated with postmodernism, *program* or *event* came to stand in for the urban in architectural terms. For many post-1968 architect/urbanists interested in the city as a social project, but wishing to avoid the architecture of the city, density of social relations came to stand as a surrogate for urbanity, even in the absence of appropriate architectural accommodations. Many of these protagonists would inform the emergence of interest in landscape as a form of urbanism, locating in landscape a particular mix of social intercourse and programmatic performance, unburdened of all that architectural baggage.

The emergence of landscape urbanist discourse and practices in this context fueled an equivalent interest in the various alternative planning practices of the twentieth century associated with social and environmental agency. One flank of the landscape urbanist agenda has been the construction of a useful history. This volume reconstructs that particular genealogy and identifies a small set of ecologically informed planning practices from the nineteenth and twentieth centuries. These precedents, most notably evident in the work of Ludwig Hilberseimer, among others, share an interest in ecological function and social equity, manifest in spatial terms. Most often these projects take the form of political or cultural critique, as in the work of Andrea Branzi. These projects, as described here, stand in contradistinction to the abject failures of many modernist planning practices to come to terms with the environmental and political crises of modernity. These antecedents to landscape urbanism also sit within a longer intellectual tradition of ecological planning. That long-standing tradition of planning the city through ecological knowledge is described here as a necessary, yet ultimately insufficient, precondition for the formation of landscape urbanist discourse in the postmodern era. The discourse and practices of landscape urbanism presuppose an intellectual and practical tradition of ecological planning as a foundation. Yet it was only through the unlikely intersection of modernist ecological planning with postmodern architectural culture that landscape urbanism would emerge. Whereas ecological planning presupposes the region as the basic unit of empirical observation and the site of design intervention, landscape urbanism inherits the region as a scale of ecological observation and analysis, yet most often intervenes at the scale of the brownfield site, which is itself the result of ongoing restructuring of industrial economies.

In reexamining the origin myth and basic claims for landscape architecture as a new profession and academic discipline in the nineteenth century, the narrative revisits the origins of landscape as a genre, locating the original impulse for landscape in the formerly urban sites of the shrinking city. These interpretations shed new light on the origins of planning in the field of landscape architecture. They also illuminate the origins of urban design and the unrealized potential for that disciplinary formation to have been housed within landscape architecture. This examination raises timely questions regarding the ongoing relevance of an architectural metaphor for urban order, as well as for the status of the architectural object in the contemporary field of planetary urbanization.

In constructing a general theory for rethinking the urban, this volume assembles a thick description of cases and conditions, sites and subjects. This layering of material from discrete disciplines and discourses, while acknowledging the significance of disciplinary boundaries, aspires to a more relational reading of the urban arts grounded on a range of claims, conditions, and cases. Taken together, these materials presuppose the ongoing act of theory making as a necessary element of disciplinary formation and reformation. The term "general theory" in the subtitle signals the aspiration to offer a coherent and broadminded, if not comprehensive, monograph-book-length account of a subject that has been previously examined through journal articles or occasional anthologies of shorter, more episodic, projects and texts.

This volume is organized in a series of nine chapters, offering an intellectual history of its subject in thematic thirds. In the first third of the book, chapters 1 through 3 rehearse the discourse and practices of landscape urbanism. These chapters situate the emergence of landscape urbanist discourse in postmodern architectural culture and critiques of modernist planning, concluding with the more recent claim to the landscape architect as urbanist of our age. In the second third of the book, chapters 4 through 6 reveal the economic and political conditions underpinning the emergence of landscape urbanism. These chapters locate the origins of landscape urbanist practices in the neoliberal economies of post-Fordist urbanization, rather than in the purported autonomy of architectural culture. In the final third of the book, chapters 7 through 9 revisit various forms of subjectivity and representation implicated in the subject. This account reframes the nineteenth-century origins of landscape architecture as an academic discipline and liberal profession responsible for the shape of the city, rather than pastoral exceptions to it.

Chapter 1, "Claiming Landscape as Urbanism," rehearses the primary assertions of the emergent neologism "landscape urbanism," providing a genealogy of the concept originating in postmodern critiques of modernist planning in the 1970s and 1980s. It further articulates the origins of the concept as embodied in critical texts and canonical projects from the 1980s and 1990s by Stan Allen, James Corner, Kenneth Frampton, Lars Lerup, Bernard Tschumi, and Rem Koolhaas, among others. This account surveys Koolhaas's interest in "congestion without matter" and Tschumi's concern with the "open work," along with Frampton's concepts of "megaform as urban landscape" and "acupunctural urbanism," and Lerup's notions of the "zoohemic canopy" and an urbanism populated by points of "stim and dross." Allen's interest in infrastructure and the performative dimensions of the horizontal surface is shown to correlate with Corner's articulation of the operational field of contemporary urbanism. Collectively these critical concepts are taken to form the intellectual groundwork for "landscape urbanism" at the end of the twentieth century.

Chapter 2, "Autonomy, Indeterminacy, Self-Organization," builds on the concept of the "open work" as discussed in the previous chapter and traces the impact of ideas from literary criticism, linguistics, and critical theory on architectural theory in the postmodern era. Landscape urbanist discourse emerged at the intersection of neo-avant-gardist architectural interest in concepts of deferred authorship, open-endedness, and indeterminacy in relationship to landscape ecology. In this formulation cultural interest in indeterminacy and delayed authorship found an analogue in the natural world conceived as a self-regulating system absent human agency. Postmodern architectural culture's rejection of function or use came to stand as a proxy for criticality, or cultural value, as seen in Peter Eisenman's 1976 essay "Post-Functionalism." These questions of authorship were appropriated from cultural practices of the historical avant-garde. The strategy of delayed, deferred, or distanced author-ship in architecture of the postmodern era became a means toward a putatively critical architecture, as these concepts were adopted by urbanists in the 1980s and 1990s, and by advocates of the nascent landscape urbanism in the 1990s and 2000s. As architects and urbanists of a certain generation espoused the critical dimension of their work through autonomy and problematized authorship, proponents of landscape as a form of urbanism articulated the potential for reading ecology as equally autonomous, open-ended, and indeterminate. This chapter surveys a short list of canonical works embodying concepts of criticality through problematized authorship in landscape and urbanism that were subse-quently supplanted by nascent landscape urbanist discourse and practices.

Chapter 3, "Planning, Ecology, and the Emergence of Landscape," outlines the relationship between contemporary practices of landscape urbanism and the disciplinary and professional commitments of urban planning. The chapter describes continuities and discontinuities between current landscape urbanist practice and antecedent planning practices informed by ecology. Particular practices of ecological or landscape planning from the twentieth century formed a necessary yet insufficient basis for the articulation of landscape urbanist discourse and practice at the close of that century. The chapter locates early and mature landscape urbanist work in relation to nontraditional planning ac-tors and agents, neoliberal development practices, and the rise of philanthropy in support of design culture and environmental performance.

The post-1968 radicalization of planning in the North American academy resulted in its effective alienation from design culture and rejection of spa-tial planning in favor of a turn toward the social sciences. This was a historic shift in relation to economic and political transformations in North America that tended toward neoliberal and laissez-faire development practices rather than traditional welfare state public planning. These transformations had particular impact on the legacy of environmentally or ecologically informed planning prac-tice, as public-sector capacity for state control of planning tended to recede in North America at precisely the moment that it was most forcefully articulated in the work of Ian McHarg and a generation of landscape planners. The chapter similarly locates landscape urbanist practice in relation to the origins and de-velopment of urban design in North America, seeing landscape urbanism as an alternative to neotraditional town planning strategies that advocated for a return to spatial patterns of the nineteenth- and early twentieth-century city. In this regard, landscape urbanism embodies an unlikely combination of pro-gressive architectural culture and environmental performance in the context of an economic transition from industrial to postindustrial.

Chapter 4, "Post-Fordist Economies and Logistics Landscape," locates recently renewed interest in landscape as a medium of urbanism in the transition from an industrial "Fordist" economy of production toward a "post-Fordist" economy of consumption. The work of David Harvey is seen to sharply articulate the role of design and planning in anticipating and enabling new forms of urban identity through spatial and cultural production. Harvey's concept of "spatial fix" explains the role of the landscape medium in the spatial transition from an industrial to a postindustrial urban economy. Also referenced is his account of stylistic change in the arts and design culture as embedded in larger structural economic transformations, which situate landscape urbanism's ascendency.

This chapter describes the formation of landscape urbanist practices in relation to the economic structure of contemporary urbanization. Recent scholarship in economic geography distinguishes between three periods of urbanization: a dense nineteenth-century "pre-Fordist" industrial economy, a decentralized twentieth-century "Fordist" economy, and a distributed twenty-first-century "post-Fordist" economy. In the nineteenth-century metropolis, landscape was conceived as an exception to the spatial structure of the city, most often as a form of park or public-realm improvement intended to ameliorate undesirable social and environmental conditions. In the decentralizing twentieth-century city, landscape was invoked as a medium of planning and was called on to provide spatial limits and structure. Finally, in the globally urbanized twenty-first-century city, landscape has taken the form of landscape urbanism, and is expected to mitigate the transition from one economic spatial order to another. In this most recent formulation, landscape remediates the formerly urban postindustrial site, animating the latent cultural, economic, and ecological potentials of derelict and distressed sites. The chapter describes the emergence of landscape urbanist practices as a structural response to the cultural conditions of advanced capitalism and, following Harvey, identifies landscape as offering a particular spatial order for our contemporary economic restructuring. In this regard, mature landscape urbanist practice is understood to be particularly relevant as a balm for the shrinking cities described in the next chapter as the "formerly urban."

Chapters 5 and 6 extend questions of economic structure and spatial order to examine another venue for landscape urbanist practice, the shrinking city. Chapter 5, "Urban Crisis and the Origins of Landscape," cites Detroit as the most legible form of advanced industrial economy in the post-Fordist era and identifies the origins of the landscape genre in the West in the articulation and representation of urban abandonment. The chapter builds on the concept of *disabitato* as referring specifically to the abandonment and reappropriation of the formerly urban. A key reference is made to the reception of Claude Lorrain's drawings and paintings by English popularizers of the modern taste in landscape gardening, and the disproportionate impact of Lorrain's images of the formerly urban in the formation of what would become landscape architecture.

Chapter 6, "Urban Order and Structural Change," continues the question of urban economy and shrinking cities to identify a proto-landscape urbanist practice of landscape planning that anticipated the decentralization of the city. The chapter examines Ludwig Hilberseimer's theory of the "settlement unit," and his single built example, Lafayette Park in Detroit. Hilberseimer's planning practice was an important antecedent to contemporary interest in landscape urbanism and a relatively underexamined exemplar of landscape as a medium of urbanism. At Lafayette Park, landscape is deployed as a driver of urban order uniquely capable of anticipating and responding to the ongoing spatial decentralization of the mature Fordist city. Further, Hilberseimer's planning concept proposed landscape to insulate populations from the worst social and environmental impacts of spatial restructuring associated with the mature Fordist economy.

Chapter 7, "Agrarian Urbanism and the Aerial Subject," revisits twentieth-century landscape planning practices as precedents for landscape urbanism, with a focus on Hilberseimer's "New Regional Pattern." Hilberseimer's planning theory is representative of a more general category of agrarian urbanism evident in twentieth-century planning. His work is read in relation to Frank Lloyd Wright's "Broadacres" and Andrea Branzi's "Territory for the New Economy," among other urban propositions. These practices postponed traditional distinctions between city and countryside in favor of a more synthetic understanding of the economic and ecological orders structuring urban life. These projects were critical responses to the economic and environmental conditions of the Fordist paradigm that implied a new form of aerial subjectivity for urban life. Rather than simply a new representational lens or analytical tool, aerial representation is understood as central to the critical position and reception of these projects. In this regard, the synoptic aerial view creates a new form of citizen-spectatorship, the agrarian aerial subject.

Chapter 8, "Aerial Representation and Airport Landscape," extends the focus on the aerial subject of twentieth-century landscape planning practice with an examination of the role and status of aerial representation in landscape urbanism. The chapter evokes the question of aerial subjectivity to account for the privileged modes of landscape urbanist representation, including the synoptic aerial oblique view and the exploded axonometric diagram, which are explained in relation to the scale and situation of landscape urbanist practices. These modes simultaneously offered continuity with particular genealogies of design culture such as flatbed painting, photomontage, and the isometric diagram, while affording legibility of the horizontal field of urban operations. These representational lenses, and their privileging of the aerial subject, foreground one of the more compelling sites in landscape urbanist practice, the airport landscape.

Perhaps as much as any other urban type, the airport has been a central concern of landscape urbanist discourse and practice, as it exemplifies the vast horizontality, near complete contamination, and abiotic function of the metropolitan regions more generally. For landscape urbanists interested in the performance of the horizontal field framed by infrastructure, the port has been found relevant, and the airport especially so, as among the most significant venues for landscape urbanist discourse. This attention is manifest in a range of cases, including the ecological and urban enhancement of operating airfields as well as the conversion of redundant airfields for use as parks and in support of renewed urbanization.

Chapter 9, "Claiming Landscape as Architecture," returns to the original aspirations and landscape architecture as a profession in which boosters of the "new art" incorporated landscape as a form of architecture in the second half of the nineteenth century. Recalling the Francophone and Francophile origins of the concept in the compound identity of the *architecte-paysagiste*, the chapter describes Frederick Law Olmsted's adoption of the term and rejection of the English formulation "landscape gardening." Acknowledging Olmsted's misgivings with the "miserable nomenclature" of landscape architecture in the English language, this account revisits the decision to found the new field on the cultural legibility of the architect, in lieu of the artist or the gardener. The new profession aspired to have primary responsibility for the organization of space and urban order through infrastructure and public realm improvements, rather than dealing with plants or the garden. In this regard, the very origins of landscape architecture reside in projects of city building through infrastructure and ecological function. As evidence, the chapter describes the first commission of a landscape architect in the modern sense. This is exemplified in Olmsted and Vaux's commission for the planning of Manhattan above 155th Street, rather than the design of a public park, pleasure ground, or private garden. Landscape architecture was thus conceived in the nineteenth century as a new profession responsible for divining the shape of the modern metropolis.

From the origins of landscape architecture in nineteenth-century Paris and New York, the chapter turns to a description of the emerging role for landscape architecture in the context of East Asian urbanization. It concludes with an account of the Chinese landscape architect Kongjian Yu and his firm Turenscape, the first private practice in landscape architecture in that country. Yu's Chinese National Ecological Security Plan embodies a form of knowledge transfer from his study of ecological planning and digital mapping at Harvard and continues a line of ecological planning nearly eclipsed in contemporary North American practices of planning.

The book's conclusion, "From Landscape to Ecology," offers a brief account of the recent formulation of an "ecological urbanism," presenting the proposition as a continuation of the landscape urbanism project in more precise terms. It also acknowledges the potential of ecological urbanism as a critique of landscape urbanism's reliance on the occasionally inscrutable category of landscape.

One: Claiming Landscape as Urbanism

Increasingly, landscape is emerging as a model for urbanism.
—Stan Allen, 2001

Since the turn of the century landscape has been claimed as a model for contemporary urbanism. Over that time the landscape discipline has also enjoyed a period of intellectual and cultural renewal. While much of the landscape discipline's renewed relevance to discussions of the city may be attributed to this renewal or to increased environmental awareness more generally, landscape has improbably emerged as a disciplinary locus for discussions historically housed in architecture, urban design, or planning.

Many of the conceptual categories and projective practices embodied in landscape urbanism and documented in this volume arose from outside those disciplines traditionally responsible for describing the city. As such, landscape urbanism presented an implicit critique of architecture and urban design's inability to offer coherent and convincing accounts of contemporary urban conditions. In this context, the discourse surrounding landscape urbanism can be read as a disciplinary realignment in which landscape supplants architecture's historical role as the basic building block of urban form. Across a range of disciplines, many authors have articulated this newfound relevance of landscape in describing the temporal mutability and horizontal extensivity of the contemporary city. Among the authors making claims for the potential of landscape in this regard was architect Stan Allen, who argued that "landscape has traditionally been defined as the art of organizing horizontal surfaces. ... By paying close attention to these surface conditions—not only configuration, but also materiality and performance—designers can activate space and produce urban effects without the weighty apparatus of traditional space making."[1]

This efficiency—the ability to produce urban effects traditionally achieved through the construction of buildings simply through the organization of horizontal surfaces—recommends the landscape medium for use in contemporary urban conditions. In many contexts, the "weighty apparatus" of traditional urban design proves costly, slow, and inflexible in relation to the rapidly transforming conditions of contemporary urban culture.

The idea of landscape as a model for urbanism was also articulated by landscape architect James Corner, who argues that only through a synthetic and imaginative reordering of categories in the built environment might we escape our present predicament in the cul-de-sac of postindustrial modernity, and "the bureaucratic and uninspired failings" of the planning profession.[2] His work critiques much of what landscape architecture has become as a professional

< Figure 1.1 Rem Koolhaas/OMA, Parc de la Villette Competition, isometric cartoon of juxtaposed programs, 1982.

concern in recent years—especially its tendency to provide scenographic screening for environments engineered and instrumentalized by other disciplines.[3] For Corner, the narrow agenda of ecological advocacy that many landscape architects profess to is nothing more than a rear-guard defense of a supposedly autonomous "nature" conceived to exist a priori, outside of human agency or cultural construction. In this context, populist environmentalism and pastoral ideas of landscape appear to Corner, and many others, as naive or irrelevant in the face of planetary urbanization.[4]

The discourse and practices of landscape urbanism builds directly upon the canon of regional environmental planning, from the work of Patrick Geddes and Benton MacKaye to Lewis Mumford to Ian McHarg, yet remains distinct from that genealogy through the synthesis of design culture, ecology, and urbanization.[5] Corner acknowledged the historical importance of McHarg's influential *Design with Nature* yet, himself a student of McHarg's, rejected the opposition of nature and city implied in McHarg's regionally scaled environmental planning practice.[6]

. . . . .

The origins of landscape urbanism can also be traced to postmodern critiques of modernist architecture and planning.[7] These critiques, as Charles Jencks and other proponents of postmodern architectural culture put forth, indicted modernism for its inability to produce a "meaningful" or "livable" public realm, for its failure to come to terms with the city as a historical construction of collective consciousness, and for its inability to communicate with multiple audiences.[8] In fact, the "death of modern architecture," as Jencks proclaimed in 1977, coincided with a crisis of industrial economy in the United States, marking a shift toward the diversification of consumer markets.[9] What postmodern architecture's scenographic approach did not, in fact could not, address were the structural conditions of industrialized modernity that tended toward the decentralization of urban form. This decentralization continues apace today in North America, remarkably indifferent to the superficial stylistic oscillations of architectural culture.

In the wake of the social and environmental challenges associated with industrialization and modernization, postmodern architecture retreated to the comforting forms of nostalgia and seemingly stable, secure, and more permanent forms of urban arrangement. Citing European precedents for traditional city form, postmodern architects practiced a kind of preemptive cultural regression, designing individual buildings to invoke an absent context, as if neighborly architectural character could contravene a century of industrial economy. The ascendance of urban design discipline in this era extended interest in the aggregation of architectural elements into ensembles of nostalgic urban consumption. During this same time, the discipline of city planning abdicated altogether, seeking refuge in the relatively ineffectual enclaves of policy, procedure, and public therapy.[10]

The postmodern *rappelle á l'ordre* indicted modernism for devaluing the traditional urban tenets of pedestrian scale, street grid continuity, and contextual architectural character. As has been well documented, the postmodern impulse can be equally understood as a desire to communicate with multiple audiences or to commodify architectural images for diversifying consumer markets.

However, the dependence on sympathetically styled and spatially sequenced architectural objects would prove difficult to sustain, given the rise of mobility and ongoing effects of economic restructuring on traditional urban form. The very indeterminacy and flux of the contemporary city, the bane of neotraditional town planning, were precisely those qualities found in emergent works of landscape urbanism in the closing years of the twentieth century. This point is exemplified in Barcelona's program of public space and building projects in the 1980s and early '90s, which focused primarily on the traditional center of the Catalan capital. More recently, Barcelona focused on redeveloping the airport, logistical zone, industrial waterfront, metropolitan riverways, and water-treatment facilities. This work had less to do with buildings and plazas than with large-scale infrastructural landscapes. These examples, along with recent work in the Netherlands, reveal the role of large-scale landscape as an element of urban infrastructure. Of course many traditional examples of nineteenth-century urban landscape architecture integrate landscape with infrastructure—Olmsted's Central Park in New York and Back Bay Fens in Boston serve as canonical examples. Contrasting this tradition, contemporary practices of landscape urbanism reject the camouflaging of ecological systems within pastoral images of "nature." Rather, contemporary landscape urbanist practices recommend the use of infrastructural systems and the public landscapes they engender as the very ordering mechanisms of the urban field itself.

.....

Landscape is a medium uniquely capable of responding to temporal change, transformation, and adaptation, as Corner, Allen, and others recalled. These qualities recommend landscape as an analogue to contemporary processes of urbanization and as a medium uniquely suited to the open-endedness, indeterminacy, and change demanded by contemporary urban conditions. As Allen puts it, "landscape is not only a formal model for urbanism today, but perhaps more importantly, a model for process."[11]

The earliest projects to reveal this potential for landscape to operate as a model for urban process were proposed by European architect/urbanists interested in program and event as surrogates for a contemporary urbanism. Among these projects claiming landscape as analogous to programmatic change were the first- and second-prize entries to the 1982 competition for Parc de la Villette in Paris. The competition invited submissions for an "Urban Park for the 21st Century" over a 125-acre site, once the site of the city's largest slaughterhouse. The demolition of the Parisian *abattoir* and its replacement with intensively programmed public activities is precisely the kind of project increasingly undertaken in postindustrial cities across the globe. Just as more recent design competitions in North America such as Downsview and Fresh Kills, la Villette proposed landscape as the basic framework for an urban transformation of what had been a part of the working city, left derelict by shifts in economies of production and consumption. The competition for la Villette began a trajectory of large public projects in which landscape was conceived as a complex medium capable of articulating relations between urban infrastructure, public events, and indeterminate urban futures for large postindustrial sites.[12]

From over seventy countries 470 entries were submitted for la Villette, the vast majority of which retraced familiar profiles for public parks and typologies for the recovery of the traditional city, while two submissions clearly signaled a paradigm shift still underway in the reconception of contemporary urbanism. The winning scheme, by the office of Bernard Tschumi, represented a conceptual leap in the development of landscape urbanism. The scheme formulated landscape as the most suitable medium through which to order programmatic and social change over time, especially complex evolving arrangements of urban activities. This proposal continued Tschumi's interest in reconstituting event and program as legitimate architectural concerns in lieu of the stylistic issues dominating architectural discourse in the postmodern era. As Tschumi put it in his proposal, "the '70s witnessed a period of renewed interest in the formal constitution of the city, its typologies and its morphologies. While developing analyses focused on the history of the city, this attention was largely devoid of programmatic justification. No analysis addressed the issue of the activities that were to occur in the city. Nor did any properly address the fact that the organization of functions and events was as much an architectural concern as the elaboration of forms or styles."[13]

Equally significant for the development of landscape urbanism was the influence of the second-prize entry submitted by Rem Koolhaas and the Office of Metropolitan Architecture (figures 1.2, 1.3). The unbuilt scheme explored the juxtaposition of unplanned relationships between various park programs. Koolhaas's organizational conceit of parallel strips of landscape, now

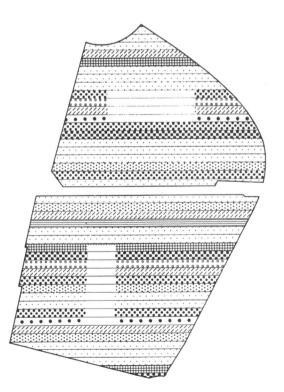

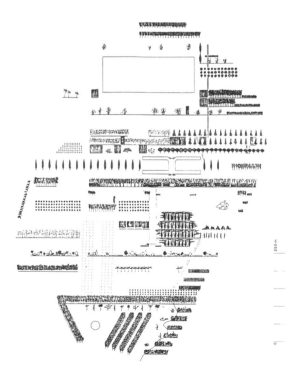

Figure 1.2 Rem Koolhaas/OMA, Parc de la Villette Competition, strip diagram, 1982.

Figure 1.3 Rem Koolhaas/OMA, Parc de la Villette Competition, isometric planting diagram, 1982.

something of a canonical cliché, radically juxtaposed irreconcilable contents, invoking the sectional juxtaposition of various programs on adjacent floors of Manhattan skyscrapers as described in Koolhaas's *Delirious New York*.[14] As conceived by Koolhaas/OMA, the infrastructure of the park would be strategically organized to support an indeterminate and unknowable range of future uses over time. As Koolhaas put it in his project text, "it is safe to predict that during the life of the park, the program will undergo constant change and adjustment. The more the park works, the more it will be in a perpetual state of revision. ... The underlying principle of programmatic indeterminacy as a basis of the formal concept allows any shift, modification, replacement, or substitution to occur without damaging the initial hypothesis."[15]

Through their deployment of postmodern ideas of open-endedness and indeterminacy, Tschumi's and Koolhaas's projects for Parc de la Villette signaled the role that landscape would play as a medium through which to articulate a layered, nonhierarchical, flexible, and strategic urbanism. Both schemes offered a nascent form of landscape urbanism, constructing a horizontal field of infrastructure that might accommodate all sorts of urban activities, planned and unplanned, imagined and unimagined, over time.

In the wake of la Villette's influence, architectural culture became increasingly aware of landscape's role as a viable framework for the contemporary city. Across a diverse spectrum of cultural positions landscape has emerged as the most relevant medium through which to construct a meaningful and viable public realm in North American cities. Consider how the thinking of architectural historian and theorist Kenneth Frampton shifted over this period of time. In the 1980s, Frampton lamented the impediments to making meaningful urban form given the power of speculative capital and the rise of automobile culture. As he put it, "modern building is now so universally conditioned by optimized technology that the possibility of creating significant urban form has become extremely limited. The restrictions jointly imposed by automotive distribution and the volatile play of land speculation serve to limit the scope of urban design to such a degree that any intervention tends to be reduced either to the manipulation of elements predetermined by the imperatives of production, or to a kind of superficial masking which modern development requires for the facilitation of marketing and the maintenance of social control."[16] Against the forces of "optimized technology," Frampton argued for an architecture of "resistance." By the following decade, however, his call for architecture as an instrument of local resistance to global culture gave way to a more resigned position that conceded the unique role of landscape in providing a modicum of urban order. In this later formulation, landscape rather than object formalism affords the greater (albeit still slim) prospect of constructing meaningful relations within the detritus of market production. By the mid-1990s, Frampton had resigned himself to this reality, arguing that "the dystopia of the megalopolis is already an irreversible historical fact: it has long since installed a new way of life, not to say a new nature. ... I would submit that instead we need to conceive of a remedial landscape that is capable of playing a critical and compensatory role in relation to the ongoing, destructive commodification of the man-made world."[17]

To invoke Frampton and Koolhaas together is perhaps curious, for Frampton's interest in local cultural resistance to globalization could not be further afield from Koolhaas's project of engagement with the very mechanisms of modernization. Despite their divergent cultural politics, by the mid-1990s, Koolhaas and Frampton had come to occupy curiously convergent positions, concurring on the fact that landscape had supplanted architecture's role as the medium most capable of ordering contemporary urbanism. As Koolhaas put it in 1998: "Architecture is no longer the primary element of urban order; increasingly urban order is given by a thin horizontal vegetal plane, increasingly landscape is the primary element of urban order."[18]

Arguably a third significant cultural position, a realpolitik of laissez faire economic development and public-private partnerships in planning processes, is articulated by Peter Rowe in *Making a Middle Landscape*.[19] Interestingly, Rowe's conclusions are not dissimilar; he advocated a critical role for the design disciplines in the making of a meaningful public realm in the exurban "middle" between traditional city center and greenfield suburb beyond. Rowe's position is summarized by Frampton, who identifies two salient points: "first, that priority should now be accorded to landscape, rather than to freestanding built form and second, that there is a pressing need to transform certain megalopolitan types such as shopping malls, parking lots, and office parks into landscaped built forms."[20]

In this context, landscape came to provide not simply a medium of design but also a cultural category—a lens through which to see and describe the contemporary city. Again, Koolhaas's position is notable for its clarity.[21] He uses Atlanta as an exemplar of the contemporary North American urban condition: "Atlanta does not have the classical symptoms of the city; it is not dense; it is a sparse, thin carpet of habitation, a kind of suprematist composition of little fields. Its strongest contextual givens are vegetal and infrastructural: forests and roads. Atlanta is not a city; it is a landscape."[22]

The tendency to view the contemporary city through the lens of landscape was most evident in projects and texts that appropriate the terms, conceptual categories, and operating methodologies of landscape ecology.[23] This reveals one of the implicit claims of landscape urbanism—namely, the conflation, integration, and fluid exchange between environmental (natural) and infrastructural (engineered) systems. While this newfound relevance for landscape in rethinking the urban first manifested itself in the work of architects, it was quickly corroborated from within the profession of landscape architecture itself. Although initially marginalized by the dominant culture of mainstream landscape architecture on both sides of the Atlantic, landscape urbanist discourse has been, more or less, thoroughly absorbed by the discipline globally. This was made possible in part given the critical reassessment that landscape architecture enjoyed as an academic discipline and cultural category. In this context, it would be useful to understand the recent renaissance of landscape in general, and the ascendance of landscape as a form of urbanism in particular, as the relatively belated impact of postmodern thought on the field.

·····

As the discipline of landscape architecture was examining its own historical and theoretical underpinnings, the general public became increasingly conscious of environmental issues, and thus more aware of landscape as a cultural category. During this time, many landscape architecture practices became proficient in professional activities that were once the domain of urban designers and planners. This allowed landscape architects to fill a professional void, as planning had largely opted out of design culture in favor of the social sciences. During this time, landscape architects were also increasingly involved in work for both postindustrial sites and the easements of various infrastructural systems such as electrical, water, and highway systems. Australian landscape architect Richard Weller describes the landscape profession's newfound relevance: "Postmodern landscape architecture has done a boom trade in cleaning up after modern infrastructure as societies—in the first world at least—shift from primary industry to post-industrial, information societies. In common landscape practice, work is more often than not conducted in the shadow of the infrastructural object, which is given priority over the field into which it is to be inserted. However, as any landscape architect knows, the landscape itself is a medium through which all ecological transactions must pass: it is the infrastructure of the future."[24]

The efficacy of landscape as a remediating practice—a salve for the wounds of the industrial age—is evident in the work of many landscape architects. Projects by Peter Latz at Duisburg Nord Steelworks Park in Germany, and Richard Haag at Gas Works Park in Seattle, are useful illustrations of this tendency. Projects by Hargreaves Associates, Field Operations, and Julie Bargmann's DIRT Studio are equally representative here, among others. Another key strategy of early landscape urbanist practice was the integration of transportation infrastructure into public space. This was exemplified by Barcelona's program of public space and peripheral road improvements, including projects such as Trinitat Cloverleaf Park by Enric Batlle and Joan Roig, among others. While this genre of work—the use of landscape in the stitching of infrastructure into urban fabrics—has well-established precedents, the Barcelona peripheral roadwork is distinct. It offers public parks conceived and constructed simultaneously with the public conveyance of the highway, subtly inflecting its design away from an optimized artifact of civil engineering toward a more complex synthesis of requirements, in which neither civil engineering nor landscape dominate.

One of the more significant embodiments of landscape as a medium of urbanism has been the work of Adriaan Geuze, principal of West 8 Landscape Architects, based in Rotterdam. West 8 has worked on projects at various scales, articulating multiple roles for landscape in the shaping of contemporary urbanism.[25] Several of these projects imaginatively reorder relationships between ecology and infrastructure, deemphasizing the middle scale of architectural or urban work and favoring instead the large-scale infrastructural diagram and the small-scale material condition.

West 8's Shell Project, for instance, organized dark and light mussel shells and the corresponding flocks of similarly shaded dark and light birds naturally adapted to feed from them (figures 1.4, 1.5, 1.6, 1.7). These surfaces formed parallel strips of shoulders along the highway connecting the constructed islands of the East Scheldt storm-tide barrier. The project organizes an ecology

Figure 1.4 Adriaan Geuze/West 8, Eastern Scheldt Storm
Surge Barrier, Zeeland, bird diagram, 1990-92.

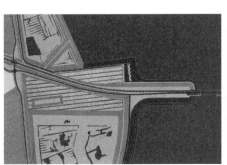

Figure 1.5 Adriaan Geuze/West 8, Eastern Scheldt Storm
Surge Barrier, Zeeland, plan, 1990-92.

of natural selection and renders it for public perception via the automobile. By contrast, historical precedents for urban parkways typically reproduce a pastoral image of "nature" without intervening in their ecological surroundings in any substantial way. Likewise, West 8's ambitious landscape planning scheme for Amsterdam's Schiphol Airport is significant here. In this project, West 8 abandoned the professional tradition of specifically detailed planting plans, deploying instead a general strategy of sunflowers, clover, and beehives (figures 1.8, 1.9, 1.10). By avoiding detailed designs and precise compositions, the project is capable of responding to future programmatic and political changes in Schiphol's planning. Another example of early landscape urbanist practice is West 8's redevelopment plan for Borneo and Sporenburg in Amsterdam Harbor. The planning and design of this large-scale redevelopment is conceived as an enormous landscape urbanist project, orchestrated by West 8, into which the work of numerous other architects and designers is inserted. The project suggests the potential diversity of landscape urbanist strategies through the insertion of numerous small landscaped courts and yards and the commissioning of numerous designers for individual housing units. Taken together, the range of West 8's recent production illustrates the potential for landscape architecture to supplant architecture, urban design, and planning as professionals responsible for reordering postindustrial urban sites in the wake of economic restructuring.

Around the turn of the century, several international design competitions for the reuse of enormously scaled industrial sites in North American cities proposed landscape as their primary medium. Downsview Park, located on the site of an abandoned military airbase in Toronto, and Fresh Kills, on the site of the world's largest landfill on Staten Island, New York, are representative of these trends and offer mature examples of landscape urbanist practices applied to the detritus of the industrial city.[26] While significant distinctions exist between these two projects, the body of work produced for Downsview and Fresh Kills

Figure 1.6 Adriaan Geuze/West 8, Eastern Scheldt Storm Surge Barrier, Zeeland, aerial view, 1990-92.

Figure 1.7 Adriaan Geuze/West 8, Eastern Scheldt Storm Surge Barrier, Zeeland, shells, 1990-92.

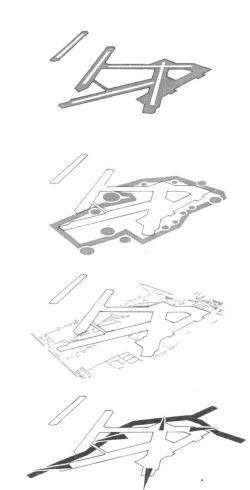

groenstructuur

Figure 1.8 Adriaan Geuze/West 8, Schiphol Amsterdam
Airport Landscape, green gaze montage, 1992-96.

Figure 1.9 Adriaan Geuze/West 8, Schiphol Amsterdam
Airport Landscape, green structure diagrams, 1992-96.

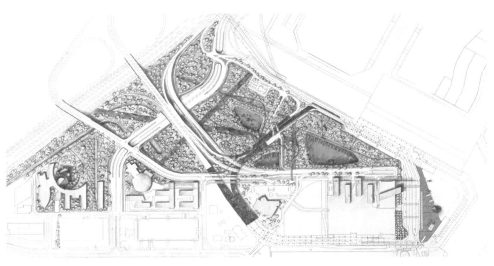

Figure 1.10 Adriaan Geuze/West 8, Schiphol Amsterdam
Airport Landscape, plan, 1992-96.

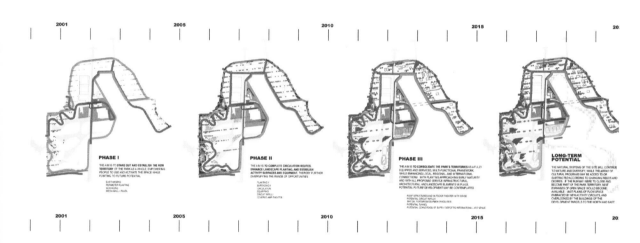

Figure 1.11 James Corner/Field Operations and Stan Allen,
Downsview Park Competition, Toronto, phasing diagram, 2000.

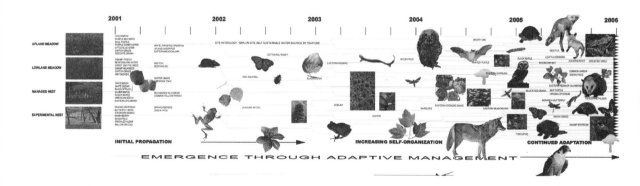

Figure 1.12 James Corner/Field Operations and Stan Allen,
Downsview Park Competition, Toronto, emergence diagram, 2000.

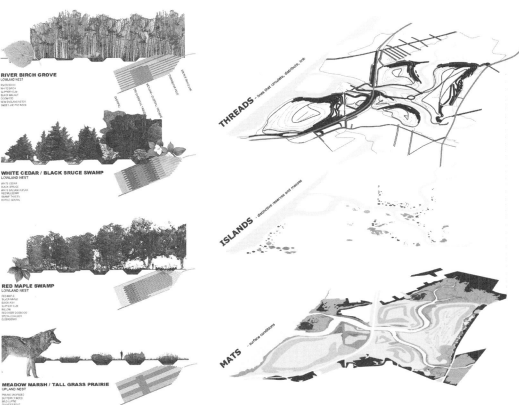

RIVER BIRCH GROVE
LOWLAND NEST

RIVER BIRCH
WHITE BIRCH
SLIPPERY ELM
BLACK WALNUT
DOGWOOD
NEW ENGLAND ASTER
SWEET JOE PYE WEED

WHITE CEDAR / BLACK SRUCE SWAMP
LOWLAND NEST

WHITE CEDAR
BLACK SPRUCE
WHITE BALSAM POPLAR
RED MULBERRY
SWAMP THISTLE
BOTTLE GENTAL

RED MAPLE SWAMP
LOWLAND NEST

RED MAPLE
SILVER MAPLE
BLACK ASH
SLIPPERY ELM
WILLOW
REDOSIER DOGWOOD
SPECKLED ALDER
ELDERBERRY

MEADOW MARSH / TALL GRASS PRAIRIE
UPLAND NEST

PRAIRIE DROPSEED
BUTTERFLY WEED
WILD LUPINE
CULVER'S ROOT
BLAZING STAR
LITTLE BLUE STEM
SWITCH GRASS

GREAT LAKES / ST. LAWRENCE FOREST PATCH
UPLAND NEST

SUGAR MAPLE
AMERICAN BEECH
RED OAK
STAGHORN SUMAC
NANNYBERRY
GOLDENROD
PURPLE MILKWEED
LITTLE BLUE STEM

SUMAC / SASSAFRAS GROVE
UPLAND NEST

STAGHORN SUMAC
NANNYBERRY
SASSAFRAS
BIG BLUE STEM
INDIAN GRASS

EASTERN SYCAMORE GROVE
LOWLAND NEST

EASTERN SYCAMORE
SILVER MAPLE
EASTERN COTTONWOOD
SPECKLED ALDER
WILD SEDGES
WHITOY GRASS

Figure 1.13 James Corner/Field Operations and Stan Allen, Downsview Park Competition, Toronto, nests diagram, 2000.

THREADS – lines that circulate, distribute, link

ISLANDS – distinctive reserves and masses

MATS – surface conditions

Figure 1.14 James Corner/Field Operations, Fresh Kills Landfill Competition, New York, isometric diagram of mats, islands, threads, 2001.

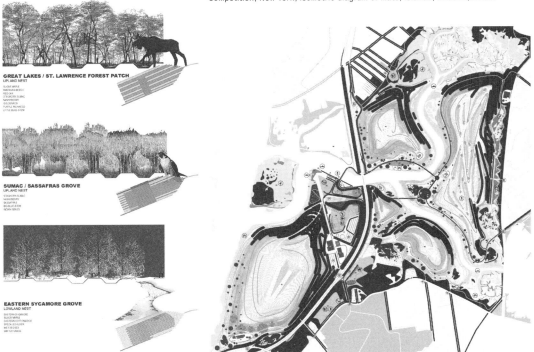

scale 1" = 500'

Figure 1.15 James Corner/Field Operations, Fresh Kills Landfill Competition, New York, plan, 2001.

represents an emerging consensus that designers of the built environment would do well to examine landscape as the medium through which to conceive the renovation of the postindustrial city. Schemes for Downsview (figures 1.11, 1.12, 1.13) and Fresh Kills (figures 1.14, 1.15) by Corner and Allen/Field Operations are exemplary in this regard, illustrating mature works of landscape urbanism through their accumulation and orchestration of absolutely diverse and potentially incongruous contents. Typical of this work, and by now standard fare for projects of this type, are detailed diagrams of phasing, animal habitats, succession planting, and hydrological systems, as well as programmatic and planning regimes. While these diagrams initially overwhelm with information, they present an understanding of the enormous complexities confronting any work at this scale. Particularly compelling is the complex interweaving of natural ecologies with the social, cultural, and infrastructural layers of the contemporary city.

More recently and equally indicative of this newfound synthesis of ecology, infrastructure, and urbanism is the work of the Boston-based Stoss LU. Stoss LU is the intellectual project and professional practice of Chris Reed. Reed was among the first students of James Corner at the University of Pennsylvania to establish an independent international identity as a designer in his own right. Reed launched Stoss in 2000 polemically addending "landscape urbanism" to his enigmatic firm name. In so doing, Reed was among the first designers to explicitly link his professional practice to the emerging discourse of landscape urbanism.[27]

In Stoss's work one can identify at least three distinguishing characteristics that are significant relative to the emergence of landscape urbanism. First is a constant consideration for water, a pervasive awareness of the potential aquatic agency of any particular site or subject. This often manifests itself through the de-engineering of the hydrologic infrastructure of a previous regime. This opening of the site to the vicissitudes of tide and time through the actions of water has the corollary effect of activating dormant or redundant ecologies. In many projects this new hydrologic surface is rendered as a complex hybrid of reengineered surface performance in a complex intermingling of porosity, stability, and opportunistic species of flora and fauna. A second obsession evident in Stoss's work has been a manifest interest in the articulation of surfaces rendered through complex nonlinear geometries, particularly ordering systems that aspire to a complexity of surface conditions through a simplicity of repetitive formal elements. These are often surfaces promising a multitude of programmatic possibilities, while affording a gradient of porosities, and permanencies. Through this device, Reed's work often aspires to an explicit open-endedness with respect to its final formal occupation. A third tendency evident in Stoss's work to date is an ongoing interest in the potentials for tension between native and invasive, between local and exotic. This reveals itself in many projects through the direct juxtaposition of regionally situated yet opportunistic species that have thrived in marginal or derelict sites. These regional natives are juxtaposed repeatedly with invasive or exotics that consciously reflect the increasingly global conditions for economy, ecology, and urbanism. These tendencies in Stoss's work effectively illustrate the potentials of landscape as a form of urbanism. They promise a more responsive, sustainable, and complex urbanism, capable of expanding the range of relationships between nature and culture.

In Stoss's 2003 Mt. Tabor Reservoir proposal, the site of an aging public works project outside Portland, Oregon, is reconsidered as a complex accommodation of architectural heritage, bird habitat, and recreational amenity. The hydrologic strategy involves the reengineering of a water reservoir so as to sectionally separate below ground storage of drinking water from a newly constructed surface reservoir for amenity and habitat. This hydrologic sleight of hand is accomplished through the insertion of a diaphragm between the old reservoir below and the new surface above, effectively protecting the precious drinking water below from the equally precious habitat water above. On top of this high-performance dynamic surface, Stoss's proposal hybridizes new habitat for native, exotic, and invasive species, commingling nesting areas for local species with stopover rest areas for birds along the Pacific flyway.

Equally telling of these commitments is Stoss's 2006 winning entry to the Erie Street Plaza competition for a small public square on Milwaukee's postindustrial lakefront at the mouth of the Milwaukee River opening into Lake Michigan. On a tight urban site, Stoss's hydrological strategy begins with cutting down into the bulkhead of the seawall, again selectively de-engineering a previous generation's attempt to keep water and land distinct, in this instance a steel sheet piling retaining wall installed by the US Army Corps of Engineers. From this opening of the seawall, the site is allowed to enter in to the daily, seasonal, and event-driven chronology of wave action, flooding, and freezing. This simple act of demolition requalifies the site's infrastructural heritage while opening the site to ongoing ecological processes. Following from this hydrological opening, the project conceives a surface strategy that

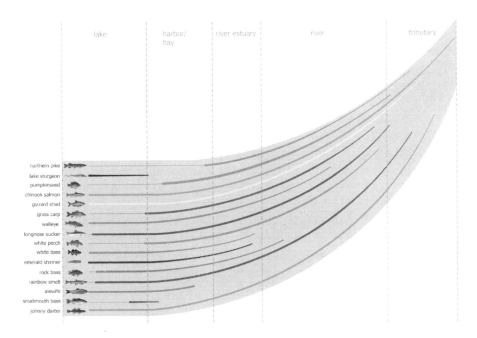

Figure 1.16 Chris Reed/Stoss Landscape Urbanism, Lower
Don Lands Competition, Toronto, fish habitat diagram, 2007.

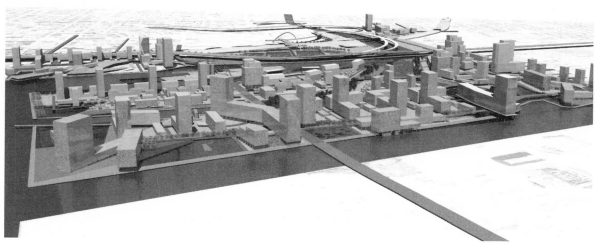

Figure 1.17 Chris Reed/Stoss Landscape Urbanism, Lower
Don Lands Competition, Toronto, aerial view, 2007.

Figure 1.18 Chris Reed/Stoss Landscape Urbanism, Lower
Don Lands Competition, Toronto, aerial view, 2007.

again deploys complex nonlinear patterns of porosity and paving through a minimum of repetitive formal elements. Stoss conceives of this hybrid surface as an
open-ended, indeterminate field of potential, equally available for programmed
events and emergent ecologies. The project explicitly delineates three zones
across this surface: the lower level directly impinged upon by lake water and
most specifically engaged in native specie s through succession process, the
middle level available for public programs, and the upper level planted with a
dense grove of exotic invasives, in this case bamboo. While the bamboo grove
also offers spatial enclosure and microclimate modification through the venting
of steam and misting of water, its primary agency is to contrast with the regional ecology of the site, invoking the ever-present global economy and the
species that invade the region through its conveyances.

A third recent competition entry by Stoss is equally illustrative of these
tendencies. Stoss's 2007 finalist entry to the Lower Don Lands competition in
Toronto persists in these obsessions, pursuing them to their urban and conceptual limits at the scale of a new urban district (figures 1.16, 1.17, 1.18). The
complex project brief called for the renaturalization of the mouth of Toronto's
Don River, the reengineering of the flood plain protection for the city's adjacent
downtown, and the design of a new district on Toronto's now redundant inner
harbor. Stoss's proposal begins with the selective de-engineering of a previous regime of flood control that had canalized the river and its mouth. From
this opening up of hydrologic process, the project calls for the construction
of a newly conceived river delta flowing over a newly conceived hybrid surface
and within which emergent, submergent, and submerged habitat are multiplied.
Stoss's project proposes a fivefold increase in surface area and watercourses
devoted to open-ended and self-regulating fluvial processes. Washed by the
hydrology of the river mouth, these surfaces afford public amenity, urban image,
and ecological performance. This strategy calibrates the relations between
emergent and submergent marshes, while focusing the city of Toronto and its
diverse constituents on the river mouth as a legitimately public venue.

These three recurring themes and their manifestation in the Stoss Landscape
Urbanism's work to date offer a promising picture of landscape as the medium
of urban order. The primary commitments of the work continue to offer a profound implied critique of the moribund and nostalgic assumptions of most urban
design and planning practice in North America. Stoss's work to date illustrates
the potentials of landscape ecology as a primary determinate of a contemporary urbanism for North America, one built on the intelligent reconsideration of
infrastructure, ecology, and urban development.

.....

As professional practices began to identity themselves with the discourse
and methods of landscape as a form of urbanism at the turn of the century,
academic programs and publications proliferated. The first such programs
were a graduate master of architecture stream in landscape urbanism at the
University of Illinois–Chicago that began in 1997 with funding from the Graham
Foundation. This program was quickly followed by the formation of a postgraduate unit in landscape urbanism in 1999 at the Architectural Association
School of Architecture in London.[28] Both of these academic initiatives led to

subsequent publications, and the English-language discourse on the topic grew internationally in the first decade of the twenty-first century.[29]

The emergence of these practices and the projects they embody collectively illustrate dramatic changes in the disciplinary and professional assumptions regarding the design of the city. Particularly significant in the formulation of landscape as urbanism was an improbable alliance of design culture with landscape ecology. As we will see in the following chapter, the landscape urbanist discourse was enabled by the confluence of architecture's late avant-gardist interest in autonomy and criticality through distanced authorship, as enabled by readings of postmodern ecology in which natural systems were understood to be open-ended, indeterminate, and self-organizing.

Two: Autonomy, Indeterminacy, Self-Organization

If there is to be a "new urbanism" it will not be based on the twin fantasies of order and omnipotence; it will be the staging of uncertainty.
—Rem Koolhaas, 1994

The discourse and practices of landscape urbanism described in the previous chapter emerged at the improbable intersection of ecological performance and design culture. Beginning in the 1990s, a generation of landscape architects and urbanists found in ecology a conceptual framework for design capable of reconciling the contradictory desires for architectural autonomy on the one hand with increasing demands for instrumental environmental engagement on the other. These designers and theorists articulated the potential for ecological systems to be seen as self-organizing and open-ended, while affording a strategic framework for urban intervention. Architecture's appropriation of the "open work" in the 1970s and early '80s informed this improbable confluence of autonomy and instrumentality. A range of cultural practices and discourses, not least among them the import of concepts from literary criticism into ar-chitectural theory, informed this interest in delayed, deferred, or distanced authorship.

For urbanists of the postmodern era wishing to avoid the style wars of the 1980s, many found urban life itself, absent its architectural accommodations, to offer a model of the open work. As we have seen, both Koolhaas and Tschumi invoked landscape as a model of programmatic change over time. As we saw in the previous chapter, these tendencies were evident in Koolhaas's and Tschumi's projects for la Villette from the early 1980s in which the open work was taken as a surrogate for the propinquity and open-endedness of urban life itself, absent the need for any particular architectural accommodation.[1]

Rem Koolhaas would develop the implication of these ideas more completely in urban form with OMA's entry to the 1987 competition for the French new town Melun-Sénart. Koolhaas's scheme for the French new town proposed a landscape framework for open space, infrastructure, and public amenity as the overall planning diagram for the town. Private laissez-faire development would grow to populate the territory left between these public easements.[2] Koolhaas's proposal for the Melun-Sénart new town competition would recall his collaboration with O. M. Ungers and their mutual interest in the city as a "green archipelago." It would also prefigure a decade of interest in urban indeterminacy by architects, urbanists, and increasingly, landscape architects.

The subsequent emergence of landscape urbanism in the late 1990s was informed by this line of work and fueled by the emancipatory potential of reading

the city as the ultimate "open work." By this time, a range of landscape architects, including James Corner and Adriaan Geuze, among others, had identified
ecology as embodying many of the putatively autonomous aspects of architectural culture, while offering an informed environmental position. Corner and
Geuze were joined by a phalanx of urban and architectural theorists in the late
1990s operating on at least three parallel tracks. First, Stan Allen and Alex Wall,
among others, developed theoretical frameworks for describing the city as a
set of horizontal surfaces. These thick two-dimensional surfaces were read as
forming larger fields of infrastructure and event in which landscape came to
occupy a privileged position.[3] Alex Wall's focus on programming the urban surface paralleled Allen's interest in the port as a site irrigated by event. Both
were informed by Koolhaas's call for a "new urbanism" organized around the
staging of uncertainty and the irrigation of territories. Second, the claims
of the "postcritical" by Michael Speaks, Robert Somol, and Sarah Whiting,
among others, advanced the potential of reconciling architectural autonomy
with renewed forms of urban agency. Speaks's formulation of the "postcritical" prompted James Corner to respond with an essay titled "Not Unlike Life
Itself," in which he articulated the parallels between a postcritical urban practice and the potentials for an open-ended, indeterminate, and self-regulating
set of ecological systems.[4] Finally, during this period, Sanford Kwinter and
Detlef Mertins, among others, explored the potential for a reading of the natural sciences to inform contemporary architectural theory. Through a series of
influential essays in the 1990s, Kwinter pursued the potential for properties
found in the natural world to be appropriated for use as models for cultural,
architectural, and urban projection.[5] The perennial project of finding models for
architecture in models of nature informed Kwinter's interests in this regard.The
reading of modern architecture's commitment to organic orders for the
city informed Mertins's work.

Contemporary interest in landscape as urbanism owes much to the critical reception of strategies for distanced authorship imported to architecture
during the 1970s and 1980s. Reports of the author's death, once greatly
exaggerated, have become extremely rare in contemporary discussions of design. While architectural discourse has been focused recently on the ongoing
relevance of criticality and the possibilities of the so-called postcritical, landscape urbanist discourse has appropriated displaced authorship and strategies
of indeterminacy, self-regulation, and autonomous emergence. In response to
these developments this chapter examines the connection between neo-avant-
gardist discourses of problematized authorship and their appropriation by landscape urbanism. Before taking up those connections, however, it is important
to convey something of the substance of these strategies of weak or displaced
authorship as they first emerged in the theory and practice of the early twentieth-century avant-gardes. Here the practices of Raymond Roussel, Marcel
Duchamp, and Max Ernst exemplify the range and spirit of these strategies.

·····

In part due to the rejection of his work by the French literary establishment
and his humiliation in front of a series of Parisian audiences, the avant-gardist
playwright and author Raymond Roussel took his own life in 1933.[6] His last

manuscript, intended for publication after his death, was a nonfiction account of his primary working methodology titled *Comment j'ai écrit certains de mes livres* (*How I Wrote Certain of My Books*).[7] This "secret and posthumous" work describes in detail his use of compositional protocols that, while resembling the aleatory strategies of surrealism and Dadaism, were distinguished by both the arduousness and the arbitrariness of the restrictions they placed on the process of creation.

Another difference between Roussel and his surrealist and Dadaist counterparts becomes apparent if we compare him with Marcel Duchamp, whose work is better known. A case in point is Duchamp's *3 stoppages étalon* (*3 Standard Stoppages*) from 1913. In this work Duchamp reportedly dropped a meter of string from a meter above a tabletop and then claimed the twisting shapes resulting from this operation as new units of measure (figure 2.2). The project exemplifies Duchamp's commitment to precision in the service of indeterminacy. In spite of the fact that both the construct itself and repeated attempts to reproduce Duchamp's practice have illustrated that the work was most likely a consciously constructed hoax, the project has come to enjoy canonical status as a model of problematized authorship in cultural production.[8]

After the posthumous publication of Roussel's explanation, his working methods became the object of intense scrutiny and interest for a range of cultural agents, including the authors and critics of the *Nouveau Roman* of the 1950s and the so-called structuralist critics of the 1960s and '70s. It was from these literary sources that the "death of the author" first entered

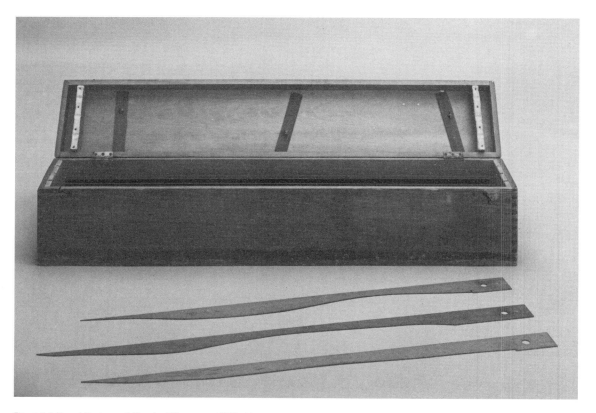

Figure 2.2 Marcel Duchamp, *3 Standard Stoppages*, 1913–14.

architectural discourse in the 1960s and '70s. Among the various texts responsible for introducing such posthumanist concepts of cultural production into architectural discussion at this time, one especially stands out, Peter Eisenman's 1976 essay, "Post-Functionalism." Eisenman's text, and the collection of essays in which it was included, proposed the subversion of the author function as one symptom of a larger cultural trajectory.[9] The absorption of architectural theory and practice into this trajectory would, on Eisenman's account, allow the discipline to abandon its obsession with motivating form functionally, so that it could then follow the other culture disciplines (music, painting, literature) in their pursuit of more willfully mediated strategies of composition.

Roussel intended his plays and novels to be read without knowledge of the working method, with the result that contemporary audiences were not inclined to read the works as manifestations of a theory. This fact distinguishes his practice from Duchamp's. For Duchamp depended upon very public claims for the method of production, so that collapsing the space of production and reception proves to be part of the work's effect. Lacking this reading of the artifact as an allegory of compositional process, Roussel's works were found unremarkable and often unintelligible. By expecting his plays and novels to be on their own, Roussel anticipates Barthes's emphasis on the reception of a work liberated from any presumed authorial intent. The result of this liberation is the "open work," a work that would also figure in contemporary architectural discourse, and that continues to inform contemporary understandings of "field" as a model of both the urban surface and those operations we apply to it.

This relationship between the reception of a cultural product and the claims of authorial intent is of particular relevance to contemporary debates about the status of criticality within architectural discourse. As architectural culture declares the ascendance of the postcritical, interest in displacing authorial intent has been in a predictable state of decline. However, even as fewer claims are being made for problematized or distanced authorship in architectural production, contemporary landscape and urbanism have provided these topics with fertile ground and newfound relevance.

As the previous chapter illustrated, the projects by Bernard Tschumi and Rem Koolhaas/OMA for the Parc de la Villette competition explicitly invoke the notion of an open work (Tschumi) or unplanned juxtaposition (Koolhaas) as necessarily posthumanist conditions for the twenty-first-century urban park. These projects variously exhibit attenuated authorship through the deferral of decisions over program, the focus of those modernist strategies they were seeking to displace. The projects equally signal the coming centrality of landscape as the medium through which an appropriately open-ended, responsive, and indeterminate urbanism might be conceived. Equally evident in this line of thought are the more recent urban projects of Stan Allen. Allen's interest in infrastructural arrangement and the notion of constructing the site for future architectural embodiment offer evidence of an ongoing engagement with questions of indeterminacy and delay.[10] Allen's proposal for the Barcelona Port or Logistical Activities Zone (1996) proposes a "thick 2-D" surface of urbanism as the locus of design attention, forming a horizontal surface or landscape of infrastructural affordance, one capable of responding dynamically to unforeseeable future conditions. Allen developed his proposal for this thickened horizontal surface as a "field condition" and drew inspiration from the study of a range of open-ended and indeterminate, yet self-regulating, forms evident in the natural world (figure 2.3). This field was often conceived as an infrastructure in its own right, one staged to accommodate any configuration of capital or logistical requirement attendant to contemporary flows. In this formulation postcritical interest in the fluidity and flux of global capital flows intersect with the necessity those flows produce for an urbanism that is responsive, efficient, and potentially abandonable. Each of these imply their own form of distanced authorship, one in which the recuperation of selective aspirations of modernist urban planning becomes desirable.

While modernist aspirations to totalizing instrumental control are distanced through an explicit interest in self-regulation and autonomy, the parallel modernist interests in an organic relation between economic, ecological, and infrastructural arrangement are seen as highly desirable. Recent interest in the diagram as a locus of architectural and urban content are equally relevant here, with the critical aspects of deferred authorship continuing in a subconscious operating system, while the desire for postcriticality articulates itself in an increasing desire for proximity to decision making, capital, and social relevance. While this line of thought is increasingly interested in models and organizations taken from natural systems and often invokes neo-organicist aspirations, more often than not it invokes natural systems as models or metaphors for infrastructural organization rather than as operating ecological regimes.

. . . . .

A variety of contemporary landscape practices employ techniques of problematized authorship and contemporary discourse around landscape, and urbanism is awash with claims of indeterminacy, open-endedness, self-regulation, and

Figure 2.3 Stan Allen, Field Conditions, diagrams, 1999.

postmodern ecological models of autonomous emergence. These practices, while multiform and various, can be summarized into two general lines of thought, each with its own specific aspirations, origins, and claims. The first of these, and the one most directly extending from the critical architectural discourse, comprises urban landscape projects designed through various automatic methods yielding highly sculpted horizontal surfaces. These projects and the architects responsible for them represent a clear extension of the neo-avant-gardist architectural project. A second distinct body of work invokes the indeterminacy and self-regulation ascribed to natural systems and attempts to transfer these qualities to the instruments of urban collectivity. Typically, this involves the employment of ecological models and natural metaphors to describe an urban landscape capable of adapting itself over time to rapidly changing conditions. Taken together, these two lines of work offer evidence that, within the discourses of landscape and urbanism at any rate, neo-avant-gardist strategies of composition, production, and reception continue to be an influence, however much faith in the criticality that originally sponsored them may have eroded.

The first such line of work is exemplified in the work of two Spanish architects and their partners, Enric Miralles (with Carme Pinós) and Alejandro Zaera-Polo (with Farshid Moussavi). The direct indexical rubbing of found lines is particularly evident in the Igualada Cemetery (1986–89) (figure 2.4) and Archery Range (1989–92) (figures 2.5, 2.6) by Enric Miralles and Carme Pinós. Both projects derive from the rubbing of drawings over the topographic lines of the Igualada site, the cemetery constructed on that same site as a representation of the site's surface, and the Archery Range constructed on a remote site on the periphery of Barcelona.[11] Both operations invoke the surrealist project and the work of Max Ernst specifically as the origin of various

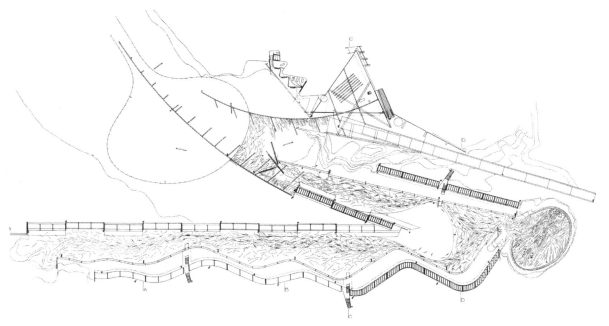

Figure 2.4 Enric Miralles and Carme Pinós, Igualada Cemetery, plan, 1986–89.

frottage and collage techniques. The resulting constructed surfaces are highly sculpted, complex forms in contrapose to their landscape sites. Both imply a thin volume of space between a highly delineated horizontal surface and architectural volumes just below (Archery Range) or behind (Igualada Cemetery) that surface. Both read as highly constructed architectonic landscapes that happen to contain some building enclosures, and both exhibit a palpable tension between the figurative gestures of their organization and the prosaic demands of their respective programs, be it the storage of cremated remains and gardening supplies (Igualada Cemetery) or the accommodation of locker rooms and Zen-like preparation spaces (Archery Range). Both projects are experienced primarily as horizontal landscapes creased by complex sectional relations between the building enclosure and the found topographic conditions of their sites. The Igualada Cemetery project predates the Archery Range project, and the latter commission simply reappropriates the already available set of complex rubbings originally produced for the cemetery. Set upon an arid plain in the peripheral territories of the Olympic site, the Archery Range deploys Igualada's automatic topography across a nearly flat site, folding it into an architectural section and vast rooftop landscape. Both projects exhibit a clear continuity with previous techniques of problematized posthumanist authorship within architectural culture, including Eisenman's obsessions with mathematics and abstract formal operations.

Alejandro Zaera-Polo, another Spanish architect laundered in Ivy League architectural theory, and his partner Farshid Moussavi have authored a range

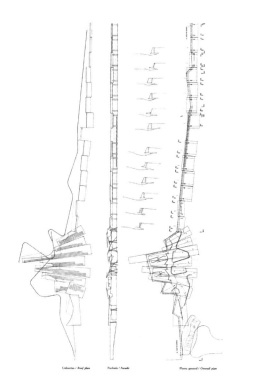

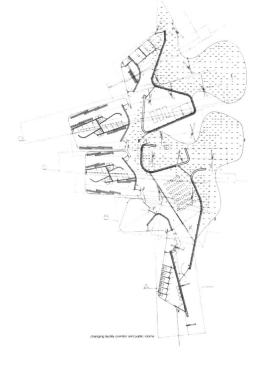

Figure 2.5 Enric Miralles and Carme Pinós, Archery Range, Barcelona, overall plan, 1989–92

Figure 2.6 Enric Miralles and Carme Pinós, Archery Range, Barcelona, partial plan, 1989–92.

Figure 2.7 Alejandro Zaera-Polo and Farshid Moussavi/Foreign Office Architects, Yokohama Port Terminal, site plan, 1995.

Figure 2.9 Alejandro Zaera-Polo and Farshid Moussavi/Foreign Office Architects, Yokohama Port Terminal, aerial view, 1995.

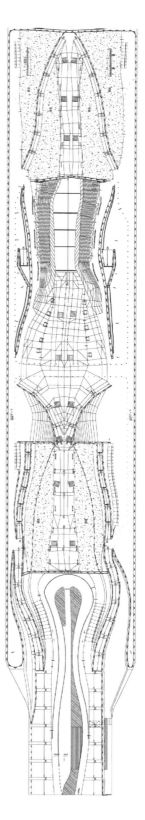

Figure 2.8 Alejandro Zaera-Polo and Farshid Moussavi/Foreign Office Architects, Yokohama Port Terminal, plan, 1995.

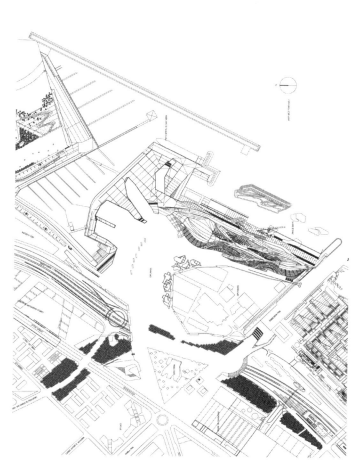

Figure 2.10 Alejandro Zaera-Polo and Farshid Moussavi/Foreign
Office Architects, Barcelona Amphitheater, site plan, 2004.

Figure 2.12 Alejandro Zaera-Polo and Farshid Moussavi/Foreign
Office Architects, Barcelona Amphitheater, aerial view, 2004.

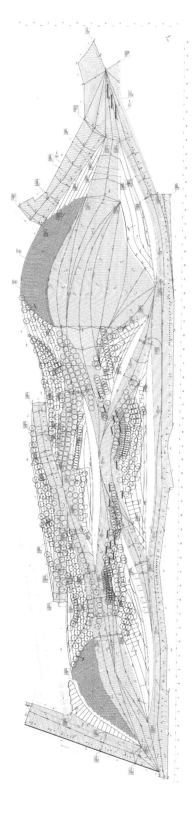

Figure 2.11 Alejandro Zaera-Polo and Farshid Moussavi/Foreign
Office Architects, Barcelona Amphitheater, plan, 2004.

of urban landscape projects over the past decade extending the neo-avant-gardist interest in subverting or displacing authorship. Zaera-Polo and Moussavi / Foreign Office Architects' Yokohama Pier Terminal of 1995 (figures 2.7, 2.8, 2.9) and Barcelona's Auditorium Park at the Forum of International Cultures of 2004 (figures 2.10, 2.11, 2.12) construct highly complex three-dimensional surfaces that perform in the first instance as urban landscapes, effectively masking larger building programs below or behind them.[12] In place of Miralles and Pinós's distinctly analogue techniques of frottage, Zaera-Polo and Farshid Moussavi fashion their horizontal surfaces from complex computer algorithms of multivariate, indeterminate inputs. Emerging from these digital parameters, their horizontal surfaces respond to a complex array of instrumental expectations, while distancing authorial control or instrumental intent from the resulting surface. While the Miralles and Pinós projects depend upon an emptying of programmatic demands in favor of an initial figuring of form and a subsequent accommodation of program, the Zaera-Polo and Moussavi projects are shaped in response to a dizzying array of programmatic demands. From this response vertiginous landscapes emerge, landscapes that afford a renewed engagement with the topography of a site as a surface for appropriation. While both projects invoke traditional park programs of theater, spectacle, and promenade, each sufficiently distances humanist expectations of authorship to maintain continuity with the aspirations of neo-avant-gardist architectural practice. With their use of frottage and autonomous digital iteration, both these lines of work eschew traditional representational devices and expectations of public reception. Equally, they reject the monumentality and verticality implicit in the traditional program of the public park buildings. In so doing, they invoke a body of landscape work colloquially known as landscape sculpture.[13]

·····

A second distinct body of work implicated in this discussion explicitly deploys and develops ecological claims for their distanced authorship, often articulating a natural process, landscape strategy, or ecological regime as the first phase of a subsequent urbanism. These projects tend to make broader claims for the relative autonomy of ecological systems and their ability to shape future urbanization. While each of these projects and their protagonists were distinct, they shared a certain intellectual terrain in progressive design culture of the 1990s. In this context ecology was most often invoked as a model or metaphor, but rarely as also a description of the natural world. It was in the work of a small number of landscape architects that these lines of thought would intersect most consequentially for the development of landscape urbanism. James Corner and Adriaan Geuze, the clearest exemplars of landscape urbanist practices in the 1990s, were originally trained in landscape ecology as an applied natural science or practice of environmental resource management. Corner studied with Ian McHarg at the University of Pennsylvania where the curriculum was centered on landscape ecology as a principle of organizing the design work of landscape architects and urbanists. To this milieu Corner brought previous educational and professional experience as an urbanist, and he subsequently immersed himself in neo-avant-gardist architectural theory, notably the work of Tschumi and Koolhaas.[14] Geuze was trained in landscape ecology as part of his curriculum in landscape architecture at Wageningen University, the preeminent Dutch school for the natural sciences. Geuze brought to his training an interest in the arts and urbanism, and subsequently was immersed in contemporary Dutch design culture and theory.[15] The combination of these experiences for both Corner and Geuze enabled them to imagine landscape ecology as simultaneously capable of critically distancing authorial intent of the architect, while embodying the potential for an environmentally progressive urban position. Both Corner and Geuze explored the theoretical implications and projective potentials for such an intersection in early, unbuilt projects.

The James Corner / Field Operations 2003 proposal for the Bridesburg neighborhood on Philadelphia's Delaware River Waterfront exemplifies this line of thought (figures 2.13, 2.14). At Bridesburg, the indeterminate spatial location of contaminated soil on site persists in the form of randomized urban voids in the context of future urbanization. In this remarkable proposal for the redevelopment of a derelict former industrial site for mixed-use urban development, Corner deploys a strategy of phytoremediation. Techniques of phytoremediation, the use of plant species, and their attendant properties to remediate contaminated sites, have been developed as part of landscape architectural practice over the past two decades. These strategies promise remediation of brownfield sites at lower costs and greater efficacy than other more industrial means. In his Delaware Waterfront project, Corner proposed that the phasing of urban development would be linked to the successful completion of remediation. As a part of the remediation process, plantations of poplar trees would be planted. Those trees that continue to absorb contaminants and die off are replaced with new plants as part of an ongoing process. The first evidence available of the successful completion of that process is the ongoing presence of healthy poplar trees, having survived their absorption of contaminants. Counterintuitively, and contrary to typical professional practice, Corner proposed that those sites would be urbanized first, through the development of block structure, urban infrastructure, and development parcels. This would occur in parallel with ongoing phytoremediation processes for the more contaminated portions of the site. Ultimately, the most contaminated sites, the plumes of subsurface contamination that resist remediation the longest, would provide the figure of the public parks and open spaces of the future development. In this way, the process of remediation remains as a legible, indexical record of the site's environmental history, and the seemingly technical process of phytoremediation would inform the shape of the city through its disposition, placement, and configuration of parks and public realm.

Similarly, Adriaan Geuze / West 8's 1995 proposal for the Dutch coastal new town of Buckthorn City imagines the urban potential of ecological processes (figures 2.15, 2.16). In lieu of the largely engineered infrastructure and planning of traditional North Sea settlements on the Dutch coast, Geuze proposed to colonize the emergent dredgeate dunescape of the polder under construction with the buckthorn plant. The invasive European buckthorn plant, generally regarded as a nuisance plant, acts as an active agent consolidating the subsurface conditions through its extensive root system and produces topsoil in advance of future urbanization. The ultimate market-driven urbanization takes

Figure 2.13 James Corner/Field Operations, Bridesburg,
Philadelphia, aerial view, 2003.

Figure 2.14 James Corner/Field Operations, Bridesburg,
Philadelphia, aerial view, 2003.

a more or less conventional (or at least market compliant) form, while the rhizomatic shape of the buckthorn colony indexes the form of future infrastructure and urban form. In this case, Geuze's proposal draws on the open-endedness of market-based development, while allowing the shape of the city to be derived from an autonomous, open-ended natural process.[16]

Both of these projects propose a dynamic and open-ended relationship between urbanization and ecological process, one in which traditional hierarchies between urban figure and landscape void are inverted in favor of a more environmentally informed, if not more sustainable, regime of urban development. Equally in each of these examples the privileging of landscape strategy and ecological process distances authorial control over urban form, while

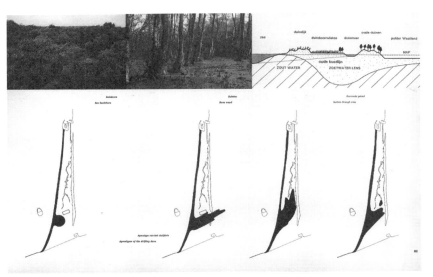

Figure 2.15 Adriaan Geuze/West 8, Buckthorn City Project, Hoek van Holland, plan and section diagrams, 1995.

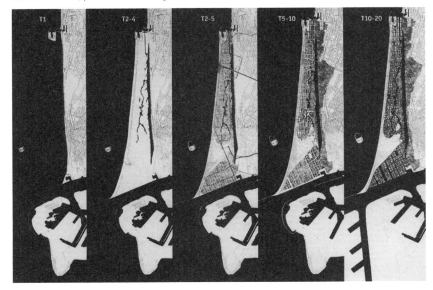

Figure 2.16 Adriaan Geuze/West 8, Buckthorn City Project, Hoek van Holland, figure-ground plan over time, 1995

allowing for specificity and responsiveness to market conditions as well as the moral high-ground and rhetorical clarity of environmental determinism.

In these early experiments with radical ecological indeterminacy, urban form is given not from planning, policy, or precedent, but through the self-regulation of emergent ecologies as curated by a landscape urbanist. In both examples the ultimate urban figure is attained not through design but rather through the agency of ecological process directed toward cultural ends. As we will see in chapter 3, the emergence of digital associative, parametric, or relational models for urban form represent the most recent manifestation of these tendencies. In parametricism, contemporary practices of landscape urbanism aspire to defer authorship of form, while specifying performative parameters for urban form. The landscape urbanism unit at the Architectural Association School of Architecture in London has been at the forefront of these experiments since the inception of its program. Drawing on relational parametric modeling techniques developed by the Design Research Lab (DRL) at the school, the landscape urbanism unit has developed a range of projects exploring associative or relational modeling as one facet of landscape urbanist strategies for reconciling the shape of the city with its performative criteria. This development of parametric tools for service in landscape urbanist projects has drawn the practice into an existing debate over the limits or dangers of "parametricism."[17] The most vocal critiques of the parametric have been voiced in response to the proclamation of parametricism by self-proclaimed parametricist Patrik Schumacher, with respect to his work with Zaha Hadid. While those critiques tended to generally stigmatize the potential of this approach to urban form, the potential for relational urban modeling to correlate formal outcomes to performative ecological criteria remains one of the more vibrant lines of investigation in recent landscape urbanist projects and pedagogy. For many, however, landscape urbanism's recent dalliance with parametricism has reinforced the perception that it is allied with elite culture, rendering it vulnerable to a long-overdue social critique. On the topic of the social, a 2007 exhibition at the Museum of Modern Art located landscape urbanism as among landscape architecture's contemporary practices and used that opportunity to open a line of social critique at precisely the moment of landscape architecture's greatest global visibility.

.....

Many of the landscape projects described in this and the previous chapter were included in a recent Museum of Modern Art exhibition program under the title *Groundswell*.[18] The *Groundswell* exhibition and catalog documented over a decade of urban restructuring projects conceived through the landscape medium for sites in North America, Europe, and Asia. For academics, design professionals, and critics engaged with the landscape medium over the past decade, the work documented in *Groundswell* can hardly be considered news. The exhibition text and accompanying catalog acknowledge that the body of work they describe has been accomplished over the past decade or two, with the earliest of the projects included (Igualada Cemetery, Miralles and Pinós, 1985–96) dating from as early as the mid-1980s. It is true that for those who have followed landscape's reemergence over the past decade there are few surprises.

Rather, the exhibition assembles a solid international sampling of relatively known, high quality quantities. Of course as is to be expected given a venue of this volume, some critics have scrutinized various curatorial decisions and their implications for the cultural currency of the various designers included. While not without its pleasures, this reading mistakes the larger value of the MOMA show. By offering contemporary urban landscape the single largest and most legible stage from which to announce its renewed relevance to broader audiences, the *Groundswell* initiative offers to nudge the field ever so slightly out of the academic and professional shadows. In this regard, the value of the MOMA show can be found in its leavening of the broader cultural context for discussions of landscape among and across a range of disciplines, not to mention with potential patrons and broader publics. In many ways, the body of work and broader themes described in Peter Reed's thorough and even-handed introductory essay can be read as a retroactive history of the recent past for the landscape medium.[19] In so doing, Reed's *Groundswell* more than adequately stands up to MOMA's previous survey of landscape, *Denatured Visions* (1991), edited by William Howard Adams and Stuart Wrede.[20] While the *Denatured Visions* catalog included a robust volume of academic essays generally converging on questions of modern landscape, the *Groundswell* exhibition and symposium was organized primarily to present individual projects and players in their own terms, as mediated (in print) and moderated (on stage) by Reed. The single exception to that structure, offering an interdisciplinary intellectual frame for the work, was David Harvey's keynote address.[21]

For some members of the *Groundswell* audience, Harvey's keynote address raised the question as to how precisely it was that a Marxist geographer interested in dialectical and materialist understandings of political economy might be invited to front a discussion of contemporary landscape architecture. This question was even more pointed for some given the fact that the remarks in question formed the primetime keynote address critically framing the most substantial exhibition of contemporary landscape architecture to be organized in North America in recent decades.

Harvey's accounts of the impact of industrial economy on cultural production have been particularly relevant to the developing discourse surrounding landscape urbanism in North America. MOMA curator Peter Reed, who instigated and orchestrated the *Groundswell* project, invoked the contemporary discourse surrounding landscape urbanism explicitly in the exhibition catalog.[22] What was significant about the *Groundswell* initiative was the invocation of David Harvey's work as relevant to the serious consideration of contemporary urban landscape. Many in the audience were puzzled, to say the least, as to why Harvey would be invited to offer the keynote, given the show's focus on contemporary urban landscape architecture internationally. Harvey's inclusion was meant to ensure that the discussion of contemporary postindustrial urban landscapes would be grounded in the economic, environmental, and political conditions attendant to their development. Harvey's remarks offered an ethical position from which to adjudicate the relevance of this body of work across disciplinary boundaries and signaled the show's availability to discussions across disciplinary and professional boundaries.

Harvey is best known for his by now canonical book *The Condition of Postmodernity* (1990), in which he describes the impact of economic and political conditions on cultural production.[23] In this work Harvey locates the origins of postmodern cultural tendencies within the larger structural collapse of the Fordist economic regime in the early 1970s. For Harvey, rather than the superficial stylistic concerns of design, the shift to postmodernist tendencies in architecture and urbanism correlate directly to a new regime of what he calls "flexible accumulation" characterized by neoliberal economic policies, just-in-time production, outsourcing, flexible or informal labor arrangements, and increasingly global capital flows. It would be hard to overstate the impact of Harvey's work on architectural discourse over the past fifteen years, as his work has come to stand as among the most durable accounts of the postmodern cultural condition and its relationship to contemporary urbanism. Given Harvey's work reading cultural production through political economy, he was uniquely suited to frame a discussion of urban landscape projects for sites largely left in the wake of global economic restructuring over the past three decades. Harvey's comments offered ethical reflections on the broader meanings of the work under consideration in relation to questions of social equity, environmental crisis, and uneven development. Harvey's attention to the social and political reminded his audience of the embeddedness of landscape practices in the structures that enable processes of urbanization. Rather than any easy moral high ground, this suggests that contemporary claims for the landscape architect as urbanist implicate the field in the very economic, social, and political structures that produce urban order.

Three: Planning, Ecology, and the Emergence of Landscape

Ecology ... provides a useful analogy for the complexity and diversity of urban processes.
—Julia Czerniak, 2001

Landscape has enjoyed a relative renaissance within design culture since the turn of the century. More recently, landscape architecture has benefited from this renaissance, with claims of the landscape architect as urbanist of our age. This well-documented resurgence of what had been described by some as a relatively moribund field of intellectual inquiry has been variously described as a recovery or renewal, and has been particularly fruitful for discussions of contemporary urbanism. Among the questions implied by this is the relative impact of landscape's newfound ascendancy for the status of urban planning. Ironically, the most compelling argument in this regard suggests that the potential for landscape to inform planning comes from its newfound status within design culture and the deployment of ecology as model or metaphor rather than through the long-standing project of regional or ecological planning. This chapter offers a reading of how practices of landscape urbanism have come to supplant the traditional role of urban planning in projecting the shape of the contemporary city through a synthesis of ecological function and design culture.

The recent recovery of landscape might be thought of as the impact of postmodernism on the field. This reading suggests that an essentially modernist positivist discourse of the natural sciences has been supplanted, if not made redundant, by the notion of nature as a cultural construct. In that formulation, landscape architecture moves from a position of positivist certainty over the mechanisms of ecological function to a culturally relativist position of ecology as a model for understanding the complex interactions between nature and culture. Of course landscape's recent cultural relevance has to do with a unique combination of broad environmental awareness in mass culture and the rise of the donor class as the means through which design is defined as culture.

The discourse and practices of landscape urbanism presuppose an intellectual and practical tradition of ecological planning as a foundation. Yet it was only through the unlikely intersection of modernist ecological planning with postmodern architectural culture that landscape urbanism would emerge. Whereas ecological planning presupposed the region as the basic unit of empirical observation and the site of design intervention, landscape urbanism inherits the region as a scale of ecological observation and analysis, yet most often intervenes at the scale of the brownfield site, which is the result of ongoing restructuring of industrial economies.

< Figure 3.1 James Corner/Field Operations and Diller Scofidio + Renfro, The High Line, New York, view, 2004.

European architects and urbanists describing the North American city first articulated landscape's newfound relevance as model for contemporary urbanism. It has come to stand for a profound critique of the perceived failures of urban design to effectively respond to the spatial decentralization, neoliberal economic shifts, and environmental toxicity found in those cities. Equally, it has come to promise a cultural alternative to the reactionary cultural politics of traditional urban form, simultaneously offering an alternative future for urbanism in which environmental health, social welfare, and cultural aspiration are no longer mutually exclusive. While it may be true that landscape architects were not the first to make such claims, the discipline has mounted spirited support for such claims as the field diversifies and grows in design literacy.

Since the turn of the century, as landscape architecture has reconceived itself, the discipline of urban design has been largely preoccupied with various alibis for traditional urban form, and has until recently been relatively slow to appreciate the import that landscape would come to have in discussions of North American urban form. These developments are not unrelated to the rapprochement between the design disciplines. Equally, they have been informed by calls for interdisciplinarity with respect to the challenges of the contemporary city as well as in design education. In this context, urban planning has been relatively slow to apprehend the import of landscape's newfound cultural relevance for discussions of urbanism.

In many ways, planning's relative immunity to these developments within landscape architecture is not surprising given the history of the two disciplines. In the context of the cultural politics of the 1960s, or so goes the conventional wisdom, many prominent planning departments (including those at Harvard University and the University of Toronto) left schools of architecture to articulate their own disciplinary identity and to distance themselves from the perceived hegemony of architecture as dominant among the design arts. Similarly, many departments of landscape architecture were radicalized on environmental issues and distanced themselves from the cultural and intellectual commitments of their architect colleagues. The combined effect of these events was to alienate the design disciplines from one another, and to disengage architecture as a discipline from the economic, ecological, and social contexts that had historically informed design. In that period of relative alienation between design culture and environmental activism, planning programs were predisposed to strike alliances with their environmentally minded colleagues in landscape architecture and to distance themselves from the seemingly subjective and self-referential commitments of the architecture discipline.

As architecture, landscape architecture, and urban design have recently enjoyed a relative rapprochement as design disciplines, the question persists as to the relative impact of that renewed disciplinary proximity on planning. This begs the question as to the status and contemporary commitments of planning, particularly in relation to design culture and ecological function. One approach to this question would be to examine the current paradigms and discourse available within urban planning. Among the myriad subjects and positions available, recent literature suggests that the present moment in planning might be summarized in three historic oppositions. The first of these concerns top-down executive authority versus bottom-up organic community decision making. A second of these supposes an opposition between planning allied with design culture as opposed to an organic vernacular. A third presupposes an ongoing opposition between planning as an instrument of the welfare state informed by environmental science and planning as real politick facilitator of laissez-faire economic development and the art of the deal. While these facile oppositions are surely reductive, they continue to inform the discourse of planning, perpetuating a return to the political context of the 1960s in which they were formalized.[1]

Of the numerous points of departure for this question, an interesting place to start would be 1956 and the origins of urban design. Urban design as formulated in the mid-1950s was conceived at least in part as a response to planning's already evident commitments to empirical knowledge, scientific method, and disciplinary autonomy. For Josep Lluís Sert, as for many "urban-minded" architects of his era, urban design was conceived as a venue for the physical design of the city. It was consciously constructed to spatialize the challenges of the modern city in response to planning's increasing interest in public policy and social science.

Equally significant in the mythical origins of urban design over half a century ago was Sert's critique of Beaux-Arts town planning (perceived as culturally reactionary) and ecologically informed regional planning (perceived as irretrievably transcendentalist).[2] While it may be tempting from our historical perspective to find original sin in the Sertian division of labor that conceived urban design, this would be both unfair and too simple. Nevertheless, it might be fair to say that after five decades of urban design, the field is in a state of some crisis.[3]

A part of that crisis might originate in the denial of various other available positions that were neglected in that 1956 formulation of urban design. Among the lines of work Sert and his colleagues abandoned was the strain of ecologically informed modernist city planning informed by the new objectivity and the new science of ecology. Among those planners embodying such a tradition was the German émigré Ludwig Hilberseimer. In the same 1956, Hilberseimer executed the plan for Detroit's Lafayette Park urban renewal public housing project. This alternative history for modernist planning is particularly relevant to our present predicament given the fact that Hilberseimer's theories of urban planning produced among the best examples of modernist public housing in North America. Hilberseimer's planning theories produced a more socially integrated, more ecologically diverse, and more culturally progressive planning project than the canonical projects that would come to embody the aspirations of urban design.

Given our current commitments, the combination of a socially engaged, environmentally informed, and culturally literate planning practice seems promising yet remote. While the perceived failures of modernist planning have been seared into our collective retinas over the past quarter century, there are indications that a tipping point has been reached. The most promising evidence of this is the numerous contemporary histories that critically reconsider modernist urbanism. Often these projects rescue specific agents and subjects from more general guilt by association. They attempt to restate the environmental, communitarian, and cultural aspirations associated with the social project of modernism. While the writing of these histories can only do so much in reconfiguring our current disciplinary commitments, the best of this work promises to reconstruct a useful past for planning, one in which the social, economic, and ecological contexts of design were meaningful and resonant.[4]

This points to another major tradition rendered redundant by Sert's formulation of urban design: the lineage of ecologically informed regional planning extending through the work of Patrick Geddes, Benton MacKaye, Lewis Mumford, and Ian McHarg. While conflating the distinct identities and specific projects of this group does some considerable damage, they shared many aspects of an identifiable intellectual tradition that Sert found fault with. Among those commonalities was a distinct taste for transcendentalist thought, and a concurrent metaphysical reverie in face of the natural world. To the extent that this tradition manifested itself in Ian McHarg's reformulation of landscape architecture as a branch of environmentally informed regional planning, McHarg can be seen to have institutionalized the disciplinary commitments of landscape architecture in the 1960s and '70s. This position has come to stand for an empirically informed planning process dependent upon a robust welfare state for implementation.

For a generation of landscape architects trained as empirical advocates, the McHargian paradigm proved to be a tragic dead end. The McHargian project of rational ecological planning came to be perceived, rightly or not, as ultimately antiurban. It was equally understood as transcendentalist, and therefore anti-intellectual. Ultimately, it also came to be seen as less than pragmatic in the context of the withering of the welfare state, and pathologically dependent upon an anachronistic notion of centralized state planning.[5]

·····

Sadly for many, ironically for some, the recent renewal of landscape's relevance for discussions of contemporary urbanism has little to do with the McHargian project. It has much more to do with an understanding of contemporary design culture. Today the challenges of the design disciplines with respect to the city and the failings of planning have seemingly little to do with the strengths of the McHargian project in empirical knowledge and scientific method. The challenges of our present urban conditions have little to do with lack of information; rather, they have more to do with the political failures of a culture that has largely abandoned welfare state expectations of rational planning. Landscape's newfound relevance for questions of urbanism, rather than originating in the tradition of environmentally informed regional and urban planning, has much more to do with landscape's recent rapprochement with design culture. For many landscape architects trained in the shadow of the 1960s, and who identify as environmental advocates, this has been a disorienting and confusing turn of events. Many of those landscape architects who identified as advocates for nature have been surprised to learn that landscape has newfound relevance for discussions of the city through design agency rather than through public process and rational planning. Ironically, in spite of decades devoted to ecological planning, much of landscape's newfound relevance for contemporary urbanism comes through a particular conflation of design culture, the donor class, and a broad-based populist environmentalism.

In many ways the interests of the landscape architects advocating for landscape as urbanism can be found to have originated within architectural discourse over the past quarter century, as if postmodernism has finally come to landscape.[6] As evidence of this, one could simply cite the formative role that prominent architects have had on those landscape designers. Not surprisingly many of those leading landscape architects began their education in landscape ecology only to have that knowledge catalyzed by architectural theory.[7] The generation of landscape architects and urbanists trained in this way exhibits a tendency to combine several seemingly contradictory uses of ecology. Among the diverse modes for deploying ecological subjects, many contemporary landscape designers deploy ecology as a model of urban forces and flows, as a medium for deferred authorship in design, and as a rhetorical device for public reception and audience participation. They also reserve recourse to the traditional definition of ecology as the scientific study of species in relation to their habitats, but often in service of a larger cultural or design agenda.

In the most intriguing of the projects conceived through this conflation, urban form is given not through planning, policy, or precedent, but through the autonomous self-regulation of emergent ecologies. In many examples the ultimate urban figure is attained not through design but rather through the agency of ecological process directed toward cultural ends. This conflation of ecology as design strategy with ecology as natural science is a source of much confusion in these discussions for urban designers, planners, and environmentalists.[8]

These tendencies were evident within landscape culture as early as the competitions for the grand projects of the 1980s described earlier. This raises a set of interesting questions with respect to the status of urban planning. What was the role of planning in the canonical projects that have come to define landscape's influence on urban design? What has been the role of the planning profession in the conception and implementation of those projects? A brief survey of contemporary landscape design practices internationally offers a provisional thesis: in many instances landscape design strategies precede planning. In many of these projects ecological understandings inform urban order, and design agency propels a process through a complex hybridization of land use, environmental stewardship, public participation, and design culture. Often in these projects a previously extant planning regime is rendered redundant through a design competition, donor bequest, or community consensus. In many of these projects, the landscape architect cum urbanist reconceives the urban field, reordering the economic and the ecological, the social and the cultural, in service of a cultural product. Finally, so goes this thesis, planning rushes into document design, and to manage public relations, legislative process, and community interests in its wake.[9]

If this holds true, what does it suggest for the planning profession? If it is true, the traditional definition of the planner as fair broker setting the ground rules for laissez-faire development may give way to other more complex roles engaging social policy, environmental advocacy, and design culture. The tacit assumption that planning is the medium through which public policy and community participation are brokered in advance of development may be open for debate. Planning's preferred position in advance of the design disciplines may ultimately be at stake. In this formulation the agency of design is invoked over a larger territorial scale as a means of circumventing, short-circuiting, or simply rendering redundant the traditional planning process. What was the role of planning in the canonical projects that have come to define landscape's influence on urban design? What has been the role of the planning profession in the conception and implementation of those projects?

A brief survey of contemporary landscape design practices internationally offers a provisional thesis: in many instances landscape design strategies precede planning. In many of these projects ecological understandings inform urban order, and design agency propels a process through a complex hybridization of land use, environmental stewardship, public participation, and design culture. Often in these projects a previously extant planning regime is rendered redundant through a design competition, donor bequest, or community consensus. In many of these projects, the landscape architect cum urbanist reconceives the urban field, reordering the economic and the ecological, the social and the cultural, in service of a cultural product. Finally, so goes this thesis, planning rushes into document design, and to manage public relations, legislative process, and community interests in its wake.

What then would be the status of planning in the body of putatively canonical landscape urbanist projects to date? As we saw in previous chapters, the early promise of landscape urbanist discourse was buoyed by built work in western Europe. These antecedent projects fit squarely in the national welfare state planning traditions that commissioned them, such as the French *grand projet* for la Villette or the French new town of Melun-Sénart.[10] Both were clearly the manifestation of planning across a variety of scales, and in both projects, their conceptual impact for landscape urbanist discourse had to do with the content of their competition entries, more so than a critique of planning practice per se. Equally, the comparable Spanish projects surrounding Barcelona in the 1980s and the subsequent Dutch projects of the 1990s read as firmly situated in their respective and distinct planning traditions.[11] While landscape emerges as a medium of particular significance in many of these moments, it emerges from a planning structure that predates that interest. Taken together these three examples offer a range of precedents for such projects from the French examples of cultural construction at the national scale, to the expression of planning as a political instrument in post-Franco Catalonia, through the Dutch tradition of national spatial planning for hydrological and transportation infrastructure.

More recently, North American precedents for landscape urbanist practice suggest a very different political economy of planning. The European precedents for landscape urbanism tend to emerge from specific conceptions of the public sector's role in enabling social welfare, regulating environmental standards, subsidizing public transport, and funding the public realm. As evidenced by projects over the past decade in New York, Toronto, and Chicago, among others, contemporary landscape urbanist practice in North America reveals a very different set of relationships to planning. Equally, these most recent examples illustrate a maturing of landscape urbanist practice and a culmination of claims to render urban form correlated to and informed by ecological processes.[12]

. . . . .

A survey of recent city building initiatives in North America's largest urban centers corroborates this reading. In recent years several North American cities have articulated a putative landscape urbanist position through a range of projects. Some of these projects deploy landscape as a medium of planning and only imply the limits of urban form, while others are more explicitly engaged in urban design by describing built form, block structure, and building height and setback in relation to landscape process. In the most legible example, Toronto's waterfront is being reconceived along explicitly landscape urbanist lines. Taken together, recent projects in New York, Chicago, and Toronto represent the emergence of the landscape architect as the urbanist of our age.

The city of New York has been among the most important venues for the development of landscape urbanist practices. Following the election of Michael Bloomberg as mayor in 2002, the city began a decade of landscape-driven urban development projects of international significance. Many of these projects emerged at the landscape urbanist intersection of ecological function, arts philanthropy, and design culture. As we have seen earlier, the competition for the remediation and reconstruction of Fresh Kills landfill on Staten Island offered an early opening to a landscape architect operating at the scale of urban development. While the James Corner Field Operations commission for Fresh Kills Park (2001–present) focused on landscape remediation and ecological function, it is also conceived as a heavily programmed urban space. The park is intended to accommodate ongoing development around the perimeter of its site, while absorbing increasing demands for recreation and tourism. In this early landscape urbanist project the claiming of a park in the public imaginary was as important as the design of a succession process to grow the park over time. In this context, the relatively rare political alignment of Republican leaders in the governor's office in Albany and the mayor's office in New York produced an equally rare project of public patronage for New York's reliably Republican Staten Island.[13]

At a more boutique and pedestrian scale of landscape architecture, yet more directly implicated in urban development and built form, is Field Operation's collaboration with Diller Scofidio + Renfro and Piet Oudolf for The High Line (2004–present) (figures 3.2, 3.3). This project was the result of community organization in opposition to a plan to demolish an abandoned elevated freight rail line cutting through Manhattan's lower west side meatpacking district. While city planners in the previous administration understood the derelict structure to be an impediment to development, the Friends of The High Line advocated successfully for the incoming Bloomberg administration to view it as a potential asset. The Friends funded an international design competition for the site's redevelopment as an elevated landscape promenade, reminiscent of Paris's Promenade Plantée. While the city invested millions of

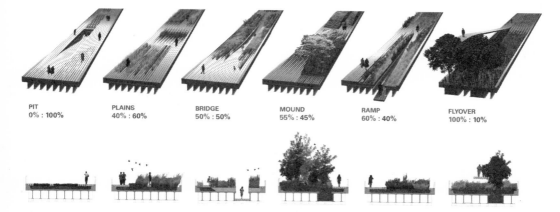

PIT
0% : 100%

PLAINS
40% : 60%

BRIDGE
50% : 50%

MOUND
55% : 45%

RAMP
60% : 40%

FLYOVER
100% : 10%

Figure 3.2 James Corner/Field Operations and Diller Scofidio
+ Renfro, The High Line, New York, landscape typologies,
2004.

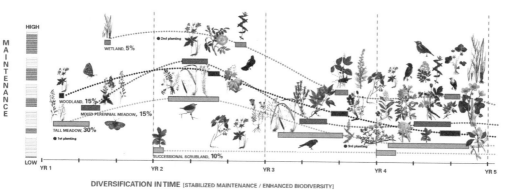

Figure 3.3 James Corner/Field Operations and Diller Scofidio
+ Renfro, The High Line, New York, diagrams of diversity over
time, 2004.

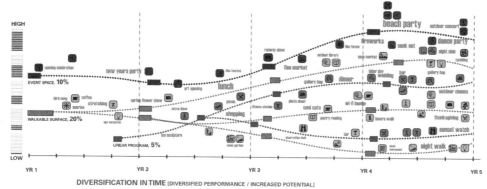

public tax dollars in the design and construction of The High Line, the tax increment return on that funding was reported to be six to one, even through the worst of the economic downturn. While the project can be described as a work of landscape architecture, the urban implications of the project are equally evident, as the intervention has catalyzed urban development and an intensity of activity equal to the densest urban destinations in North America, yet not through traditional urban form, but rather through landscape. The High Line's particular mix of arts and design culture, development, and public space offers a robust argument in favor of the landscape architect as urbanist.[14]

During the past decade New York has also pursued a range of public landscapes through a variety of planning mechanisms. Among these, the project for the East River Waterfront, Ken Smith Workshop with SHoP (2003–present) is notable. Equally notable has been the development of Hudson River Park by Michael Van Valkenburgh Associates (2001–12). Across the East River, Michael Van Valkenburgh Associates' Brooklyn Bridge Park (2003–present) offers a mature work of landscape urbanism, convening community, catalyzing development, and remediating environmental conditions for a newly conceived public realm (figures 3.4, 3.5, 3.6). More recently Adriaan Geuze / West 8's plan for Governors Island (2006–present) portends an equally significant confluence of landscape amenity, ecological enhancement, and urban development.[15]

Chicago offers another example of North American landscape urbanist practice. Mayor Richard M. Daley championed a number of highly visible landscape projects coincident with the rise of landscape urbanist discourse and practice. The earliest of these projects, Millennium Park, was originally designed by Skidmore, Owings & Merrill to offer an on-time, on-budget faux Beaux-Arts public park over the site of a long-abandoned rail yard within Grant Park. Following intervention by several of Chicago's notables advocating on behalf of design culture and the arts, the project evolved into an international destination for design culture. The subsequent hybrid plan juxtaposed the destination landscape of the Lurie Garden by Kathryn Gustafson with Piet Oudolf

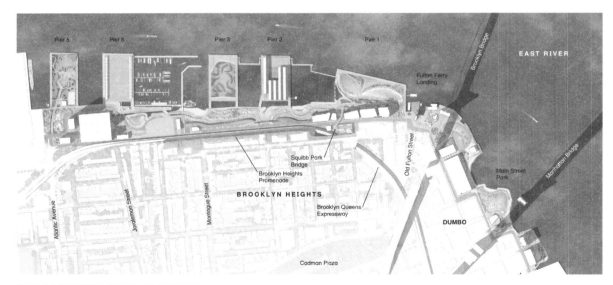

Figure 3.4 Michael Van Valkenburgh Associates,
Brooklyn Bridge Park, New York, site plan, 2014.

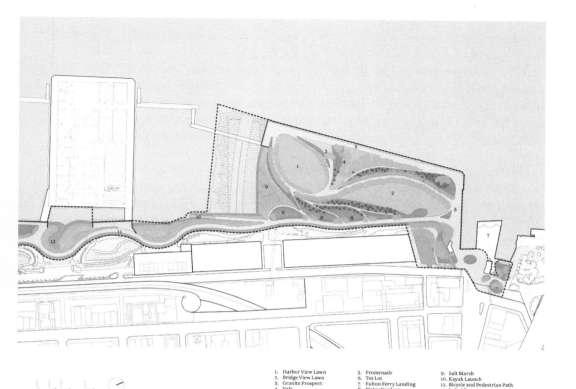

1.	Harbor View Lawn	5.	Promenade	9. Salt Marsh
2.	Bridge View Lawn	6.	Tot Lot	10. Kayak Launch
3.	Granite Prospect	7.	Fulton Ferry Landing	11. Bicycle and Pedestrian Path
4.	Vale	8.	Water Gardens	12. Spiral Ramp

Figure 3.5 Michael Van Valkenburgh Associates,
Brooklyn Bridge Park, New York, plan, 2010.

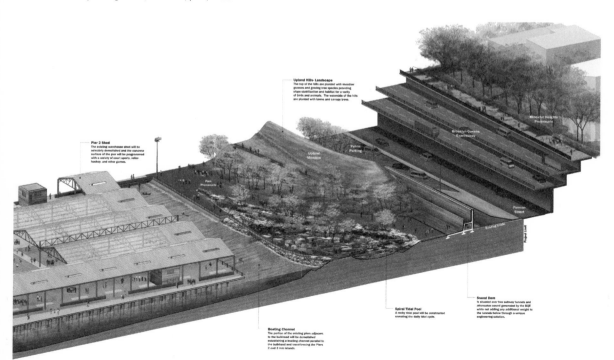

Figure 3.6 Michael Van Valkenburgh Associates,
Brooklyn Bridge Park, New York, isometric site section, 2006.

(2000–2004) with architectural projects by Frank Gehry, Renzo Piano, as well as installations by Anish Kapoor, Jaume Plensa, and others (figures 3.7, 3.8).[16] More recently, Chicago's own abandoned elevated rail line, the Bloomingdale Trail, is being reconceived by Michael Van Valkenburgh Associates (2008–present) as a more equalitarian and diverse equivalent to New York's High Line. Comparable projects for the redevelopment of Chicago's Navy Pier by James Corner Field Operations (2012–present) and Northerly Island by Studio Gang Architects (2010–present) suggest an ongoing commitment to landscape as a medium of the city's public lakefront.

Contemporary Toronto offers perhaps the most legible and robust example of the landscape architect operating as urbanist of our age. The postindustrial waterfront of Canada's most populous city is being redeveloped by Waterfront Toronto, a public crown corporation. Waterfront Toronto has commissioned a cohort of leading landscape architects, including Adriaan Geuze, James Corner,

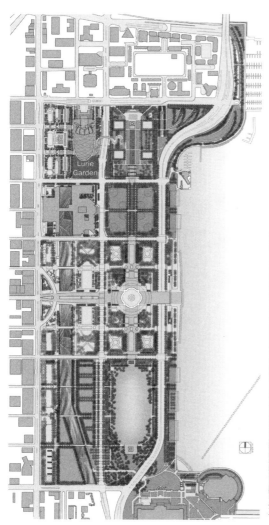

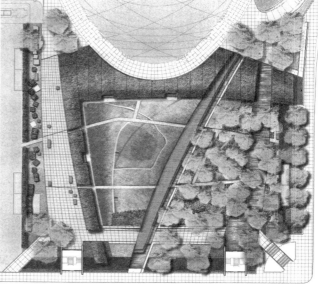

Figure 3.7 Kathryn Gustafson/Gustafson Guthrie Nichol, Lurie Garden, Millennium Park, Chicago, site plan, 2000.

Figure 3.8 Kathryn Gustafson/Gustafson Guthrie Nichol, Lurie Garden, Millennium Park, Chicago, plan, 2000.

and Michael Van Valkenburgh, among others, to shape the redevelopment of the city's waterfront. In these projects the public realm and built form of new urban districts are being specified in relation to the recuperation of the lacustrine and riverine ecologies that shaped the city's growth (figure 3.9). The first such commission was for Adriaan Geuze / West 8 with DTAH for the development of the Central Waterfront (2006–present) (figures 3.10, 3.11, 3.12).[17] Beginning with an explicitly ecological argument for urban form, Geuze's proposal was premiated from among a shortlist of international architects, as the only project that expressed the spatial and cultural implications of fish habitat, zero carbon transit, and spatial legibility. Presently under construction, Geuze's project promises infrastructural continuity, storm-water management, and a renewed cultural image for Toronto. At the eastern end of Geuze's plan, James Corner Field Operations have been commissioned to design a nearly 1,000-acre public park. Lake Ontario Park (2006–present) proposes new recreational amenity and lifestyle landscapes in the context of severely degraded industrial sites as well as several of the most biologically diverse and attractive bird habitats in the region. In between Geuze's Central Waterfront and Corner's Lake Ontario Park, the Lower Don Lands are presently the site of an ongoing development effort led by Michael Van Valkenburgh Associates with Ken Greenberg (2005–present) (figures 3.13, 3.14, 3.15). The project for the Lower Don is the result of an international design competition for the renaturalization of a completely compromised riverine estuary at the mouth of the Don River, and for the development of new neighborhoods housing up to 30,000 residents. This unique program for simultaneously managing flood control, recuperating ecological function, and accommodating urban development offers a clear case study in landscape urbanist practice. While several of the finalist schemes for the Lower Don Lands competition advanced the discourse of landscape urbanism as we have seen previously, the team and scheme assembled by Michael Van Valkenburgh represents the finest example of the integration of built form and landscape process evident in North America today. As such, it embodies the promise of contemporary landscape urbanist practice, in which the landscape architect orchestrates a complex multidisciplinary team of urbanists, architects, ecologists, and other specialists toward the reconciliation of dense, walkable, sustainable communities in relation to diverse, functioning urban ecosystems.[18]

.....

While practices of landscape urbanism have reshaped the planning and development of North American cities, these practices can be found increasingly commonly in cities and cultures around the world. From an international perspective, two tendencies are evident. The first example would be various initiatives that deploy cultural installations as part of a larger program of landscape and infrastructure, including the Bat Yam (Tel Aviv) Biennale of Landscape Urbanism (2007–8), the Toledo ArtNET Public Art Landscape competition (2005–6), and the Syracuse (New York) Cultural Corridor competition (2007–present). Another genre of work deploys landscape strategies as the pretext for a broadly conceived program of water management and economic development. These include Alex Wall and Henri Bava / Agence Ter's Green Metropolis planning proposal for the metropolitan regions spanning the Rhine River (2006–7)

Figure 3.9 Waterfront Toronto, Central Waterfront, East
Bayfront, Lower Don Lands, and Lake Ontario Park, aerial
photomontage, 2007.

Figure 3.10 West 8 and DTAH, Central Waterfront
competition, Toronto, site plan, 2006.

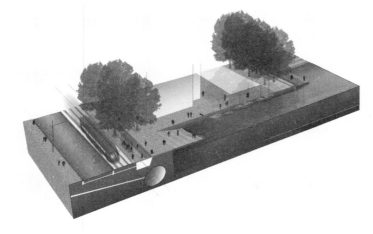

Figure 3.11 West 8 and DTAH, Central Waterfront
competition, Toronto, isometric site section, 2006.

as well as Christopher Hight's recent planning project for the Harris County Regional Water Authority (2007–9) in Houston.[19]

In recent years East Asia has been particularly fecund for the development of landscape urbanist practice. A number of landscape architects have been engaged in a range of projects for cities across the region. Many landscape architects and urbanists have made plans for the redevelopment of Singapore Bay, as well as for the development of landscape strategies in and around Hong Kong. Over the past decade, a range of design competitions for sites in Korea and Taiwan have premiated landscape urbanist strategies for complex urban and environmental problems. On the Chinese mainland, Shenzhen is among the most committed to landscape urbanist projects of city building in recent years.

The design competition for the Longgang Town Center offers an international case study in the contemporary landscape urbanist practices. The urban proposal for Longgang Town Center premiated by the Shenzhen Planning Bureau was the work of a collaborative group from the Architectural Association's Landscape Urbanism unit including Eva Castro and Alfredo Ramirez/Plasma Studio with Eduardo Rico et al./Groundlab (2008–present) (figures 3.16, 3.17, 3.18).[20] In their proposal for Longgang, Castro, Rico, et al., propose a relational digital model through which urban form, block structure, building height, setbacks, and the like are correlated to desirable environmental metrics as outcomes. Rejecting the competition brief's requirement for an enormous physical model, the Groundlab team substituted a dynamic relational or parametric digital model capable of correlating ecological inputs, environmental benchmarks, and development targets through specific formal outcomes. The development of associative or relational digital models is at the forefront of landscape urbanist practice and promises to more precisely calibrate ecological process with the shape of the city. More recently in Shenzhen, the competition for the Qianhai Port City represents an ongoing investment in landscape ecology as a medium through which to articulate the development of the megacity. All three finalist projects by Rem Koolhaas OMA, James Corner Field Operations, and Joan Busquetts proposed to organize the new town of one million residents first

Figure 3.12 West 8 and DTAH, Central Waterfront competition, Toronto, aerial view, 2006.

in relation to the recuperation of ecological function and environmental health in the river tributaries flowing to the sea. The premiated project by James Corner Field Operations (2011–present) and the other two finalist projects give shape and substance to an otherwise unremarkable urban field informed through landscape ecology. In this regard all three finalist projects began from a comparable position relative to the watershed and overall urban morphology, before diverging on the question of how best to order and articulate the urban field itself. This symmetry of approach is remarkable, coming from teams led by an architect, landscape architect, and urban planner, respectively.

What do these practices have in common? Collectively they represent the landscape architect acting as urbanist of our age. Landscape urbanist practices are reconceiving the shape of the city in relation to economic, ecological, and

Figure 3.13 Michael Van Valkenburgh Associates and Ken Greenberg, Lower Don Lands, Toronto, site plan, 2007.

Figure 3.14 Michael Van Valkenburgh Associates and Ken Greenberg, Lower Don Lands, Toronto, plan, 2007.

Figure 3.15 Michael Van Valkenburgh Associates and Ken
Greenberg, Lower Don Lands, Toronto, aerial view, 2007.

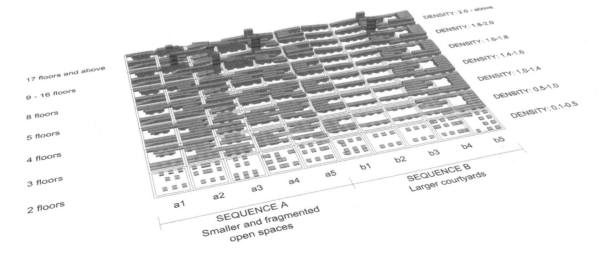

Figure 3.16 Eva Castro and Alfredo Ramirez/Plasma Studio
and Eduardo Rico/Groundlab, Deep Ground, Longgang Town
Center, Shenzhen, International Urban Design competition,
relational urban model, 2008.

infrastructural orders. What might this mean for urban planning? While it is still early in these developments, the fundamental assumption that planning is the medium through which public policy and community participation are brokered may also be open for debate, as in many of these examples design agency and environmental claims precede the traditional planning process. In this regard planning's historically preferred position in advance of design may be at stake.

Contemporary urban practice is often characterized by flexibility and fluidity of professional roles and responsibilities. Most often these projects are the result of complex multidisciplinary teams in which the landscape urbanist plays a formative role at the level of urban strategy. Equally often these projects articulate contemporary forms and scales of urban development in relation to ecological performance and design culture. In this milieu there is no doubt that planning will continue to play a variety of vital roles. Equally, it suggests that these roles and relationships may be fluid over time.

What does this particular formation suggest for the discipline of urban planning? First, it suggests that planning should commit to the reconstruction of its modernist history with the goal of recovering a useful past, one in which social equity, environmental health, and cultural literacy were not mutually exclusive. This implies that the discipline of planning would be well served to revisit the best cases in the history of modernist planning, those in which ecological and social knowledge is applied through, rather than the expense of, the agency of design. Without abandoning their disciplinary identity and core values, planners might be cross-trained to be literate consumers of and commissioners

Figure 3.17 Eva Castro and Alfredo Ramirez/Plasma Studio and Eduardo Rico/Groundlab, Deep Ground, Longgang Town Center, Shenzhen, International Urban Design competition, plan, 2008.

Figure 3.18 Eva Castro and Alfredo Ramirez/Plasma Studio and Eduardo Rico/Groundlab, Deep Ground, Longgang Town Center, Shenzhen, International Urban Design competition, aerial view, 2008.

of design. This corroborates the well-established notion that planners are uniquely positioned to broker the complex entanglements between individual landowners, local community concerns, and collective ecological agendas at the regional scale. While planners will continue to serve as advocates and interlocutors of public participation in design, they might seek to enhance their unique expertise as brokers between real estate markets, the emerging donor class, and design leaders. Planners will continue to be called upon to act as sponsors of and advocates for design. In those cases the planning process will likely continue to precede the agency of the designer. In many other cases however, design process might be found to precede planning. This is particularly true in those contexts where the intersection of landownership, community interest, public policy, and ecological benefit are so completely enmeshed as to render the traditional planning process ineffectual. To respond to that eventuality, planners and the institutions that educate them might benefit from a reevaluation of landscape as a medium for urbanism. This also recommends the critical reconsideration of the best models of modernist planning practice, particularly those that anticipated contemporary interests in landscape as a medium of urbanism. The next several chapters take up that question directly and situate the emergence of landscape urbanism in the economic restructuring associated with the shifts from Fordist to post-Fordist models of industrial economy.

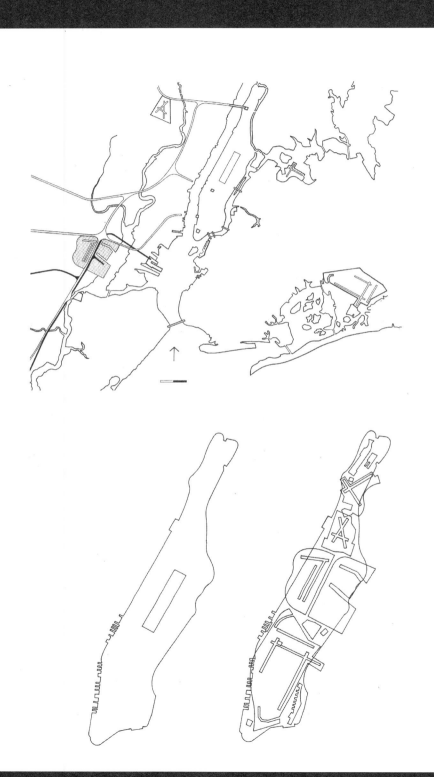

Four: Post-Fordist Economies and Logisitics Landscape

> The dystopia of the megalopolis is already an irreversible historical fact: it has long since installed a new way of life, not to say a new nature.
> —Kenneth Frampton, 1990

Landscape urbanist practices emerged in relation to sites left in the wake of the restructuring of industrial economy. In this regard, landscape has been called on to absorb the shocks of economic restructuring and to insulate urban populations from the worst social and environmental impacts of these transformations. As changes in the industrial economy left previous urban forms redundant in its wake, landscape has been found relevant to remediate, redeem, and reintegrate the subsequent form of development. Rather than a simply stylistic or cultural question, this suggests a structural relationship between landscape as a medium of design and transformations in the industrial economies that underpin processes of urbanization. This chapter repositions landscape urbanist practices in relation to the neoliberal post-Fordist economies that have shaped them.

Cities are historically bound up in, and shaped by, economic processes.[1] Many accounts of the origins of the city in Western culture cite transitions from nomadism to agriculture, a division of labor between agricultural and artisanal, and the accumulation of surplus labor as necessary preconditions for dense human settlement. Equally significant in these accounts are the invention of the money economy, the articulation of banking systems, and the emergence of markets. This complex set of social and economic processes has corollaries in the physical transformation of natural environments into built environments (or indigenous into artificial), the colonization of territories, and the construction of cities. In the West this pattern produced the classical military encampment and trading port, the medieval village, the Enlightenment city, and the industrial metropolis. Recent accounts of the history of urban form in the West have stressed the dependence of settlement patterns on particular forms of exchange. The increasing scale and scope of those patterns of exchange, fueled by liberalized market economies and democratic forms of governance during the Industrial Revolution, produced unprecedented densities in European and American cities simultaneous with unprecedented concentrations of private wealth, social pathologies, and environmental contaminants.

The construction and development of these metropolitan conditions in the late nineteenth and early twentieth centuries depended on systems of transportation and communication that facilitated and fueled their explosive growth in

< Figure 4.1 Alex Wall and Susan Nigra Snyder, Newark Airport and Port Newark–Port Elizabeth superimposed on Manhattan, plan diagram, 1998.

urban form. An early sociologist of that modern city, Georg Simmel, attributed the psychology of the metropolitan experience to the impersonal money economy, anonymous social relations, and the repetitive labor associated with industrialization.[2] For Simmel, the anonymity experienced in the modern metropolis came at the expense of more proximate familial and social relations of the smaller settlements of rural and agrarian life. In the modern era this psychological condition came to be associated with a sense of alienation and loss of personal identity, largely as a result of migrations of rural populations to urban centers. These conditions of human subjective experience were formed in response to industrialization and the growth of the city as a dense collection of diverse populations. This traditional understanding of metropolis is unthinkable absent the migrations, rural and transoceanic, that fueled it with relatively cheap labor.

. . . . .

It has become commonplace within contemporary design culture to associate the metropolitan with this specific form of the industrial city, the subjective psychological conditions of the metropolitan experience persist, outliving the specific physical and spatial arrangements that were associated with it. With the rise of post-Fordist service economies based on information, education, and entertainment, North American cities now find themselves competing for population, not through expanding industrial employment, but rather through the delivery of services, experiences, and quality of life. Increasingly, these intangible quality of life issues form the basis for increasingly flexible employment arrangements.[3]

Rather than a sense of alienation and anonymity, the urban territories constructed in response to these economic and social conditions intend to produce the reassuring familiarity of reliable brands, known commodities, and reproducible routines. As the prosperity of metropolitan regions has come to depend on the attraction of increasingly mobile capital and markets, two tendencies have become evident: the ongoing decentralization of metropolitan urban form, and the identification of themed districts distilling the commodified experiential qualities of the industrial metropolis, without the historical ills attributed to it. These zones, aimed equally at tourist and immigrant alike, constitute much of the contemporary public realm. Among the salient qualities of contemporary metropolitan life in these districts are the collapse of historical distinctions between the tourist class and the immigrant class, between private capital and public space, between culture and commerce, education and entertainment.[4]

The role of contemporary landscape architecture as a scenographic staging for these destination environments for consumption has been well documented.[5] The role of contemporary landscape architecture in the remediation and redemption of abandoned industrial sites left in the wake de-industrialization and disinvestment has been equally well documented.[6] Less attention has been given to the new landscapes necessitated by the growth of logistical networks and their attendant infrastructure.

. . . . .

Geographers have distinguished between three distinct historical configurations of industrial economy: concentrated, decentralized, and distributed.[7] Each of these eras constructed a distinct spatial organization and shaped urban form in particular ways. The shifts between these modes of production are most evident as ruptures in the urban form that preceded them, leaving previous spatial modes obsolete and abandoned in their wake. The first of these shifts, from the dense concentrated industrial model to a decentralized model, took place in the middle of the twentieth century and is closely associated with the decentralization of urban form. It has been described as a shift from an early concentrated Fordism to a mature decentralized Fordism. The second shift, currently underway, is transforming industry from nationally decentralized organizations to an internationally distributed one. The first transition, from a dense urban industrial base to a suburban decentralized one, was characterized by the growth of national highway systems, suburbanization, and the depopulation of many urban centers. Although decentralized from traditional urban centers, national markets and industries characterized this period. The more recent second transition to a global economy could be characterized by its increasing reliance upon international trade and neoliberal economic policies.[8]

As we have seen in chapter 2, David Harvey locates the origins of postmodern cultural tendencies within the larger structural collapse of the Fordist economic regime in the early 1970s.[9] For Harvey, rather than the superficial stylistic concerns of design, the shift to postmodernist tendencies in architecture and urbanism correlate directly to a new regime of what he calls "flexible accumulation" characterized by neoliberal economic policies, just-in-time production, outsourcing, flexible or informal labor arrangements, and increasingly global capital flows.[10] It would be hard to overstate the impact of Harvey's work on architectural discourse over the past fifteen years, as his work has come to stand as among the most durable account of the postmodern cultural condition and its relationship to contemporary urbanism.

Harvey's reading of the economic underpinnings of postmodern cultural conditions has recently been appropriated by the design disciplines, particularly landscape architecture.[11] Harvey's accounts have come to be particularly effective in articulating the relationship between the themed destination environments that have come to be the stock in trade of contemporary urban design and the mass industrial economies of production, consumption, and exchange that enable them.[12] Harvey argues that in the second half of the twentieth century a global restructuring of the industrial economy and the construction of new infrastructures of mobility, communication, and exchange realigned patterns of urbanization across North America.

Harvey's formulation of "flexible accumulation" is intended to describe the new modality of urban consumer culture fed by post-Fordist networks of global integration, flexible labor relations, and neoliberal economic policies. Following the oil shocks of 1973–74 and 1979, the deregulation of many sectors of the US economy indicated a breakdown of the Fordist order of Keynesian welfare state regulation. This period also marked the greatest crisis in industrial economy, with the near collapse of the US automobile industry in the face of growing international competition. The effects of these transformations on urban form are complex and still unfolding. They include the ongoing abandonment of formerly dense, well-capitalized industrial sites, with vestigial populations, those least equipped for mobility, left in the wake. They also include the branding of destination tourism, recreation, and entertainment venues in cities, as well as the ongoing gentrification of particular urban neighborhoods within an increasingly diffuse fabric of the former city.[13]

This shift to a distributed model depends on global systems of transportation, communication, and capital. One aspect of the distributed model has been its reliance upon "just-in-time" production models. Many of these strategies are intended to reduce the overhead costs associated with keeping large inventories of raw materials or parts in advance of their integration into finished goods. Equally these strategies are interested to produce a consumer good at precisely the time when it is purchased, and not before. Both of these tendencies derive from an interest to reduce costs associated with storing on site the raw materials, components, and completed products of industrial production. When combined with competitive global markets for labor, materials, and capital, these tendencies have fueled the internationalization of industrial production.

These tendencies have had three direct consequences. First, it has become commonplace for the components of any industrial process to come together from various locations across the planet, arriving just in time for their integration into a final product that is itself only ordered when sold to the customer. Second, industrial concerns are increasingly interested in storing materials or components of the final assembly in the shipping system or supply chain. Third, the final product itself is shipped out as quickly as possible after manufacture. Taken together, this system places more materials, components, and products in a global shipping system for longer and longer journeys between increasingly remote locations.[14]

The impact of these transformations includes cheaper consumer goods and the entrance of many emerging labor markets into the global economy. It also includes the abandonment of many industrial sites made redundant by these transformations and the construction of new industrial forms increasingly dependent upon global supply chains. Consequently, they have produced a logistics landscape in which more land area is given over to accommodate the shipment, staging, and delivery of shipped goods. This landscape is arguably among the most significant transformations in the built environment since the turn of the century, one that has yet to be fully described or theorized. It is not coincidental that two of the authors who first published on the subject of logistics for audiences in the design disciplines each claimed landscape as having a particular relevance to the subject. Both authors have also contributed in significant ways to the discourse surrounding landscape urbanism. Alejandro Zaera-Polo's 1994 essay, "Order out of Chaos: The Material Organization of Advanced Capitalism," was one of the first attempts to articulate the relationship between otherwise opaque aspects of globalization and their all too visible impacts on urban form.[15] Citing the work of David Harvey as a primary referent, Zaera-Polo's essay attempts to theorize the spatial implications of Harvey's economic analysis. Unfortunately, Zaera-Polo's otherwise serviceable effort is not fully realized, particularly as it takes a perplexing tangent toward a discussion of chaos theory and scientific models for complexity that were fashionable in 1994. Susan Snyder and Alex Wall's 1998 essay, "Emerging Landscapes of Movement and Logistics," offers a much clearer argument that has proven to be more durable over time.[16] As the first essay to deal specifically with the increasing role of logistics within advanced capitalism, the article anticipates the spatial and disciplinary implications for these new conditions and offers an underappreciated argument that helps to structure future lines of work on the topic. This was certainly the case with Wall's subsequent 1999 essay "Programming the Urban Surface," which has come to be regarded as seminal in its anticipation of current discussions of landscape and the material economy of contemporary urban form.[17]

Zaera-Polo and Wall effectively anticipated contemporary interest in the organization of global capital, its flows and forces, as well as the increased relevance for discussions of landscape in the wake of those capital flows. Among the more significant shifts this work implies is the priority afforded to sites of transportation and network infrastructure, the space of the flows of material goods, information, and capital. These sites are privileged in Wall's and Zaera-Polo's accounts and have displaced the sites of material production, which had figured prominently in discussions of urbanism over the previous century. While those sites persist in various states of abandonment, disinvestment, and decay, contemporary interest focuses more fully on the sites of highway infrastructure, intermodal exchange, and logistical staging. Recent scholarship on the topic by Keller Easterling, Neil Brenner, Alan Berger, and Clare Lyster suggests that this remains a productive topic for contemporary urban theory.[18]

Among the clearest example of these sites are the ports that accept, redirect, and stream the contemporary flow of consumer culture. The transition from a Fordist regime of mass consumer goods to a post-Fordist regime of flexible accumulation has witnessed a new scale of port operation, one that has left many historical ports vacant. This transition has also revealed new forms of urbanization. Each of these transformations bears distinct implications for the landscape medium.

·····

In 1956, two fundamental components of a new spatial order associated with logistics were launched, coinciding with the first conference proposing "urban design" at Harvard. The first of those was the US Interstate and Civil Defense Highway System. The second was the standardized shipping container.[19] In 1956, the first such shipping containers left the New York / New Jersey Port Authority bound for the Panama Canal. They were the invention of a North Carolina trucker and shipping innovator, Malcom Purcell McLean. His conception of a single container that could be easily transferred between modes, from ship to train, from train to truck, and back to ship, came to be among the most significant transformative technologies in the shipping industry in the second half of the twentieth century. What had been the backbreaking work of longshoremen and stevedores, the so-called break bulk method of cargo transfer, was replaced with an internationally standardized transfer by crane from the hold of a ship to a tractor trailer in a fraction of the time. This saved much of the time, expense, and inefficiency associated with the individual transfer of countless items from a ship to the port docks, to a warehouse, and into individual train cars or trucks.[20]

Figure 4.2 Alan Berger, Port of Los Angeles/Long Beach,
Long Beach, California, aerial photograph, 2003.

Figure 4.3 Alan Berger, Alliance Airport and Free Trade Zone,
Alliance, Texas, aerial photograph, 2003.

In place of that ancient model of port activity, McLean's new container afforded a more or less seamless continuity from point to point, regardless of mode. This innovation greatly sped port operations, increased volumes, decreased costs, and drastically cut the time required for international shipping. This newfound ease of transfer opened international markets for consumer goods deeper into foreign continents and shaved the friction costs associated with getting them there. It also eased the identification and security of goods, reduced pilferage, and ultimately changed the culture of port operations. It had equally profound impacts on the size, organization, and spatiality of ports, effectively accelerating the growth of East and West Coast superports.[21] The Port of Los Angeles/Long Beach, California, is representative of these tendencies (figure 4.2). This superport includes an onsite Foreign Trade Zone (FTZ), established in 1994. The Los Angeles/Long Beach FTZ comprises about 2,700 acres including warehousing facilities compatible with global distribution and shipping operations. The United States has over 230 such FTZs in fifty states.

The shipping container also greatly accelerated the growth of interstate trucking as the primary means of connecting East and West Coast seaports with inland markets and sources. It increased efficiency as well as the size and number of ships. The new economies of scale attendant to international shipping through the use of standardized shipping containers led to the development in the United States of new inland ports serviced by private international airports, typically surrounded by new industrial parks within foreign trade zones, for example, as found in Alliance, Texas (figure 4.3). The Fort Worth Alliance Airport is an 11,600-acre, master-planned, international trade and logistics complex built for handling new, globalized, flexible manufacturing and distribution. It is a 100 percent industrial airport, including intermodal hub facilities and status as a Triple Freeport Inventory Tax Exemption and Foreign Trade Zone. This new mode of inland airport and logistical operations facility facilitated the development of free trade routes within North America under the North American Free Trade Agreement (NAFTA). It also played a significant role in the articulation of border town industrial networks such as along the US-Mexico border in Texas and California. In addition to putting untold numbers of longshoremen out of work, the shipping container and the practices it privileged effectively hastened the demise of many older, smaller ports that the new system found inefficient, inconvenient, or simply unnecessary. This was particularly the case with ports in traditional city harbors or waterfronts that lacked the necessary space for expansion in the new era. Equally, it hastened the redundancy of ports that lacked the necessary capital-intensive investment in new technologies. It also facilitated the demise of ports that were left in cities where populations had long ago dispersed.

In response to the redundancy of old ports these practices hastened, many former port sites were redeveloped internationally. Among the approaches evident is a specific line of work by landscape architects. At the port of Qianhai in Shenzhen, an international design competition won by James Corner Field Operations accommodates a million residents in a new urban center, built over the site of what had been the new port of Shenzhen, constructed only a decade prior (figures 4.4, 4.5). In Amsterdam Harbor, the master planning work of Frits

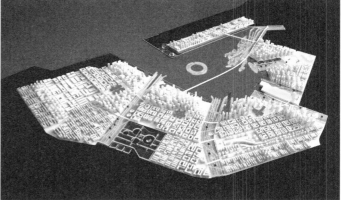

Figure 4.4 James Corner/Field Operations, Qianhai Water City, Shenzhen, site plan, 2010.

Figure 4.5 James Corner/Field Operations, Qianhai Water City, Shenzhen, model, 2010.

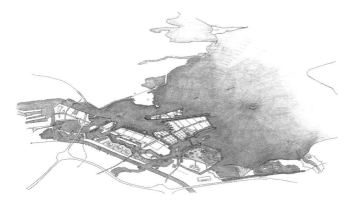

Figure 4.6 Frits Palmboom/Palmbout Urban Landscape, Ijburg, Amsterdam, sketch plan, 1995.

Figure 4.7 Frits Palmboom/Palmbout Urban Landscape, Ijburg, Amsterdam, model, 1995.

Palmboom and Jaap van den Bout of Palmbout Urban Landscapes (figures 4.6, 4.7) paralleled the development of the Borneo and Sporenburg docks as a residential district in the Eastern Harbor District by Adriaan Geuze/West 8 (figure 4.8).[22] West 8's project for Borneo/Sporenburg represents an antecedent to contemporary landscape urbanist practice in which the landscape architect is made responsible for not only ecological function, but equally for built form. In the Dutch planning tradition, this leadership role was historically unremarkable, as landscape architects have often played such a leadership role. West 8's work in Amsterdam Harbor prefigured and in some ways enabled their broader project for the reconceptualization of Toronto's central waterfront a decade later.

As we saw in the previous chapter, redundant port sites have been central to the development of mature landscape urbanist practices internationally. Beginning with a range of canonical projects in western Europe, these practices have now been embodied through waterfront redevelopment projects in North America and East Asia, led by landscape architects responsible for the block structure, building envelope, and built form profile of the contemporary city. These factors had enormous consequences for shipping, ports, and cities across the Great Lakes in particular. Shipping historically had made the long journey up the Saint Lawrence River from the North Atlantic, into the interior of the continent through the Great Lakes and the complex system of locks forming the Saint Lawrence Seaway. This added significantly to the length of any international shipping. Thus, among many other forces, the shipping container and the new era of supercontainer ships hastened the redundancy of many ports in the region. In the older economy of break bulk loading and unloading, the extra length of voyage was compensated by the fact that unloading and warehousing occurred at or near the final market for many goods. In the new era of standardized shipping containers, it was much more efficient to simply transfer containers at East Coast ports to train or truck for the remainder of their journey to interior destinations. The easy transfer from ship to train or

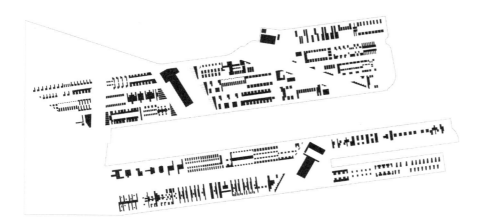

Figure 4.8 Adriaan Geuze/West 8, Borneo and Sporenburg, Amsterdam Harbor, figure-ground diagram, 1993–96.

truck with one or two crane operations consolidated the industry into a smaller number of larger ports, while simultaneously feeding trucks and trains to increasingly decentralized markets far from traditional city centers. It also necessitated the development of so-called intermodal sites, for the orderly transfer of containers from one mode of transport to another, such as train to truck or vice versa. This new model of intermodal freight and logistics facilities can be found just outside the largest US metropolitan areas, including New Rochelle, Illinois, and Midlothian, Texas. The Midlothian Railport in Midlothian, Texas, serves as an intermodal logistical support facility incorporating train-truck intermodal connections and its own electrical plant.

·····

The contemporary postindustrial economic regime as described by Harvey, its attendant infrastructures, and the new social relations they afford, also manifest themselves in the built environment as landscapes of infrastructure and logistics. These logistical zones are hardly recognizable as city forms yet produce and provide a base for the economic activity that supports contemporary urban development.[23]

In the context of the post-Fordist economic era, landscape has been found uniquely useful in addressing the vacancy and toxicity of former industrial sites abandoned as production moves offshore. The inverse of those postindustrial brownfields, the sites that capital continues to flow through, "irrigated" with new potentials and economies, have received less critical attention in discussions of contemporary landscape, yet they are equally helpful in clarifying the relations between industrial economy and urban form. In this sense, logistics landscapes might be profitably thought about as the inverse of the abandoned postindustrial brownfield site. Both are the result of global economic restructuring, and both are more legible as forms of landscape than as either urban or architectural forms. Some theorists have proposed these contemporary economic networks and their infrastructures as capable of offering symbolic meaning to spatial forms in times of indistinguishable "generic" urban landscapes.[24] When revealed to their public constituents, infrastructural networks make a connection between provision and consumption, use and neglect, waste and conservation, on an everyday scale and on a monumental region-wide experience. Rather than a marginal absence, vacancy, or undervalued void, these surfaces are among the most productive, efficient, and specific, albeit generic and reproducible, of places. These landscapes, the spaces of the new logistics economy, are designed and built. Rather than being the unconscious by-product of economic development or the unconsidered remnants of preceding generations of inhabitation, these landscapes are among the most engineered and optimized of spaces.

The potential for these spaces of infrastructure and logistics to stage and stimulate urban activity has been explored in a spate of projects that informed the emergence of landscape urbanist practices from just before the turn of the century. Adriaan Geuze / West 8's 1991 Schouwburgplein (Theater Square) in Rotterdam leveraged that city's status as global shipping hub to transform an undercultivated corner of the Theater District into a highly programmed urban surface. At Schouwburgplein West 8's operable interactive lighting towers recall

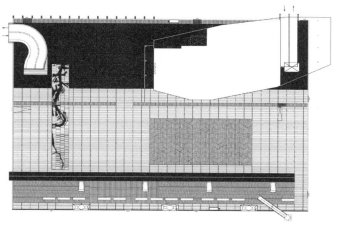

Figure 4.9 Adriaan Geuze/West 8, Schouwburgplein,
Rotterdam, plan, 1991–96.

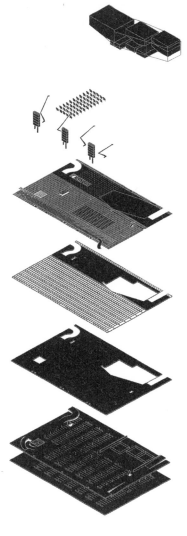

Figure 4.10 Adriaan Geuze/West 8, Schouwburgplein,
Rotterdam, isometric diagram of layers, 1991–96.

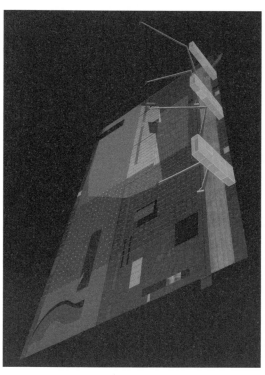

Figure 4.11 Adriaan Geuze/West 8, Schouwburgplein,
Rotterdam, aerial view, 1991–96.

the port's enormous shipping cranes while the thickened two-dimensional surface of the square itself anticipates and enables a range of public programs over the subterranean parking deck below (figures 4.9, 4.10, 4.11).

As we saw previously, Stan Allen's interest in the thick two-dimensional programmed surface was evident in his 1996 proposal for the Logistical Activities Zone in Barcelona (figure 4.12). In this project for the conversion of the old port made redundant by increasing scale in shipping, Allen borrows concepts and diagrams from landscape ecology, most notably from Richard Forman's concepts of patch, corridor, matrix, and mosaic. Allen's proposal embodies the improbable intersection of Tschumi's interest in event with Forman's diagrams of ecological structure. Another comparable project would be James Corner's 1996 proposal for the reanimation of Greenport, Long Island's redundant harborfront (figure 4.13). In this competition-winning yet ultimately unrealized proposal, Corner imagines the derelict harborfront of a former fishing village as destination entertainment and event surface orchestrating a choreography of spectacle and event. Finally, as we will see in chapter 7, Andrea Branzi's master plan for the Strijp Philips district in Eindhoven (1999–2000) developed comparable interest in the thickened two-dimensional surface of landscape below a generalized repetitive infrastructural array. Branzi's Strijp Philips proposal generalizes from the logic of the contemporary logistics landscape and extrapolates from that origin to produce a postutopian image of a "territory for the new economy" (figures 4.14, 4.15, 4.16).[25]

As a provisional schema, the following accounts describe three emergent categories of logistics landscape: distribution and delivery, consumption and convenience, and accommodation and disposal. Each of these provisional categories implies a range of landscape types that are themselves the subject of the representations and descriptions included here. These cases are by no means exhaustive, nor even completely contextualized. Rather, they pose an initial introduction and multiple lines of future research into the specifics of each logistical mechanism and corresponding landscape type.

.....

Distribution and delivery refer to the basic functions of the supply chain, fundamental infrastructure, and organizational ideology of the new economy. They are among the first and most ubiquitous material activities of the new economy. Easy access to international intermodal transportation networks and the communication infrastructures that enable them has become a central assumption of the new economy.[26] Ports and telecommunications networks occupy privileged positions in this new organization, with international aviation and cell phone networks enjoying explosive growth following deregulation of a formerly Keynesian welfare state system of control. Following deregulation, airports and cell phone networks grew rapidly and have come to serve as fundamental transportation and communication networks in the post-Fordist economy of logistics and distribution.

The speed and surety of a global distribution system has fostered larger economies of scale in the selling of consumer goods, as evidenced by the phenomenon of the big-box retail store. More significant than the size and shape of these retail outlets are the vast digital infrastructures of communication and

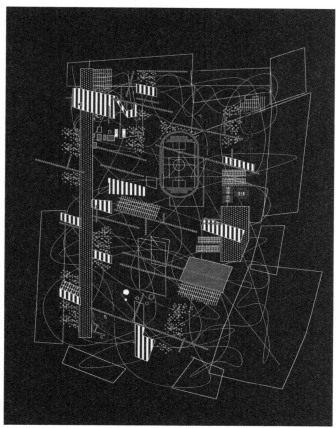

Figure 4.12 Stan Allen, Logistical Activities Zone, Barcelona,
plan diagram, 1996.

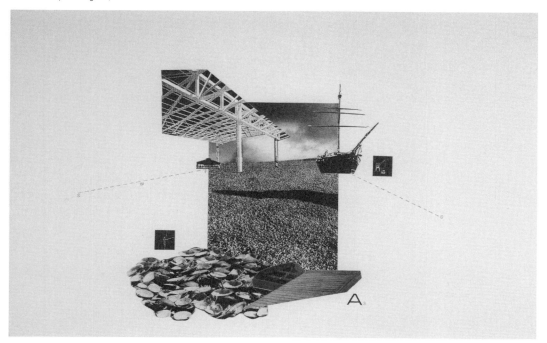

Figure 4.13 James Corner, Greenport Harborfront, Long
Island, New York, ideogram montage, 1996.

Figure 4.14 Andrea Branzi, Lapo Lani, and Ernesto Bartolini,
Masterplan Strijp Philips, Eindhoven, model, 1999–2000.

Figure 4.15 Andrea Branzi, Lapo Lani, and Ernesto Bartolini,
Masterplan Strijp Philips, Eindhoven, model, 1999–2000.

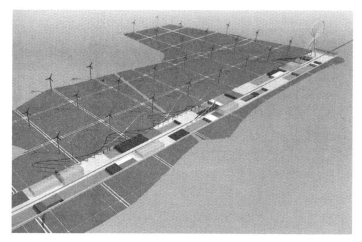

Figure 4.16 Andrea Branzi, Lapo Lani, and Ernesto Bartolini,
Masterplan Strijp Philips, Eindhoven, aerial view, 1999–2000.

control that facilitate their existence. Among the clearest of these systems is the symbiotic partnership between Dell Computer and United Parcel Service (UPS). Dell and UPS have integrated operations to effectively deliver parts from Dell suppliers just in time to the Dell factories producing computers. These completed consumer goods are then shipped through UPS with components of a consumer's order being streamed together mid-shipment. Often UPS stores one component, say monitors, at its own warehouses near major markets, bringing them together with the computers they are sold with just prior to delivery. This pushing of material and inventory up into the supply chain shortens waiting and production times, reduces costs, and effectively outsources much of the warehousing functions into the distribution chain itself and onto public infrastructure. This parallels a broader trend to reclassify what had historically been understood as costs of production, into "externalities" to be offloaded onto the consumer, a supplier, a strategic partner, or the public sector. One aspect of this transformation has been increased demand for public investment in transportation infrastructure. Another aspect of this trend has seen companies shifting the costs associated with their buildings and grounds from capital assets to considering them as annual operating expenses. This shift, implicit in the concept of treating overhead costs as externalities, has the effect of rendering formerly valuable buildings and grounds semidisposable. The corollary, of course, is that these semidisposable buildings and grounds require less of an initial capital investment in construction as they are considered only an ongoing annual expense that can be written off and abandoned at any moment. This trend has equal impact on reducing the investment made in design services attendant to those buildings and grounds. Wal-Mart and Home Depot are illustrative of many of these trends and have become basic building blocks of the new posturban consumer landscape. While most critiques of this form of development regard it as chaotic, without order, or even unplanned, these spaces are highly engineered and continually reconfigured around shifting organizations of capital and material.

·····

Consumption and convenience represent the easy abundance and cheap calories of strip retail urbanism and the fast-food culture it is organized to serve. The economies that fuel retail development of this sort depend upon enormous, unseen off-site operations of resource extraction, harvesting, and staging that are embedded in natural environments. These often-out-of-site operations afford "standing reserve" for the ready appearance of consumable products into the supply chain. The convenience of this environment is organized around the ready, cheap availability of a verifiable and reproducible product. *Economist* magazine has developed its own "Big Mac index" as a global cost-of-living index, arguing that the Big Mac aspires to be a global commodity, available at once, every way, for all, and that the price difference between this integer of fast-food retail consumption in various markets is a telling indicator of the general cost of living differential.[27]

The logistics landscapes that organize natural resources for this convenience are themselves organized around transportation infrastructure: highways in the case of beef, and the vast prairie feed lots in which the beef is fattened while still in cow form. While the cows carrying that beef may begin life in any number of US locations, they will inevitably converge by truck and train upon the enormous feedlots of the central plains of Oklahoma, Nebraska, Kansas, and Iowa. The corn-based agricultural economy of Iowa offers a case study in the industrialization of a formerly natural process. What appears to the naked eye as a carbon-fixing economy transforming sunlight into sugar is in reality a petroleum economy whose economies of scale depend completely on unsustainable agricultural practices. This ironic condition has led to the recent conundrum expressed by Michael Pollan that one is increasingly left to choose between foods that are organic, yet come from enormous distances and produce negative environmental consequences, and food that is not organic per se, but is grown locally.[28]

The retail fronts of the global food supply chain, the locations where the various agriculturally derived and preprocessed products converge, whether it is McDonald's or Whole Foods, is primarily conceived as a speculative real estate investment. As such, it depends on the generic, universal availability of its commodities and functions as an anchor tenant to strip development surrounding it. The spatial organization of McDonald's restaurants within new strip developments, the distribution of organic foods to retail outlets, and the "malling" of retail space itself as a speculative real estate investment by Real Estate Investment Trusts (REITs) are all examples of these conditions.

·····

Accommodation and disposal describe the staging, storage, and disposition of the increasingly short-lived consumer goods that constitute much of the contents of the logistics networks described here. Like fast food, these consumer goods begin life as embedded energy and raw materials harvested at industrial scales across the country. The attendant networks of industrial softwood lumber harvesting and replanting are essentially agricultural operations, feeding an insatiable demand for the raw material of housing. The interlocking networks of manufactured housing plants, industrially managed forest farms, and land for manufactured housing communities reveal much about this economy dependent upon ease of mobility and economies of distribution.

The off-site corollary to our expanding houses and appetites for consumer consumption is the by-now-ubiquitous self-storage facility. Accommodating the excesses of our affluence in a sort of purgatory for impulse purchases and outdated models, these highly profitable yet temporary ghost towns occupy the periphery of every major market. They have come to be quite effective low-cost markers of low-stakes development, allowing REITs to cover costs of land acquisition and maintenance while waiting for newly urbanizing areas to increase in land value. These installations converge on the same easy access to regional transportation infrastructure and low-cost land that draw retail strip malls, McDonald's, Home Depot, and Wal-Mart. Each of them depends equally upon access to public high-speed highways providing access for both consumer goods and consumers themselves. This can be understood as off-loading transportation costs from producers to consumers, as more Americans spend more time driving longer distances to regional big-box stores. Of course the end of this food chain is equally significant here, that is, the disposal of the waste streams of contemporary consumer culture. As the volume of this waste increases, as the waste originates at residential locations spread farther and farther across the urbanized region, as the waste travels farther distances to its accommodation in landfills, incinerators, or other dumps, more and more trash is spending more and more time on the road. This suggests that not only are the raw materials, consumer products, and consumers themselves dependent upon networks of distribution and communication, but also that the ultimate disposal of those materials and products are equally and increasingly dependent upon them.

While much of the landscape, and the logistics that organize it, is shaped by speculative capital, private interests, and individual choices, the environment that landscape produces is, for better and worse, the contemporary North American urban realm. In the context of recent discourse around a putatively "planetary urbanization," it is arguably the global realm as well. By describing this logistics landscape in spatial and economic terms, it may be possible to apprehend the forms that it takes, to anticipate the priorities that it pursues, to understand the hyper-rationality behind its seemingly unconscious construction, and to acknowledge our embeddedness in the culture it represents. The case of logistics infrastructure also reinforces the role of landscape in relation to the cultural conditions of advanced capital. This is a topic that will be developed further in the following chapter, specifically in relation to the origin of landscape as a cultural category in the wake of urban abandonment, depopulation, and decay.

Five: Urban Crisis and the Origins of Landscape

> Landscape in the West was itself a symptom of modern loss, a cultural form that emerged only after humanity's primal relationship to nature had been disrupted by urbanism, commerce, and technology.
> —Christopher Wood, 1993

Landscape is a medium structurally related to transformations in the spatial manifestation of particular economic orders. Rather than the autonomous expression of cultural forces, or the stylistic concerns of taste culture, landscape urbanist practices emerged directly in response to structural transformations in the industrial economy of urbanization. Among the more legible cases in this relationship is the emergence of landscape as a medium of design in the context of the postindustrial social and environmental crises associated with shrinking cities.

At the turn of the twentieth century, as the claims of landscape as urbanism were first manifest, at least seventy urban centers in the United States were engaged in an ongoing processes of abandonment, disinvestment, and decay. The scale and scope of these conditions raise fundamental and timely questions for those engaged in the urban arts and allied design disciplines concerned with the contemporary city.[1] Limits to the inevitability of growth implied in the urban disciplines also raise questions regarding the relations between the design professions. The limits of growth raise fundamental questions about the historical formation and current commitments of architecture, urban design, and planning. The origins and epistemologies of the design disciplines reveal foundational ideological investments in models of growth, expansion, and ongoing development. Architecture plays a particularly significant role here as the ur-discipline of the urban arts, as the field's professional identity has been bound up in an ideology dependent on ongoing growth. This professional bias in favor of architecture as the progenitor of urbanism produces an ideological blind spot as urban decline, decay, or demise are rendered meaningless through an inability to conceive of them.

The French philosopher Michel de Certeau has referred to this disciplinary blind spot as a professionally constructed inability to articulate the conditions outside the limits of one's sphere of action. In a chapter of *The Practice of Everyday Life* titled "The Unnamable," Certeau describes the medical profession's inability to think beyond its ostensible object of study: "The dying man falls outside the thinkable, which is identified with what one can do. In leaving the field circumscribed by the possibilities of treatment, it enters a region of meaninglessness."[2]

This condition of professionally constructed meaninglessness is particularly evident in the inability of architecture to offer meaningful frameworks for describing or intervening upon the city in the context of urban abandonment, disinvestment, and decay. Over the past decade this inability to imagine the end of growth has fueled a range of alternative or critical discourses in the design disciplines responsible for the city. Among them, the contemporary discourse around so-called shrinking cities has emerged as particularly relevant and timely.[3] The more recent formulation of the "formerly urban" promises to augment and extend that discourse with particular relevance for a range of disciplinary formations and cultural conditions attendant to contemporary urbanism in North America. In this context, Detroit has emerged as an international exemplar of the decentralization, dispersal, and decay of the dying postindustrial city.[4]

.....

In the second half of the twentieth century, the city of Detroit—once the fourth-largest city in the United States—lost over half its population (figure 5.2). The Motor City, synonymous with the automobile industry, began a process of decentralization as early as the 1920s, catalyzed by Henry Ford's decision to relocate production outside the city. While similar conditions can be found in virtually every industrial city in North America, Detroit recommends itself

1916

1950

1960

1994

Figure 5.2 Richard Plunz, Detroit figure-ground plan diagrams, 1996.

as the clearest, most legible example of these trends evidenced in the spatial and social conditions of the postwar American city.

In August 1990, Detroit's City Planning Commission authored a remarkable and virtually unprecedented report.[5] This immodest document proposed the decommissioning and abandonment of the most vacant areas of what had been one of the most prosperous cities in the United States. With the publication of the Detroit Vacant Land Survey, Detroit's city planners documented a process of depopulation and disinvestment that had been under way since the 1950s. With an incendiary 1993 press release based on the City Planning Commission's recommendations from the 1990 report, the city ombudsman, Marie Farrell-Donaldson, publicly called for the discontinuation of services to, and the relocation of vestigial populations from, the most vacant portions of the city: "The city's ombudsman ... is essentially suggesting that the most blighted bits of the city should be closed down. Residents would be relocated from dying areas to those that still had life in them. The empty houses would be demolished and empty areas fenced off; they would either be landscaped, or allowed to return to 'nature.'"[6]

What was remarkable about the 1990 Detroit Vacant Land Survey was its unsentimental and surprisingly clear-sighted acknowledgment of a process of postindustrial de-densification that continues to this day in cities produced by modern industrialization. Equally striking was how quickly the report's recommendations were angrily dismissed in spite of the fact that they corroborated a practice of urban erasure that was already well under way. Also remarkable about the Detroit Vacant Land Survey and the city of Detroit's plan to

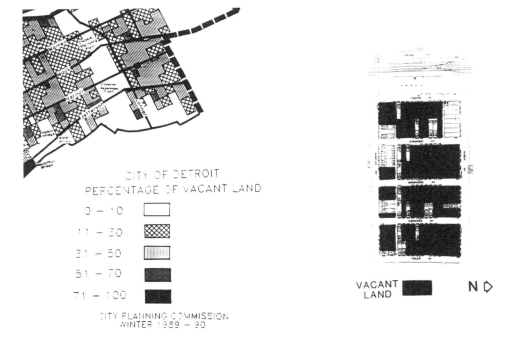

CITY OF DETROIT
PERCENTAGE OF VACANT LAND

0 – 10
11 – 30
31 – 50
51 – 70
71 – 100

CITY PLANNING COMMISSION
WINTER 1989 – 90

VACANT LAND   N ▷

Figure 5.3 Survey and Recommendations Regarding Vacant Land in the City, City of Detroit, Detroit Planning Commission, August 24, 1990.

decommission parts of itself was not its impossibility but rather the simple fact that it dared to articulate for public consumption the idea that the city was already abandoning itself. In a graphically spare document featuring maps blacked out with marker to indicate areas of vacant land, Detroit's planners rendered an image of a previously unimaginable urbanism of erasure that was already a material fact (figure 5.3).

. . . . .

"One last question must now be asked: during a crisis period, will the demolition of cities replace the major public works of traditional politics? If so, it would no longer be possible to distinguish between the nature of recessions (economic, industrial) and the nature of war."[7] Over the course of the 1990s, the city of Detroit lost approximately 1 percent of its housing stock annually to arson, primarily due to Devil's Night vandalism. Publicly, the city administration decried this astonishingly direct and specific critique of the city's rapidly deteriorating social conditions. Simultaneously, the city privately corroborated the arsonists' illegal intent by developing, funding, and implementing one of the largest and most sweeping demolition programs in the history of American urbanism. This program continued throughout the '90s, largely supported by the city's real estate, business, and civic communities. This curious arrangement allowed both the disenfranchised and the propertied interests to publicly blame each other for the city's problems while providing a legal and economic framework within which to carry out an ongoing process of urban erasure. Vast portions of Detroit were erased through this combination of unsanctioned burning and subsequently legitimized demolition. The combined impact of these two activities, each deemed illicit by differing interests, was to coordinate the public display of social unrest with administration attempts to erase the visual residue of Detroit's ongoing demise.

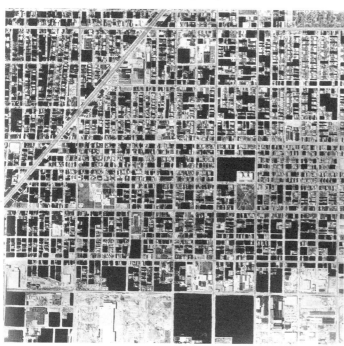

Figure 5.4 Dan Hoffman, *Erasing Detroit*, 1991.

For the architectural profession, the city of Detroit in the '90s entered a condition of meaninglessness because it no longer required the techniques of growth and development that had become the modus operandi of the discipline. Without the need for these tools, Detroit became a "nonsite" for the architect in the same sense that Certeau's dead body ceased to operate as a "site" for the physician's attention. As the city decommissioned itself, it entered a condition that could not be thought by the architectural and planning disciplines. As Dan Hoffman put it, in the early '90s "unbuilding surpassed building as the city's primary architectural activity"[8] (figure 5.4).

In spite of decade-long attempts to "revitalize" the city with the construction of theaters, sports stadiums, casinos, and other publicly subsidized, privately owned, for-profit destination entertainment, Detroit continued to lose population and building stock (figure 5.5). In spite of a massive federally funded advertising campaign and a small army of census takers, the 2000 census showed Detroit's population continuing to shrink. More recently, the city was the largest in US history to declare bankruptcy. As such, Detroit offers one of the more legible examples of conditions that can be found throughout the contemporary urban world in the context of advanced capital.

Reconsidering the "formerly urban" as a unique framework for thought suggests the need to develop models, cases, theories, and practices for these sites and subjects. It also recommends the requisite disciplinary and professional realignments implied in the topic. Among these, architecture as the building block of the traditional city finds itself incapable of responding in the wake of the decreased density and friction of social interaction, the increased horizontality and dispersion of urban events, and the attenuation and deterioration of building fabric as the traditional city recedes. As building

Figure 5.5 Alex MacLean, Brush Park, Detroit, aerial photograph, ca. 1990.

fabric, street wall, and traditional public space recede as the primary determinants of urban order, landscape emerges as uniquely capable of restoring some form of spatial or social order. For this reason, for many across a range of disciplines the medium of landscape has emerged as uniquely suited to the description of and intervention in the formerly urban. As we will see bound up in the very origins of landscape, it offers a cultural milieu and medium of design equally at ease with natural succession and cultivation, existing description, and new intervention. In this regard, landscape has emerged in recent years as offering a new disciplinary framework for approaching sites of the formerly urban.

•••••

It has been long established that landscape as a cultural form emerged at the same moment in two of the most urban, densely settled, and economically developed regions in western Europe.[9] Landscape is by definition an urban cultural construct, necessarily dependent on a complex division of labor and mature markets for cultural production and consumption. It has equally been established that landscape emerged in the West as a genre of painting and theatrical arts, well before it was adopted as a way of seeing or mode of subjectivity and long before it became concerned with physical interventions in the built or natural environment.

While there is a vigorous ongoing debate as to the first paintings to be considered landscapes, the first written reference to landscape was in a 1521 record of a Venetian collection containing several Flemish paintings.[10] As a product of highly evolved mercantile economies, landscape painting emerged in the context of the Italian Renaissance, nearly a century prior to its first usage in English, as an embodiment of ornamental work devoted to the elaborate depiction of backgrounds. In so doing, landscape paintings allowed for the representation of technical virtuosity and distinction of the artistic capability of individual painters. This development of the painted background as evidence of the painterly mastery of a particular artist formed a necessary precondition for the acquisition of status value and enhanced exchange value of the painting as a commodity.[11]

The very origins of landscape have equally been informed by and are historically bound up with the depopulation, abandonment, and decay of previously urbanized territories. Rather than a recent topic of limited scope or marginal value, landscape's engagement with urban abandonment has a long history, one that goes directly to the origins of landscape as a cultural form in the West. This rereading of the history of landscape has the potential to reposition contemporary debates on landscape as a medium of urban order, particularly in the context of ongoing urban and economic restructuring, globally.

In his canonical essay "The Word Itself," J. B. Jackson described the etymology of "landscape" in the English language. Jackson found that "a landscape is a 'portion of land which the eye can comprehend at a glance.' Actually when it was first introduced ... into English it did not mean the view itself, it meant a picture of it."[12] The Oxford English Dictionary corroborates Jackson's account with an early seventeenth-century reference to landscape as a "picture representing natural inland scenery, as distinguished from a sea picture, a portrait, etc." It was over a century later, in 1725, before a second definition had emerged, in which landscape had become a "view or prospect of natural inland scenery, such as can be taken in at a glance from one point of view; a piece of country scenery."[13] In this sequence of events, landscape emerged as a genre of painting first, and only a century later came to refer to a view comparable to those found in painting. Through this account, landscape becomes a way of seeing, or mode of subjectivity informed by the production and consumption of painterly images. Only from this origin can one refer to landscape in the English language as having to do with the ground itself, as seen in a particular way, and ultimately as something to be done to that ground.

By the beginning of the sixteenth century, landscape had been established in the English language as a genre of painting imported from the continent. By the seventeenth century, landscape in English migrated from a genre of painting and stage decoration into a way of seeing the world or a mode of subjectivity associated with the tour. By the eighteenth century, landscape in English had come to refer to the land looked at in this way. And by the nineteenth century, it could be used to describe the activity of refashioning the land so as to allow it to be looked at as if it were a painting. In this way, the emergence of landscape in English was to a great extent formed by the depiction of the formerly urban.

·····

In the long cultural history of the formerly urban, Rome must surely be among the most significant examples available in the West. While both Detroit and Rome lost over a million residents, Detroit lost more than 50 percent of its population over just half a century. Rome lost more than 95 percent of its population over a millennium. During this time, what had been the former capital of much of the ancient world devolved into lawless wilderness before being reordered through landscape into a formerly urban interior hinterland of cultivation and succession. The city that had been host to over a million citizens at the height of its empire slumped into several centuries of decline and decay without benefit of a census. By the time the population was recorded again in the ninth century, the city's population had collapsed to less than 5 percent of its second-century peak. At its nadir, what was left of the capital was barely a medieval village clustered along the banks of the Tiber for the available water. As Howard Hibbard described it, "In the Middle Ages and Renaissance, Rome lay like a shrunken nut within her shell of antique walls."[14]

The Bufalini map of 1551 (reprinted by Nolli in the eighteenth century) illustrates the extent to which the vast territory of Rome within the Aurelian wall circuit had been given over to a formerly urban condition conflating wilderness, ancient ruins, and agricultural lands (figure 5.6). In hot summers, carefully cultivated vineyards alongside abandoned monuments would offer grapes; in cold winters, wolves would traverse the ramparts of the Vatican gardens in search of food. By the time of Bufalini's depiction of this territory, the term *disabitato*, which had entered the language in general usage in the fourteenth century, had come to serve as a specific place-name designating the formerly urban territory within the Aurelian walls. The fact that the generic Italian term for abandoned urban land in the fourteenth century would predate its usage as a specific place-name for Rome in the sixteenth century suggests that there would have been many other formerly urban sites being reinhabited as part of the intellectual and political project of the Italian Renaissance, as well as its economic and cultural corollaries. Equally significant is the idea that while the abandoned formerly urban territory of Rome within the walls persisted in various states of depopulation for well over a millennium, a specific place-name (and attendant conceptual framework) for this territory was relatively late in coming. Ultimately, *disabitato* came to refer to the specific territory inside the Roman walls in the sixteenth century that served as a site for the papal reconstruction of Rome's urban structure as pilgrimage destination and capital of the Catholic Church in the sixteenth century.[15]

In his classic account of Rome from Christian antiquity through the Middle Ages, *Rome: Profile of a City, 312–1308*, Richard Krautheimer described the *disabitato* as an enormous interior agrarian hinterland that endured as late as the 1870s when it was denuded of its verdancy in favor of the modern archaeological imperative. "Beyond the populous quarters and the big mansions, the *disabitato* extended north, east and south to the Aurelian Walls, given over mostly to fields, vineyards, and pastures."[16]

In his account, Charles L. Stinger described the experience of a traveler having traversed the Roman Campagna and entering the ancient walls: "Once safely within the walls of the Eternal City, the mid-fifteenth century traveler saw before him a cityscape not remarkably different from the countryside he had just traversed. The Aurelian Walls, built for a population in excess of one million, still defended the city, but vast stretches (the disabitato) were given over to gardens, vineyards, and orchards, and much simply lay overgrown and abandoned."[17]

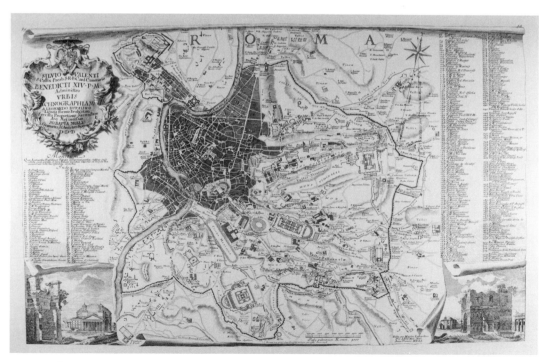

Figure 5.6 Leonardo Bufalini, *Pianta di Roma*, 1551;
reprinted by G. Nolli, 1748.

The available visual evidence of the state of the Roman *disabitato* is ample and predates the development of specific landscape paintings of the territory. As early as the mid-sixteenth century, Maarten van Heemskerck's sketches provided visual evidence of the Roman *disabitato*, as did those of Hieronymus Cock, among others. By the end of the sixteenth century, following the political consolidation and urban reconstruction projects of the Counter-Reformation Catholic Church, no fewer than four ambitious maps of Rome had been executed (by Du Pérac-Lafrérly, Cartaro, Brambilla, and Tempesta), each depicting the extent and character of the *disabitato*.[18]

These various sketches, views, and maps described the Roman Forum as invaded with kitchen gardens and livestock, while the less populous periphery of the *disabitato* persisted as wilderness in spite of the aggressive urban sanitization campaign of the church. In between the rapidly revivifying urban core and the formerly urban wilderness beyond, a kind of suburban villa landscape was interspersed with pilgrimage sites, agricultural lands, infrastructural fragments, and ancient monuments despoiled of their stone. As John Dixon Hunt described it: "Maps of both sixteenth and seventeenth centuries showed Rome as an intricate mixture of gardens and cultivated land … Falda's 1676 map of Rome … shows gardens filling not only the bastions of the city fortifications but the open spaces between ruins of classical baths and temples. Everywhere that travelers looked in the Eternal City gardens, modern gardens, seemed part of a larger classical landscape."[19]

Figure 5.7 Giovanni Battista Falda, *Pianta di Roma*, 1676.

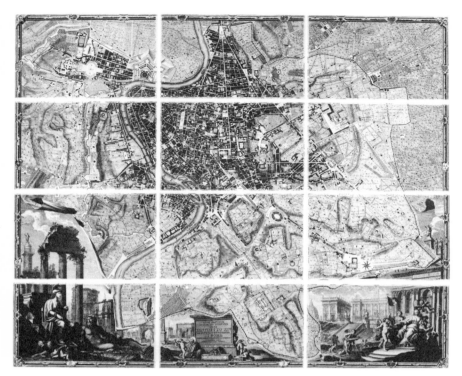

Figure 5.8 Giovanni Battista Nolli, *Nuova Topografia di Roma*, 1748.

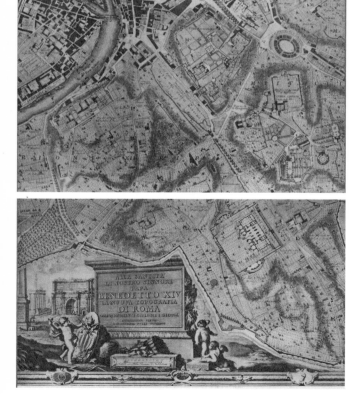

Figure 5.9 Giovanni Battista Nolli, *Nuova Topografia di Roma*, detail, 1748.

The particular landscape described by the term *disabitato* at the time of its coinage as a specific place-name might best be characterized as the juxta-position, commingling, and ongoing competition between cultivation and succes-sion. Cultivation of gardens, groves, and vineyards could be described by the Roman concept of *villeggiatura*, or the culture of summer retreat to an agricul-tural setting. A century after Pope Sixtus V's ambitious urban restructuring of the capital, Falda's *Pianta di Roma* in 1676 (figure 5.7) and subsequent pub-lication of *Li Giardini di Roma* in 1683 documented in great detail the domes-ticated landscape of cultivated gardens and managed agricultural landscapes that the *disabitato* of the baroque period had become. An example of this would be Falda's detailed depiction of the modern improvements by the Duke of Parma to the gardens of the Orti Farnesiani on the Palatine Hill.[20] Taken together, Falda's map and plates contribute to an overall sense of the *disabitato* in the seventeenth century as a largely cultivated suburban realm in which modest villas and vast private gardens contribute to an increasingly domesticated ag-ricultural realm. By the time of Nolli's *Nuova Topografia di Roma* in 1748, vine-yards, orchards, vegetable gardens, nurseries, and other agricultural uses came to occupy a large and growing majority of the parcels of land in the *disabitato* (figures 5.8, 5.9).[21]

In contrast to this cultivated landscape, much of the *disabitato* persisted well into the nineteenth century as a site of spontaneous natural succes-sion and the dynamic interplay between aggressive exotic species and their well-adapted local counterparts. As late as 1855, the English botanist Richard Deakin was able to document 420 species of plants growing spontaneously in and around the ruins of the Colosseum. In his *Flora of the Colosseum of Rome*, Deakin described over fifty varieties of grasses and dozens of wildflowers. He accounted for the presence of several exotic species through their per-sistent reproductive potential borne through the digestive tracts and upon the fur of animals brought to the site to take part in gladiatorial combat.[22] For many English tourists of the eighteenth and nineteenth centuries, the juxtaposition of classical ruins with spontaneous and adaptive plant communities and culti-vated gardens came to embody the classical tradition itself. For many who made the tour to Rome, and for many, many more who could not make the tour but would consume its contents through representations, the cultural construction of landscape came to be shaped by paintings of the Roman *disabitato*. As often as not, these paintings were made by resident French painters, who worked on site to document the juxtaposition of cultivated gardens and successional plant material set among classical ruins. The English-language formulation of the term "landscape," first articulated in 1603, would come to be disproportionately represented by a painter of Roman landscapes born to the name Claude in the Duchy of Lorrain one year later.[23]

·····

Claude Lorrain's landscape paintings came to construct the visual image of classical Rome abandoned and overgrown. In a range of paintings produced in Rome between the late 1620s and early 1680s, such as *Caprice with Ruins of the Roman Forum* (ca. 1634), Claude came to shape the English-language con-struction of landscape in the eighteenth and nineteenth centuries. Historian

Richard Rand goes further, arguing that Claude "revolutionized painting in the western tradition. During a lengthy career spent almost entirely in Rome … Claude perfected a form of landscape painting that would remain influential well into the nineteenth century."[24]

Claude was orphaned by age twelve and traveled to Italy to pursue apprenticeships as an ornamental designer and pastry chef. Following apprenticeships with artists in Naples and Rome, Claude produced his first drawings from nature between 1627 and 1628 and dates his first landscape painting, *Landscape with Cattle and Peasants*, in 1628. Both his early drawings and paintings are informed by sketching tours in the *disabitato* and Roman Campagna. In the early 1630s, he lived in Rome near the Piazza di Spagna as part of the immigrant artist community and was admitted to the Accademia di San Luca, the official guild of Italian painters and sculptors. By 1635 he began the practice of recording detailed drawings of each painting he executed to form his *Liber Veritatis (Book of Truth)*, which he maintained as evidence of the provenance of his original paintings until his death in 1682.

Figure 5.10 Claude Lorrain, *An Artist Sketching with a Second Figure Looking On*, ca. 1635–40.

Figure 5.11 Claude Lorrain, *View of the Palatine*, ca. 1650.

Figure 5.12 Claude Lorrain, *View of the Campo Vaccino*, ca. 1636.

Figure 5.13 Claude Lorrain, *View of the Campo Vaccino*, 1638.

By the late 1630s, Claude's patrons represented the political leadership of the day from princes to kings as well as the hierarchy of the church from cardinals to popes. As Claude's reputation grew, his paintings were sought after, acquired, and commissioned by international collectors across Europe. By the time of his death, his work was held in many of the elite collections across the continent. Over the century following his death, Claude's landscape paintings and drawings would come to be disproportionately acquired by English connoisseurs for their private collections, and many of those private holdings would eventually be bequeathed to public institutions, such as the British Museum where Claude's *Liber Veritatis* is housed today.

Among Claude's innovations in landscape painting was his practice of sketching from nature in the open air (figures 5.10, 5.11). Claude developed this technique to inform the spatial motifs for larger paintings and to provide detailed depictions of plant material and qualities of light. Often these studies from subjects in the *disabitato* would come to form a portion of more elaborate painting subjects completed in his studio, and the sketches that informed those paintings would come to contribute to engravings and drawings from the same subject matter.[25] From his house near Piazza di Spagna, Claude regularly made day trips to numerous sites in the Roman *disabitato* and the immediate Roman Campagna outside its walls. Claude made frequent use of visits to sites in the immediate vicinity of Saint Peter's, the Colosseum, Circo Massimo, Palatine Hill, and the sites of ancient ruins that were available throughout the *disabitato*. He would also walk along the ancient routes of the Via Appia Antica and Via Tiburtina, en route to sites in the Roman Campagna. Claude would often be in

Figure 5.14 Claude Lorrain, *A Study of an Oak Tree* (*Vigna Madama*), ca. 1638.

the company of other artists for these excursions, as well as an armed escort.[26]

The site of the Roman Forum or Campo Vaccino was a particular favorite of Claude's, and in the mid-1630s he produced a range of related images in service of a painting, including a drawing with brown ink and brown wash on paper, an etching of the drawing on white paper, and a sketch in red chalk with brown ink and brown wash (figures 5.12, 5.13). He was also particularly adept at using pencil, ink, and wash on site to capture the line and texture of trees and other details—often details that would inform future larger works executed in the studio. Claude's *A Study of an Oak Tree* (figure 5.14) and *Trees in the Vigna of the Villa Madama*, both ca. 1638, are indicative of his on-site work. Claude's landscape paintings of the Roman *disabitato* would come to provide a model for English picturesque designers, but many also emulated his drawings. Richard Payne Knight, a proponent of picturesque landscape theory, owned an impressive collection of Claude drawings that he gave to the British Museum in 1824. Claude scholar Richard Rand described the acquisition and reception of Claude's paintings and drawings by popularizers of English landscape gardening: "Of the nearly 1200 extant drawings by Claude, some 500, including the *Liber Veritatis* ... are owned by the British Museum. Such is the splendor of the collection that Thomas Cole, while visiting London in the late 1820s, spent a day at the Museum looking through them. This would have been shortly after the bequest of Richard Payne Knight, whose collection of more than 261 drawings by or attributed to Claude is particularly rich in nature studies."[27]

For many consumers of Claude landscapes, the paintings and drawings in English collections served as the inspiration for a tour of the classical sites of Rome. For these English taking the grand tour, Claude's landscapes provided the itinerary and subject matter for their trips through the *disabitato* and into the surrounding Campagna. According to Jeremy Black, for these grand

Figure 5.15 Claude Lorrain, *(Self) Portrait of Claude Lorrain (frontispiece of Liber Veritatis)*, ca. 1635–36.

Figure 5.16 Thomas Gainsborough, *Artist with a Claude Glass*, ca. 1750–55.

tourists "shifting and contrasting views of Britain interacted with the complex presentation of Italy that drew on the strong influence of a classical education and of a public ideology that was heavily based on Classical images and themes. ... These contrasts were interpreted, even 'contexted,' not only in the debate about tourism, but also in terms of another cultural product for which eighteenth-century Britain was famous: landscape gardening."[28] For Black this Anglicization of classical motifs of retreat and beauty interpreted through the Roman led to English landscapes that directly emulated the classical sites of the tour. In this context, the new landscape design "derived in large part from artistic models, especially the presentation of the landscapes of Roman Italy in the paintings of Claude Lorrain."[29]

John Dixon Hunt corroborates this account, claiming that Claude's works "would have been known to travelers long before they were copied by artists like John Wooton in the 1720s or circulated later in engravings. These landscapes from Italy were mainly idealized scenes. ... whether the pastoral landscapes of Claude or the wilder scenes with banditti. ... This ideal art was particularly attractive to those who advocated a new style in gardening, for it provided apt visual images for the ideas of paradise and the golden age, with which gardens were associated."[30]

In *The Picturesque Garden in Europe*, Hunt elaborates on the reception of Claude's seventeenth-century images for English landscape tastes in the eighteenth century. Hunt argues that with the work of William Kent "the picturesque begins to play a major and an acknowledged role in garden design. ... [Kent] knew his Claude Lorrain—both from Lord Burlington's 1727 purchase of the *Liber Veritatis* and presumably from his own sighting of Claude paintings and drawings during his years in Rome."[31] The reception of Claude's work would go on to inform the development of English picturesque landscape tastes through the eighteenth and into the nineteenth century. From William Gilpin's understanding of picturesque principles for landscape gardens, through Thomas Gray's advocacy for picturesque travel, to Uvedale Price's theory of the picturesque, the English picturesque landscape garden was conceived and perceived through the lens of Claude's paintings of Roman abandonment.[32]

·····

One enduring example of the impact of Claude's images of the formerly urban in the origins and development of English landscape is found in one of the more obscure objects attendant to touring culture and landscape experience. This eighteenth-century invention took the form of a small handheld dark convex mirror. The device was intended to allow the artist (and tourist alike) to view a landscape in accordance with picturesque principles so as to allow it to more closely emulate a painting of Claude. As Ernst Gombrich described, the device aided in the "transposition of local colour into a narrower range of tones. It consisted of a curved mirror with a toned surface that was appropriately often called the 'Claude glass.'"[33] The frontispiece of Claude's *Liber Veritatis* presents a self-portrait of the artist rendered in just such a darkly curved mirror (figure 5.15). Thomas Gainsborough's undated pencil sketch *Man Holding a Mirror* (figure 5.16) shows the intended use of the glass in the mid-eighteenth century, as a landscape tourist sits with his back to the view and peers at the landscape reflected through its darkened reflection in a mirror so as to more fully apprehend the view. "So convincing was his example and so great was his influence that, by the late nineteenth century, landscape would become arguably the dominant genre of painting in Europe and America. ... There is ... an obvious relationship of mood and sensibility, if not theme, between Claude's serene and idyllic vision of Italian countryside and the edenic landscape tradition of nineteenth-century American culture."[34]

Claude's representations of the Roman *disabitato*, through the reception of his work in discussions of English landscape gardening, came to stand for the very image of landscape as a cultural form in much of the West. This particular form, this image of landscape, and all that it implies about contemporary design culture, continue to exert an enormous ambient influence on the discipline to this day. The status of the "formerly urban" recommends a rereading of the origins of landscape in the West. As a cultural category uniquely available to the problematic of sites and subjects of abandoned urbanity, landscape has been found particularly useful in coming to terms with the social, environmental, and cultural conditions left in the wake of traditional architectonic models. Landscape has had a long history in the context of decreasing urban density and shrinkage. In the following chapter we will see how progressive practices of modern planning deployed landscape to insulate urban populations from the worst social and environmental impacts of ongoing transformations in industrial economy.

Six: Urban Order and Structural Change

The structure of the city is wrong.... Only a structural change of the city could bring about the necessary order.
—Ludwig Hilberseimer, 1949

At least one project of modern planning effectively anticipated Detroit's depopulation through design and claimed landscape as a medium of urbanism for the modern metropolis. In contrast to the worst failures of modernist planning, this project deployed landscape as a medium uniquely capable of anticipating the decentralization, depopulation, and dissipation of architectural fabric that Detroit would experience in the second half of the twentieth century. In anticipating the impact of mature Fordist decentralization on North American urbanization processes and patterns, Ludwig Hilberseimer conceived of a radical planning proposition equally informed by ecological and infrastructural considerations, half a century prior to more recent claims for landscape as a form of urbanism.

In 1955, just six years after publishing an impassioned argument for structural change in Detroit, Ludwig Hilberseimer was commissioned to plan the urban "renewal" of one of the city's deteriorating downtown neighborhoods. At the beginning of a half century of urban exodus from the city of Detroit, Hilberseimer's plan applied the theoretical principles he had developed in the first half of the century as an urban planner, architect, and educator. His plan fundamentally reconceived the urban pattern for this portion of the Motor City and provided the urban diagram orchestrating the contributions of a uniquely talented interdisciplinary design team assembled for the project. A federally underwritten urban renewal project that would come to be known as Lafayette Park produced a continuously viable and still vibrant mixed-income, mixed-race community of people living in publicly subsidized housing in the midst of Detroit's ongoing deterioration.[1] In light of recently renewed critical interest in the superblock as a strategy of modernist urban planning, the ongoing demolition of modernist housing projects nationally, and the popular acceptance of "new urbanist" models for the reconstruction of the city, Lafayette Park offers a unique counterpoint, recommending a thoughtful reconsideration of the received failures of modern architecture and urbanism.[2]

In this work landscape and transportation infrastructure replace architecture as the spatial and organizational media through which urban order is constructed. Caldwell's landscape design is significant here, as is the social vision of developer Herbert Greenwald. Mies van der Rohe's architecture of

< Figure 6.1 Ludwig Hilberseimer, "Detroit Area," planning diagram, ca. 1945. Reprinted from Ludwig Hilberseimer, *The New Regional Pattern: Industries and Gardens, Workshops and Farms* (Chicago: Paul Theobald, 1949), 173, Figure 114.

high-rise apartment slabs, two-story townhouses, and ground-level courtyard houses, not insignificant in their own right, benefit from the social and environmental context created by Hilberseimer's planning, Caldwell's landscape, and Greenwald's development.

To the extent that Lafayette Park, in spite of its obvious merits and cultural pedigree, has been neglected by the history of twentieth-century architecture and urbanism, recent interest in landscape as a medium of urbanism offers an opportunity to revisit its optimistic and alternative modernist planning. From the perspective of contemporary interests in landscape as the ordering element for decentralized urbanism, Hilberseimer's plan for Lafayette Park offers an extraordinary case study in the radical reconception of the industrial city.

.....

Following the race riots of World War II, just prior to what would become a half century of urban dispersal, a group of Detroit's civic types—boosters, planners, and politicians—conspired to renovate one of the city's downtown neighborhoods. "Black Bottom," as it was called, had come to be known as a "slum" in the professional term of art favored by urban planners of the day. This meant that the neighborhood was the site of countless "social pathologies." This meant that the residents of Black Bottom, primarily African Americans lured to industrial jobs in the north over several waves of great migrations from the south, would have to go (figure 6.2).[3] In their place, the leaders of Detroit's political and business communities imagined a decentralized, suburban enclave. The development was intended to reproduce those qualities of suburban living that were luring greater and greater numbers of whites of European descent to leave the city for the suburbs: decreased density, more open space, and the easy accommodation of the automobile.[4] Following the evacuation of its residents and demolition of buildings in 1951, the site sat vacant for four years. In spite of an award-winning plan for the site prepared by Stonorov, Yamasaki,

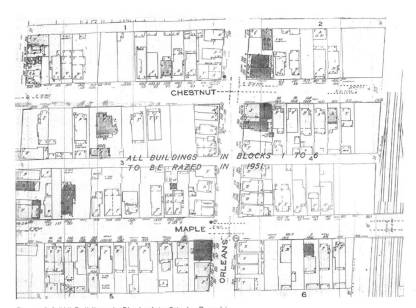

Figure 6.2 "All Buildings in Blocks 1 to 6 to be Razed in 1951," Sanborn Fire Insurance Map of Detroit's Black Bottom neighborhood, ca. 1950.

and Gruen, and approved by the city, the project lacked a local development team willing to or capable of financing it. During this time it was derided as "Mayor Cobo's fields," derisively referring to the failure of the city to develop the project. In addition to enduring the racist redlining and slum clearance process associated with urban renewal, residents of Black Bottom now faced years of abandonment, prefiguring Detroit's fate later in the century. Lacking a local developer who could manage the project, the city of Detroit ultimately agreed in 1955 to work with Chicago developer Herbert Greenwald to develop the site (figures 6.3, 6.4).

As conceived by Chicago developer Herbert Greenwald in association with Samuel Katzin, the Lafayette Park project was developed as a mixed-income and mixed-race development. Over half a century from its conception Lafayette Park continued to enjoy many original residents, high relative market value, and greater racial, ethnic, and class diversity than both the city and suburbs that surround it. Greenwald's original conception of the neighborhood remains remarkably viable today, as the site continues to provide central city housing to a middle-class group of residents with the perceived amenities of the sub-urbs, including decreased density, extensive landscaping and public parks, easy access by automobile, and safe secure places for children to play.[5]

Greenwald enlisted the services of architect Ludwig Mies van der Rohe for the design of the project, with whom he had previously worked on the develop-ment of the 860–880 Lake Shore Drive Apartments in Chicago. Mies brought to the team Ludwig Hilberseimer, to plan the site, and Alfred Caldwell, to execute

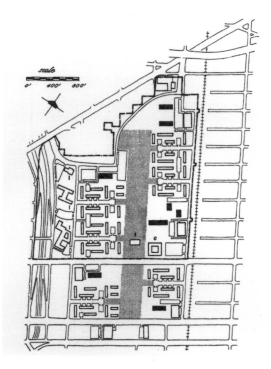

Figure 6.3 "Site Plan for Gratiot by Greenwald, Redeveloper, van der Rohe, Architect, and Hilberseimer, Planner," 1955. Reprinted from Roger Montgomery, "Improving the Design Process in Urban Renewal," *Journal of the American Institute of Planners* 31, no. 1 (1965): 7–20.

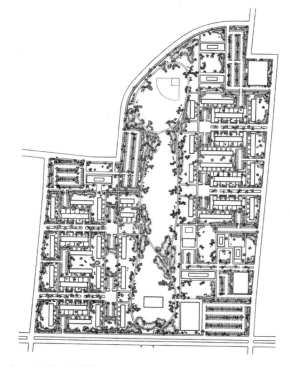

Figure 6.4 Ludwig Hilberseimer with Mies van der Rohe, Lafayette Park, Detroit, site plan, 1956.

the landscape design (figures 6.5, 6.6, 6.7, 6.8). Based largely on his previous academic projects in Germany and the United States, Lafayette Park provided the most significant application of Hilberseimer's conception of the "settlement unit" as well as the most important commission of his career. Hilb's settlement unit was particularly apt as an aggregation of planning principals and types appropriate to the decentralizing North American city (figure 6.9).[6]

·····

Hilberseimer's plans for the site proposed landscape as its primary material element. The commission offered both sufficient acreage and budget for what could have otherwise been an uninspired urban void. Central to this was Greenwald's finance and marketing scheme, which positioned landscape as the central amenity in the form of a 17-acre park bisecting the site and providing a much sought after social and environmental amenity in the midst of Detroit. By contrast, note the relatively anemic planting, absent sectional development and lack of automobile integration of the IIT campus plan, Mies's most comparably scaled urban project. This suggests that IIT would have benefited greatly from the kind of attention to planning and landscape design that Lafayette Park profited from (figures 6.10, 6.11).[7]

Displaying a superficially similar nonhierarchical organization of sliding bar buildings on a tabula rasa site (as at IIT), the Lafayette Park plan removed the vestiges of the obsolete nineteenth-century street grid in favor of a lush, verdant and extensive green *tabula verde*. By rendering the primary spatial structure of the site in a lush verdant layer of landscape, Hilberseimer accommodated the automobile completely at Lafayette Park, in relation to the residential units, yet rendered it secondary to the primary public spaces of the site. He accomplished this by delimiting the encroachment of the street to the perimeter of the site, restricting the impact of the automobile on the overall figure of the public landscape. In so doing, he avoided the necessity for any resident to cross the street and reduced pedestrian and automobile intersections to a minimum. While Hilberseimer worked through these relationships in plan, Mies van der Rohe elevated the primary residential level above the street elevation so as to further reinforce the insulation of pedestrian from street. In elevating the ground plane of the public landscape one meter above the surface streets, Mies effectively insulated the community from the most immediate impacts of automobility (figure 6.12).[8]

Figure 6.5 Gratiot Redevelopment (Lafayette Park), Detroit, site razed, aerial photograph, 1955.

Figure 6.6 Gratiot Redevelopment (Lafayette Park), Detroit, aerial photomontage with model, 1955.

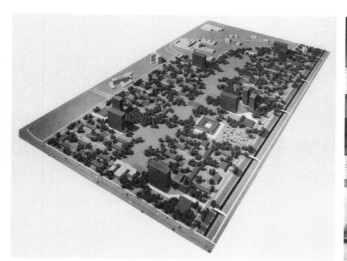

Figure 6.7 Gratiot Redevelopment (Lafayette Park), Detroit, site model, 1955.

Figure 6.8 Presentation of Gratiot Redevelopment (Lafayette Park), Detroit, 1955.

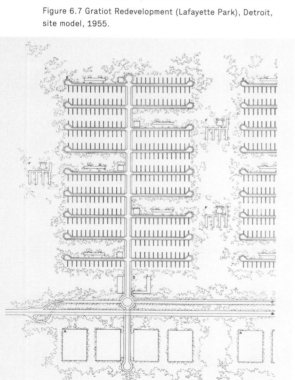

80. A NEW SETTLEMENT UNIT. A—Industry. B—Main highway. C—Local highway. D—Commercial area. E—Residential area. F—Schools in the park area.

Figure 6.9 Ludwig Hilberseimer, Settlement Unit, plan, ca. 1940.

Figure 6.10 Mies van der Rohe, Illinois Institute of Technology,
Chicago, aerial photomontage with model, 1940.

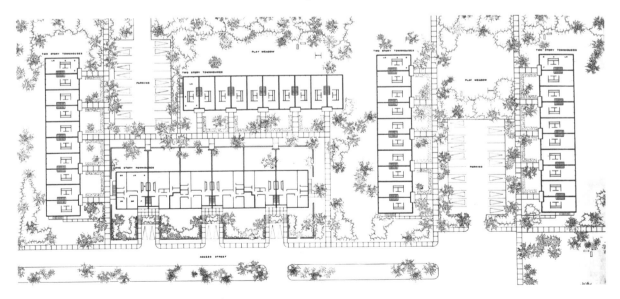

Figure 6.11 Hilberseimer with Mies van der Rohe, Lafayette
Park, Detroit, site plan of planning module with townhouses and
courtyard houses, 1956.

The landscape planting formed the primary framework for the development of the site at the scale of planning as well as at the scale of the individual residences. Caldwell's landscape also provided the exterior spaces with a regionally and seasonally inflected counterpoint to Mies's attitude regarding the universality of space and his austere industrially standardized building facades.[9] The now-mature landscape continues to form the primary framework for the spatial organization and coherence of the site, with larger communal landscapes giving way to shared yards and private courts. These landscape spaces pinwheel around a tripartite architectural ensemble of townhouses, courthouses, and apartment slabs, each rendered in a palette of standardized industrial building components.

The standardized building components of Mies's residential buildings allowed for speed of construction, hence reduced costs, while the material quality of the buildings was clearly rendered secondary to the relationship between the interior of each unit and the exterior space that serves it, both spatially and visually. This strategy effectively decreases the perceived density of the site by carefully massing the largest number of inhabitants in thin slabs, up out of the way of light, air, and access to the ground plane. Each of the housing types—apartment, townhouse, and courthouse—presents a different relation of interior to exterior, with the landscaped exterior spaces providing the spatial clarity and definition only implied in other Miesian plans (figures 6.13, 6.14).

·····

An architect and art critic immersed in *Der Neue Sachlichkeit* (New Objectivity), Hilberseimer first came to prominence for his unbuilt urban design projects from the 1920s. Hilberseimer was most notoriously known for totalizing rationally planned schemes of modernist planning such as Hochhausstadt (Highrise City, 1924) and Groszstadtarchitektur (Metropolis or Big City Architecture, 1927). Referring to this earlier work as producing "more a necropolis than a metropolis,"[10] Hilberseimer quickly abandoned those schemes in favor of projects that

Figure 6.12 Lafayette Park, Detroit, first phase, aerial photograph, 1957.

explored decentralization and landscape as remedies to the ills of the industrial city. This was evident as early as 1927 in a sketch titled "The Metropolis as a Garden-City."[11] Hilberseimer's work over the course of the 1930s was clearly influenced by European precedents for the garden city and evidenced a strategy for the use of landscape and mixed-height housing in a low-density pattern. This is a pattern that would continue to appear in his work in the United States over the following decades. Particularly formative in this regard were Hilberseimer's project for Mischbebauung (Mixed-Height Housing, ca. 1930) (figure 6.15) and for the University of Berlin (1935), the principles of which would inform the balance of his career.[12] Hilberseimer's preference for landscape and mixed-height housing in a low-density pattern would continue to appear in his work in the United States. While Hilb's early work was immersed in German planning circles of the day and notions of *Stadtlandschaft*, it was also influenced by the then-evident reality that mature industrial production would tend toward the decentralization of traditional urban form. This sentiment was apparent to Hilberseimer as early as the 1920s in Henry Ford's commitment to the decentralization of industrial production.[13]

Given Ford's well-documented sympathies with Nazism, the infrastructural and logistical logics of the German war machine provided an essential case study in the virtues of Fordist mobility. Not simply a model of production but an essential Fordist precept, mobilization was understood not only as a preparation for the projection of military power but also the retooling of the very industrial process itself.

In contrast to Ford's political commitments, Hilberseimer was a committed socialist, having been radicalized by the social conditions of the 1920s and '30s. In Germany he espoused a public socialist position informed by traditional Marxist social critique. Hilberseimer's planning projects from the late 1920s and '30s were informed by these commitments, and are imbued with his sense of "fairness."[14] Hilberseimer's commitment to equity informed planning projects that embodied equal conditions for all, most notably through equitable access to healthful housing. For Hilberseimer this suggested the necessity of equitable distribution of land as well as access to sunlight throughout the year.

Figure 6.13 Lafayette Park, Detroit, promotional photograph, 1959.

Figure 6.14 Lafayette Park, Detroit, aerial photograph, 1963.

By correlating social equity to arable land and access to sunlight Hilberseimer proposed a proto-ecological urbanism.[15] By the time of his immigration to Chicago in 1938, Hilberseimer's planning projects had explored the spatial and urban implications of these issues. While he maintained his social commitments, he eschewed a public position on socialism in the United States, most often relying on his colleagues and students to take more critical public positions.[16]

By the mid-1940s, Hilberseimer's notion of the Settlement Unit took clearer form, anticipating the development of an interstate highway system, articulating precise relationships between transportation networks, settlement units, and the regional landscape. Hilberseimer's interest in an organic urbanism for the North American continent was further fueled by civil defense imperatives toward decentralization in the years following the war. In the wake of Hiroshima, Hilberseimer adapted his proposals to anticipate the construction of the interstate highway system as a civil defense infrastructure and an extension of Fordist production logics. In this context, and conversant with Wright's Broadacre City as well as the progressive TVA project and its proponents in the Regional Planning Association of America, Hilberseimer developed his New City planning proposal for the urbanization of a low-density North American settlement pattern based on regional highway systems and natural environmental conditions (figures 6.16).

In a 1945 article titled "Cities and Defense," Hilberseimer called for the post–World War II dissolution of cities and their dispersal across the landscape as a strategy of civil defense (figure 6.17).[17] Hilberseimer proposed an organic American urbanism dispersed across the landscape with infrastructure and environment commingling so as to make the identification of city apart from countryside virtually impossible. The dispersal of population across the landscape in a thin ex-urban settlement pattern was useful not only in reducing the casualties from a potential nuclear attack but also, just as importantly, in preventing the attack in the first place by frustrating attempts at target acquisition by aerial observation. This example of an urbanism of dispersal and reduced density finds its corollary in the construction of the interstate highway system in the United States as a part of the nation's civil defense infrastructure. Using

Figure 6.15 Ludwig Hilberseimer, Mixed-Height Housing (*Mischbebauung*), aerial view, 1930.

similar arguments, the formation of the highway transportation system as an engine of dispersal across the landscape had an incalculable effect on postwar settlement patterns.

Hilberseimer's proposals for a radically decentralized pattern of regional infrastructure for postwar America simultaneously optimized Fordist models of decentralized industrial production and dispersed large population concentrations that had become increasingly obvious targets for aerial attack in the atomic age. Hilberseimer's drawing of an atomic blast in central Illinois renders a clear imperative for the construction of a civil defense infrastructure capable of transporting dense urban populations away from the dangers of the city and toward the relative security of suburban dissolution.[18] This model of the highway as a civil defense infrastructure afforded a form of insulation through camouflage. Not coincidentally, the depopulation of urban centers in response to the Cold War argues quite effectively for precisely the kind of decreasing density that his previous work had been predicated on in the name of efficient industrial production and optimized arrangement.

·····

Between 1944 and 1955, Hilberseimer authored three major English-language books on his theories and methods of planning. While the three books overlap and share fundamental material with each other, they each advance Hilb's arguments in consequential and distinct ways. The first of these, *The New City: Principles of Planning* (1944) introduced Hilberseimer's commitments to an Augustinian sense of order, as an organic relation of equal and unequal parts, each in their own relation to the whole. In this regard, Hilberseimer and Mies shared a commitment to architecture and planning as embodiments of culture, rather than mechanisms of reform. Mies authored the introduction to *The New City* and described Hilberseimer's city planning as a work of order: "Reason is the first principle of all human work. Consciously or unconsciously Hilberseimer follows this principle and makes it the basis for his work. ... City planning is, in essence, a work of order."[19]

The New City incorporates much of the analytical and methodological underpinnings for Hilberseimer's *The New Regional Pattern* (1949). Hilberseimer's planning proposals in *The New Regional Pattern* were organized around the distribution of transportation and communication networks across an essentially horizontal field of landscape. Within this extensive horizontal territory, housing, farms, light industry, commercial buildings, and civic spaces formed variously scaled networks across a field of decentralized distribution. *The New Regional Pattern*'s organizational structure did not defer to the abstraction of the grid, but rather was informed by the natural environment: topography, hydrology, vegetation, wind patterns, and the like. It conflated infrastructural systems with built landscapes and found environmental conditions to produce a radically reconceived settlement pattern for the North American continent. In this regard, the project offers a profound critique of traditional urban form and the inadequacy of traditional city planning discourse to deal with the social and technological conditions of the modern age.

Hilberseimer cites Ford directly in arguing for accelerating decentralization as the mature depiction of North American settlement patterns. Hilberseimer

Figure 6.16 Ludwig Hilberseimer, planner, with Alfred Caldwell delineator, Settlement Unit with Commercial Area, aerial perspective, ca. 1942.

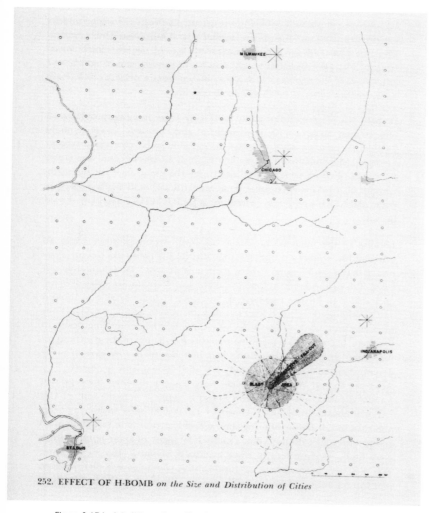

252. EFFECT OF H-BOMB *on the Size and Distribution of Cities*

Figure 6.17 Ludwig Hilberseimer, Plan for Decentralization, showing the effect of an atomic bomb on the distribution of cities, map diagram, ca. 1945.

argues that only a "structural change," a complete erasure and restructuring of traditional urban form, would bring about the necessary order. In this context, Hilberseimer proposed the replanning of Detroit. Consistent with his planning principles, Hilberseimer's analysis of Detroit focuses on the incompatibility of a nineteenth-century street grid with contemporary commitments to social equity and proto-ecological performance.

Hilberseimer extended this argument specifically to the Gratiot (Lafayette Park) site in Detroit as part of his preliminary project notes for Lafayette Park. In those project notes Hilberseimer identifies the "ancient" street grid as the primary anachronism: "Our existing street system is going back to ancient times; however motor vehicles have rendered this once perfect system obsolete. Therefore we construct highways but usually forget the pedestrian for whom each street corner is a death-trap. To avoid this there should be no through traffic within a residential area but it should also be possible to reach each house or building by car."[20]

Hilberseimer found in Herbert Greenwald a developer client equally committed to making "structural change" in the American city. Greenwald's commitment to making Lafayette Park a mixed-race, mixed-class community was equally progressive. While the overwhelming majority of federally funded urban renewal projects tended toward single-race, single-class concentrations, Greenwald argued for a mixed-race future for the American city through a mix of class and tenancy. Both Greenwald and Hilberseimer imagined a new spatial structure, built upon landscape, that would enable such a radical social transformation. In this regard, Hilberseimer and Greenwald imagined the Gratiot project would become a national model for a decentralized urbanism principally shaped by landscape. In his presentation of the project to Mayor Cobo and the Detroit Common Council, Greenwald argued: "The Gratiot development offers a major challenge not only to Detroit, but to the entire nation. ... The city must be liberated from its confinement so that it may be linked to the open space of the landscape."[21]

Tragically, this progressive vision of an American urbanism based in landscape was thwarted with Greenwald's untimely death when his American Airlines flight from Chicago crashed upon approach at New York's LaGuardia Airport in February 1959. Following his death, Greenwald's successor partners divided up the remaining parcels of the Lafayette Park site and commissioned a range of architects, including Mies, to execute buildings, absent Hilberseimer's planning. Lafayette Park would be the single planning project in his entire career that Hilberseimer would acknowledge as representing his planning theories in built form.[22] Because more extensive built examples of Hilberseimer's planning theories are lacking, one needs to look internationally for comparable progressive precedents of landscape as a medium of urban order. Among those, Lucio Costa's cotemporaneous "pilot plan" as executed for Brasilia offers compelling corroboration. Costa's capital exhibits similar successes on both environmental and social scores, while deploying landscape as the primary ordering element of a progressive urban order. While the case of Brasilia is deserving of fuller attention in this regard, at a minimum, it reveals the potentials for Hilberseimer's social and ecological agendas at the larger scale, a topic we will take up in the following chapter.[23]

At Lafayette Park, Hilberseimer's plan produced one of the most successful examples of publicly subsidized social housing through a radical reconsideration of both spatial and social structure for the American city. In his teaching Hilberseimer continued to draw upon the lessons of Lafayette Park, and often presented it as an alternative to Levittown and the ongoing automobile-based decentralization that became the dominant spatial order of the postwar era.[24] In spite of Lafayette Park's social and environmental successes, Hilberseimer's planning was largely ignored, and later discredited as evidence of the "failures of modernist planning." By the late 1960s, Mies van der Rohe lamented the relative lack of recognition for Hilberseimer's work in the context of increasing attention to energy conservation, solar orientation, and environmental topics.[25]

The completion of Lafayette Park in 1959–60 was widely reported in both popular and professional presses, with a range of racial and cultural intersections. One Detroit newspaper referred to the architect of the project as one "Miles van der Rohe." Several American professional journals documented the project through a range of formats. The May 1960 issue of *Architectural Forum* included a multiple-page spread on the project titled "A Tower plus Row Houses in Detroit," with photographs, plans, and interviews. The article describes Lafayette Park as a social and urban experiment in a new kind of living, in response to "the urban murk around Detroit's strangling downtown."[26]

Many architects and critics found much to admire in Lafayette Park. Alison Smithson and Peter Smithson cited the "self control and reticence now needed by an architect" in finding Lafayette Park "calm as an ideal." Kenneth Frampton echoed those sentiments and described it as "self-effacing and unfamiliar."[27] On the other hand, nothing in the coverage of Lafayette Park would come near the searing editorial authored by Sybil Moholy-Nagy in *Canadian Architect*. With her critique of Lafayette Park, Moholy-Nagy began a disturbing trend to misspell Hilberseimer's name, while dismissing him as a "theoretical" planner and mere teacher. Moholy-Nagy argued that Lafayette Park suffered from a "total lack of civic coherence" and that it offered "no urban environment."[28]

With her attack in *Canadian Architect*, Moholy-Nagy opened a line of critique from the left, arguing that Greenwald's mixed-class strategy was nothing more than a speculative intrusion of the middle and upper classes into what should have been low-cost housing. Manfredo Tafuri argued a comparable critique. While admiring much in Hilberseimer's theoretical planning work, Tafuri dismissed Lafayette Park as a "bourgeois" speculative development that displaced low-cost housing.[29]

Ultimately the most enduring narrative of Hilberseimer's plan for Lafayette Park would come from Charles Jencks. In a May 1966 article immodestly titled "The Problem of Mies," in the *Architectural Association Journal*, Jencks, then a graduate student, begins what would be a two-decade attack on Mies and Hilb. Jencks uses Lafayette Park as an exemplary case where "the purity of form leads to an inarticulate architecture, or one extraneous element, a bathroom vent, leads to monumental bathos."[30] A decade later in a series of issues of *Architectural Design*, Jencks would launch a headlong assault on the failures of postmodern architecture and urbanism, with Hilberseimer the surrogate for attacks against Mies. Infamously, Jencks ultimately declared the "death of modern architecture," on April 22, 1972, with the televised demolition of the public housing project in Saint Louis (figure 6.18).[31] The most common claim in Jencks's line of attack was the notion that Hilberseimer had fallen "out of fashion." Jencks's collaborator George Baird referred to Hilberseimer as the "least fashionable modern architect" in his 1977 essay on the work of Rem Koolhaas. As we will examine in chapter 7, Baird would go on to devote an entire chapter in his 1995 book *The Space of Appearance* to an extended critique of the organicist tradition in urban thought. While not mentioning Hilberseimer directly, Baird argues that the organicist strain of urban exhibits a "mistrust of any extant form of the public realm."[32]

By the early 1980s, Joseph Rykwert concluded that Hilberseimer's success was astonishing, given the obvious lack of merit in the work. Further, Rykwert argued that Hilberseimer's plans were worse than anything that modernist planning had wrought. "Looking back, one can only take note in astonishment of Ludwig Hilberseimer's success. His barren, gloomy, menacing drawings prophesy

Figure 6.18 Demolition of Pruitt-Igoe, Saint Louis, reprinted from Geoffrey Broadbent, "The Language of Post-Modern Architecture: A Summary," book review of Charles Jencks, *The Language of Post-Modern Architecture*, *Architectural Design*, no. 4 (1977): 261.

a city without streets, even worse, if that's possible, than that which has already been realized. This success is a sociological phenomenon of the strangest kind."[33] By this time, Hilberseimer's planning projects had been relegated to a subject of ridicule on both sides of the Atlantic. This was largely accomplished by ignoring the merits of Hilberseimer's single built project, and returning to his "Grossstadtarchitektur" of the 1920s, work that Hilberseimer had abandoned as more a "necropolis" than a metropolis. By 1989, in the context of a review of the Art Institute of Chicago's Hilberseimer symposium, "In the Shadow of Mies," Peter Blundell Jones reiterated the by then commonly held position that Hilberseimer was hopelessly out of fashion.[34] Jones's review was published only three years before the publication of K. Michael Hays's critical recuperation of Hilberseimer as an icon for the critical theory flank of postmodernism.[35]

In light of recently renewed critical interest in the superblock as a strategy of modernist urban planning, the ongoing demolition of modernist housing projects nationally, and the popular acceptance of "new urbanist" models for the reconstruction of the city, Lafayette Park offers a unique counterpoint, recommending a thoughtful reconsideration of the received failures of modern architecture and urbanism. The largest collection of Mies van der Rohe's buildings, and Ludwig Hilberseimer's most significant planning commission, Lafayette Park in Detroit is also the most fully realized US example of a superblock strategy for the decentralizing postwar city. At Lafayette Park, Hilberseimer's planning and Alfred Caldwell's planting conspire to create a significant precedent for contemporary interest in landscape as urbanism.

For contemporary readings of landscape as urbanism, *The New Regional Pattern* offers a number of significant insights that we will take up in the following chapter. Among these is the notion of program or plan as a social agenda. This was manifest, at least in part, in response to the social pathologies, economic injustices, and unhealthful conditions of the traditional city in the industrial age. Equally compelling for contemporary questions of landscape urbanism, *The New Regional Pattern* raises the role of representation, particularly the role of the diagram. Hilb's diagrams of the Pattern offer an analogue to contemporary interests in landscape representation and the synoptic view in imaging emergent forms of urbanism. Hilb's use of diagram alludes to the synthetic, synoptic, and planometric aspects of the aerial view, illustrating perhaps imperceptible relationships across scale and between ecological and infrastructural systems. At the largest scale, the drawings illustrate the large-scale distribution of nationally scaled highway systems relative to natural resources, existing population centers, and hypothetical atomic blasts. At the smallest scale, they reveal a subtly constructed landscape of parkways, parking lots, farms, and fields, within which the domestic garden forms the basis for private life. In between, Hilberseimer and Caldwell illustrate an urbanism almost wholly reconceived, unburdened of the "weighty apparatus" of traditional urban form, in which landscape provides the medium of social and spatial order.

Seven: Agrarian Urbanism and the Aerial Subject

Industry will decentralize itself. If the city were to decline, no one would rebuild it according to its present plan.
—Henry Ford, 1922, as quoted by Ludwig Hilberseimer, 1949

Hilberseimer's decentralized planning proposals for an organic American urbanism centered on a radical reconceptualization of the urban in relationship to landscape. Central to Hilberseimer's concept of "structural change" in the American city was the role of the region as an economic and ecological order. Hilberseimer's concept of a new "regional pattern" for urbanization was conceived in reference to a range of precedents including the English garden city movement and the French *desurbanist* tradition. It also referenced Frank Lloyd Wright's Broadacre City project and Petr Kropotkin's conflation of the fields and factories.[1] In so doing, Hilberseimer proposed the commingling of the agrarian and the urban.

The agrarian and the urban are two categories of thought that have more often than not been opposed to each other. Across many disciplines, and for many centuries, the city and the country have been called upon to define each other through a binary opposition. Contemporary design culture and discourse on cities are, by contrast, awash in claims of the potential for urban agriculture. This chapter revisits the history of urban form conceived through the spatial, ecological, and infrastructural implications of agricultural production. In the projects that form this tentative counterhistory, agricultural production is conceived as a formative element of the city's structure, rather than being considered adjunct to, outside of, or inserted within traditional urban forms. This alternative history of the city seeks to construct a useful past from three urban projects organized explicitly around agricultural production as inherent to the economic, ecological, and spatial order of the city.

·····

Many projects of twentieth-century urban planning explicitly aspired to construct an agrarian urbanism. Often these agrarian aspirations were an attempt to reconcile the seemingly contradictory impulses of the industrial metropolis with the social and cultural conditions of agrarian settlement. In many of these projects, agrarianism came to stand as an alternative to the dense metropolitan form of industrial arrangement that grew from the great migrations from farm village to industrial city in the nineteenth- and early twentieth-century cities of western Europe and North America. The agrarian aspirations of many modernist urban planning proposals lie in the first instance in the relatively decentralized model of industrial order Henry Ford and other industrialists favored

< Figure 7.1 Ludwig Hilberseimer, the city in the landscape, aerial view, ca. 1945.

as early as the 1910s and '20s.[2] Following Ford's organizational preference for spatial decentralization, industrial organizations tended to spread horizontally and abandon the traditional industrial city. In part as a response to the social conditions of the Depression era, agrarianism came to be seen as a form of continuity between formerly agrarian populations based on subsistence farming and the relatively vulnerable industrial workforce of the modern metropolis. By mixing industry with agriculture, many modernist urban planners imagined a rotational labor system in which workers alternated between factory jobs and collective farms. Most often these new territorial spatial orders were understood as vast regional landscapes. Equally often, these projects conflated aerial views and maps and implicated the ascendancy of an aerial viewing subject.

The emergence of these tendencies in the twentieth century might be read through a range of projects advocating a decentralized agrarian urbanism: Frank Lloyd Wright's "Broadacre City" (1934–35); Ludwig Hilberseimer's "New Regional Pattern" (1945–49); and Andrea Branzi's "Agronica" (1993–94).[3] Three very different architects produced these projects three decades apart, yet taken collectively they illustrate the implications for urban form of agricultural production as inherent to the structure of the city. These projects also form as a coherent genealogy of thought on the subject of agricultural urbanism, as Branzi explicitly references Hilberseimer's urban proposals, and Hilberseimer's work was informed by familiarity with Wright's urban project. Each of the projects presented their audiences with a profound reconceptualization of the city, proposing radical decentralization and dissolution of the urban figure into a productive landscape. This dissolution of figure into field had the effect of rendering the classical distinction between city and countryside irrelevant in favor of a conflated condition of suburbanized regionalism. From the perspective of contemporary interests in urban agriculture, both projects offer equally compelling alternatives to the canonical history of urban form.

Implicit in the work of these three urbanists was the assumption of an ongoing process of urban decentralization led by industrial economy. For Wright, Hilberseimer, and Branzi, the decreased density urbanism produced through the new industrial logic of decentralization came to depend upon landscape as the primary medium of urban form. These suburban landscapes were embodied and fleshed out with agricultural lands, farms, and fields. These projects proposed large territorial or regional networks of urban infrastructure bringing existing natural environments into relationship with new agricultural and industrial landscapes.

Each of the projects presented its audiences with a profound reconceptualization of the city, proposing radical decentralization and dissolution of the urban figure into the landscape. This dissolution of figure into field had the effect of rendering the classical distinction between city and countryside irrelevant in favor of a conflated condition of agrarian industrial economy. From the perspective of contemporary interests in landscape urbanism, both projects offer equally compelling alternatives to the canonical history of urban landscape, from progressive garden city models to the tradition of urban parks as exceptions to the industrial city. These projects reconceptualize the fundamental distinctions between city and countryside, village and farmland, and urbanism and landscape are dissolved in favor of a third term, a proto-ecological landscape urbanism for industrialized North American modernity. This brief review of historical precedents from midcentury is recommended by contemporary interest in landscape as urbanism. In this formulation, landscape supplants architecture's traditional role as the dominant medium for contemporary urban form. This is particularly relevant as the emergence of an aerial subject in midcentury modernist planning discourse parallels the enhanced role of landscape as the primary medium of decentralized urban form.

·····

In the depths of the Depression, lacking reasonable prospects for a recovery of his once towering stature as the dean of American architects, Frank Lloyd Wright persuaded his lone remaining patron to fund a traveling exhibition of Wright's conception of an organic American urbanism. Broadacre City, as it was referred to, consisted of a large model and supporting materials produced by student apprentices at Taliesin in the winter of 1934/35. While the premises underpinning the project were evident in Wright's lectures as early as the 1920s and fully informed Wright's 1932 publication of *The Disappearing City*, the Broadacre model and drawings were first debuted in a 1935 New York City exhibition (figures 7.2, 7.3, 7.4, 7.5). Subsequently, the traveling exhibition toured extensively, and the remarkably durable project was further disseminated in subsequent publications, including *When Democracy Builds* (1945) and *The Living City* (1958).[4]

Broadacre City offered American audiences the clearest crystallization of Wright's damning critique of the modern industrial city, positing Broadacre as an autochthonous organic model for North American settlement across an

Figure 7.2 Frank Lloyd Wright, Broadacre City, plan, 1934–35.

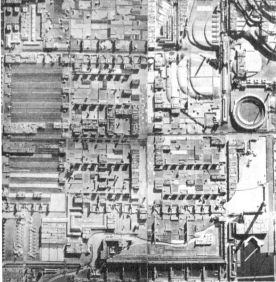

Figure 7.3 Frank Lloyd Wright, Broadacre City, model, 1934–35.

essentially boundless carpet of cultivated landscape. Eschewing traditional European distinctions between city and countryside, Broadacre proposed a network of transportation and communication infrastructures using the Jeffersonian grid as its principal ordering system. Within this nearly undifferentiated field, the county government (headed by the county architect) replaced other levels of government administering a population of landowning citizen-farmers. Wright was clearly conversant with and sympathetic to Henry Ford's notion of a decentralized settlement pattern for North America, and the closest built parallel for Wright's work on Broadacre can be found in Ford's instigation of what would become the Tennessee Valley Authority (TVA). The TVA was charged with the construction of hydroelectric dams and highways along the Tennessee River in the electrification of an entire region as a seeding process for future urbanization.[5]

Enjoying ownership of one acre of land per person as a birthright, residents of Broadacre (or Usonia, as Wright would come to refer to it) were to enjoy modern houses set in relation to ample subsistence gardens and small-scale farms. This basic pattern of variously scaled housing and landscape types was interspersed with light industry, small commercial centers and markets, civic buildings, and of course the ubiquitous highway. In spite of the project's extremely low density, most of the ground was cleared and cultivated. Occasionally this constructed and maintained landscape relented in favor of extant waterways, topographic features, or other preexisting ecologies. Presumably the extrapolation of Broadacre City from its chiefly middle-western origins to the margins of the continent would have been accomplished with varying degrees of accommodation to local climate, geography, and geology, if not cultural or material history. The status of previously urbanized areas existing outside of Wright's Broadacre remained an open question; presumably, these would be abandoned in place, again following Ford's lead in this regard.

Wright's critique of private ownership, conspicuous consumption, and accumulation of wealth associated with cities was no small part of the explicit social critique Broadacre offered, as the worst of the Depression forced bankrupt family farmers to flee their mortgaged farms in the Midwest for protest in the east or California in the west.[6] Ironically, given his anxiety over the corrosive

Figure 7.4 Frank Lloyd Wright, Broadacre City, aerial view, 1934–35.

Figure 7.5 Frank Lloyd Wright, Broadacre City, aerial view, 1934–35.

effects of accumulated wealth and speculative capital, Wright found in Ford's notion of regional infrastructure the basis for an American pattern of organic urban development. Wright's Broadacre provided a respite from the relentless demands of profit associated with the industrial city, even as the American city was well on a course toward decentralization, itself driven by the decentralizing tendencies of Fordist production.

. . . . .

Four years after Wright's Broadacre exhibition opened to the public, the 1939 New York World's Fair featured an exhibition of the "World of Tomorrow" sponsored by General Motors. The centerpiece of GM's Highway and Horizons pavilion, the "Futurama" exhibition illustrated a decentralized American urbanism as the result of a rationally planned and technologically optimized highway system. The Futurama, designed by American industrial and theatrical designer Norman Bel Geddes, was by far the most popular attraction at the fair, drawing more than twenty-five million visitors over two seasons.[7] The Futurama offered audiences in 1939–40 an aerial view of a decentralized midwestern metropolis circa 1960. Bel Geddes's aerial audience viewed an enormous scale model of the midsection of North America from moving cars suspended aloft, effectively simulating the aerial approach to what most closely resembled a future Saint Louis. Bel Geddes's strategy of viewing the model from above made effective use of the designer's extensive research into aerial photography of the North American landscape and simultaneously offered the most promising image of a decentralized urbanity based on the promise of individual automobility. For Futurama visitors still living out the effects of the Great Depression, this simulation of mass air travel was itself a utopian image of access to a mode of travel still understood by many as elitist and excessive. This particular mode of spectatorship made technological progress and individual freedom tangible through the roving supervisory gaze of the aerial viewer. Millions of visitors to Futurama were rendered complicit in a decentralized territorial urbanization that they at once apprehended from above, and ultimately opted for below. Both forms of subjectivity, the aerial and the terrestrial, promised greater individual freedom through technology and progress, all sponsored by GM's corporate benevolence.[8]

The aerial image of urbanity Bel Geddes offered was of a decentralized system of automobile transportation made possible through a national system of high-speed multilane highways. These highways bypassed city centers in favor of the coming suburban peripheries, enhanced safety with well-engineered systems of on-ramps and off-ramps, and separated lanes of traffic by speed and direction. In short, Futurama offered a prescient image of what would become much of the US interstate highway system constructed as a civil defense and military infrastructure following World War II. The following year, Bel Geddes published his vision in *Magic Motorways* (1940), documenting the Futurama exhibition for mass audiences and advocating the construction of a national highway system.[9] This publication explicitly linked technological progress (through efficiency, safety, and freedom of mobility) to an ultimately decentralized North American settlement pattern. As in Wright's Broadacre, Bel Geddes's Futurama is significant not simply for its advocacy of future decentralization, but equally for offering a mode of aerial subjectivity through which to apprehend and popularize its proposals. Both Broadacre and Futurama portend the coming age of easy and economical passenger air travel. In both exhibitions, Depression-era audiences were invited to inhabit an exotic aerial subjectivity. In so doing, both projects linked the aerial view to technological progress and democratic values, rendering audiences complicit in imagining a decentralized future that they subsequently enacted on the ground.[10]

· · · · ·

While the long-standing tradition of regionally informed planning practice from Patrick Geddes through Ian McHarg certainly points to this potential, Hilberseimer's *New Regional Pattern* diverges from that lineage in affording priority to a complex cultural conflation of civil engineering and ecological artifact. Hilberseimer's organic conception of urban order rendered basic distinctions between city and countryside irrelevant, critiquing the industrial city and its attendant social ills. Hilberseimer's Pattern drew heavily on the garden city tradition as well as the progressive tradition of regional planning in advocating for the reordering of the metropolitan region (figures 7.6, 7.7, 7.8).[11]

As we have seen, Hilberseimer's *New Regional Pattern* was constructed out of and depended upon the smaller scale Settlement Unit, a semiautonomous collective comprising housing, farming, light industry, and commerce. The Settlement Unit formed the basic module of development, constituting a virtually self-sufficient pedestrian social unit in the form of a cooperative live/work settlement. This scalar grain of the horizontal field embedded the pedestrian-scaled Settlement Unit within larger automobile-based infrastructures, which were in turn organized by the larger environmental systems in which they were situated. This scale shift between pedestrian walking distances and the larger dimensions covered by the automobile differs markedly from Wright's essentially

Figure 7.6 Ludwig Hilberseimer, planner, with Alfred Caldwell, delineator, the city in the landscape, aerial view, 1942.

scale-less framework within which the social and civic relations between neighbors are articulated in contractual relations, rather than in the physical disposition of dwellings. Bel Geddes's Futurama, by contrast, illustrated a decentralized urban field faithfully reproducing the most readily available contemporary landscape typologies and augmented with numerous high-rise ex-urban clusters. These distinctions are best understood as political distinctions between the commitments of the three author/architects. Hilberseimer's proposal advocated complex social arrangements and forms of spatial collectivity while Bel Geddes's Futurama offered a form of corporate propaganda through popular advertising and political advocacy. Wright's project envisioned the autonomous, proto-anarchic, citizen-farmer accommodated as an individual resident of a larger organic order, relatively unmediated by intervening scales of social order. The symmetry of aerial subjectivity as the most appropriate mode of democratic citizenship invoked by a decentralized North American settlement pattern is particularly striking given the diverse political and cultural commitments of Wright, Bel Geddes, and Hilberseimer. While Wright's *disurbanist* fantasy informed many of his subsequently realized residential projects, Broadacre was never executed except as a general contextual precept for subsequent residential commissions or as a representational setting for individual building projects. Likewise, Hilberseimer's proposals for an organic urbanism at the scale of the region were never fully realized, save the single case study of Lafayette Park in Detroit, where Caldwell's landscape defines the public realm.[12]

Wright's and Hilberseimer's projects for an organic American agrarian urbanism have been read by many as respectively prefiguring or collaborating with the postwar project of suburbanization. In this regard, as we saw in

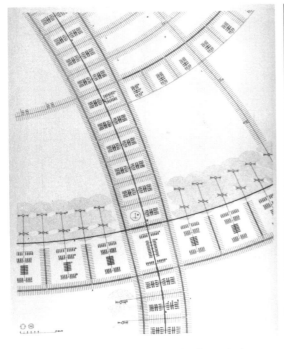

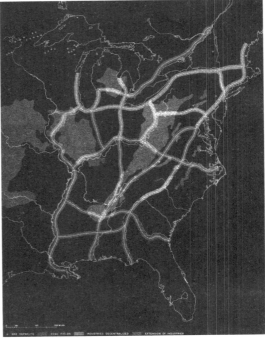

Figure 7.7 Ludwig Hilberseimer, Urban Planning System (variation), planning diagram, reprinted from *The New Regional Pattern* (Chicago: Paul Theobald, 1949), 163, Figure 107.

Figure 7.8 Ludwig Hilberseimer, New Regional Pattern, planning diagram, reprinted from *The New Regional Pattern* (Chicago: Paul Theobald, 1949), 142, Figure 93.

chapter 6, postmodern critics of modernist planning attacked Hilberseimer's proposals for a landscape-based urban pattern as ultimately antiurban, often labeling any landscape-based urban proposal as insufficiently committed to the reconstruction of the nineteenth-century structure of street wall and block structure. Among these critics, George Baird has been among the most articulate. Baird's *The Space of Appearance* includes a chapter on this subject titled "Organicist Yearnings and Their Consequences." For Baird, the organicist tradition evident in Hilberseimer's regional projects can be traced to the lineage of regional progressive planning from the Scottish planner Patrick Geddes to Geddes's influence on Lewis Mumford, and perhaps as late as Ian McHarg's 1969 *Design with Nature*.[13]

.....

The work of the Italian architect and urbanist Andrea Branzi might be found equally relevant to an understanding of the contemporary potentials for an agrarian urbanism. Branzi's work reanimates a long tradition of using urban project as social and cultural critique. This form of urban projection deploys a project not simply as an illustration or "vision," but rather as a demystified distillation and description of our present urban predicaments. In this sense, one might read Branzi's urban projects as less a utopian future possible world, but rather a critically engaged and politically literate delineation of the power structures, forces, and flows shaping the contemporary urban condition. Over the course of the past four decades, Branzi's work has articulated a remarkably consistent critique of the social, cultural, and intellectual poverty of much laissez-faire urban development and the realpolitik assumptions of much urban design and planning. As an alternative, Branzi's projects propose urbanism in the form of an environmental, economic, and aesthetic critique of the failings of the contemporary city.[14]

Born and educated in Florence, Branzi studied architecture in a cultural milieu of the operaists and a scholarly tradition of Marxist critique as evidenced through speculative urban proposals as a form of cultural criticism. Branzi first came to international visibility as a member of the collective Archizoom (mid-1960s) based in Milan but associated with the Florentine *Architettura Radicale* movement. Archizoom's project and texts for "No-Stop City" (1968–71) illustrate an urbanism of continuous mobility, fluidity, and flux. While "No-Stop City" was received on one level as a satire of the British technophilia of Archigram, it was received on another level as an illustration of an urbanism without qualities, a representation of the "degree-zero" conditions for urbanization (figures 7.9, 7.10, 7.11, 7.12).[15]

Archizoom's use of typewriter keystrokes on A4 paper to represent a nonfigural planning study for "No-Stop City" anticipated contemporary interest in indexical and parametric representations of the city. Their work prefigured current interest in describing the relentlessly horizontal field conditions of the modern metropolis as a surface shaped by the strong forces of economic and ecological flows. Equally, these drawings and their texts anticipate current interest in infrastructure and ecology as nonfigurative drivers of urban form. As such, a generation of contemporary urbanists has drawn from Branzi's intellectual commitments. Many of the architect/urbanists influenced by Branzi's work would come to shape the intellectual underpinnings of landscape urbanist discourse, from Stan Allen and James Corner's interest in field conditions to Alex Wall and Alejandro Zaera-Polo's interest in logistics.[16] Equally, Branzi's urban projects are available to inform contemporary interests within architectural culture and urbanism on a wide array of topics as diverse as animalia, indeterminacy, and genericity, among others.

As a form of "nonfigurative" urbanism, "No-Stop City" renewed and disrupted a minor tradition of nonfigurative urban projection as socialist critique. In this regard, Branzi's "No-Stop City" draws upon the urban planning projects and theories of Ludwig Hilberseimer, particularly Hilberseimer's New Regional Pattern, and that project's illustration of a proto-ecological urbanism.

Not coincidentally, both Branzi and Hilberseimer chose to illustrate the city as a continuous system of relational forces and flows, as opposed to a collection of objects. In this sense, the ongoing recuperation of Hilberseimer, and Branzi's renewed relevance for discussions of contemporary urbanism, render them particularly relevant to discussions of ecological urbanism. Andrea Branzi occupies a singular historical position as a hinge figure between the social and environmental aspirations of modernist planning of the postwar era and the politics of 1968 in which his work first emerged for English-language audiences. As such, his work is particularly well suited to shed light on the emergent discussion around ecological urbanism.

Branzi's Agronica project (1993–94) illustrated the relentlessly horizontal spread of capital across thin tissues of territory, and the resultant "weak

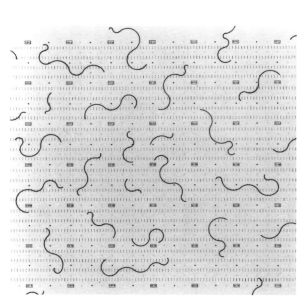

Figure 7.9 Archizoom Associati, Andrea Branzi, et al., No-Stop City, plan diagram, 1968–71.

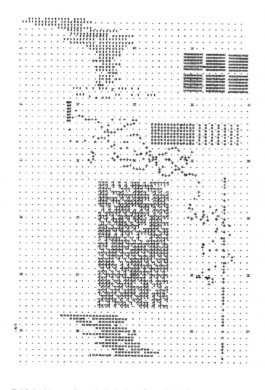

Figure 7.10 Archizoom Associati, Andrea Branzi, et al., No-Stop City, plan diagram, 1968–71.

urbanization" that the neoliberal economic paradigm affords (figure 7.13). Agronica embodies the potential parallelism between agricultural and energy production, new modalities of post-Fordist industrial economy, and the cultures of consumption that they construct.[17] Six years later in 1999, Branzi (with the Milanese postgraduate research institute Domus Academy) executed a project for the Strijp Philips district of Eindhoven. This project for the planning of the Strijp Philips portion of Eindhoven returned to the recurring themes in Branzi's oeuvre with typical wit and pith, illustrating a "territory for the new economy" in which agricultural production was a prime factor in deriving urban form (figure 7.14).[18]

Branzi's "weak work" maintains its critical and projective relevance for a new generation of urbanists interested in the economic and agricultural drivers of urban form. His call for the development of weak urban forms and nonfigural fields has already influenced the thinking of those who articulated landscape urbanism over a decade ago and promises to reanimate emergent discussions of ecological urbanism.[19] Equally, Branzi's projective and polemic urban propositions promise to shed light on the proposition of agrarian urbanism.

More recently Pier Vittorio Aureli and Martino Tattara / Dogma's project "Stop-City" directly references Branzi's use of nonfigurative urban projection as a form of social and political critique (figures 7.15, 7.16).[20] Aureli's interest in autonomy in architecture brings him to the potential of the nonfigurative and a tradition of critical thought. Like Baird, Aureli has remained committed to a position of criticality through architecture as a political project, and has remained skeptical of the claim of landscape as a medium of urbanism. In spite of this position, and his concern that landscape is too often deployed as a medium of greenwashing, Aureli too draws upon a European tradition of the project of the city as a political project. Equally he maintains an enduring interest in typology as a means of formal and morphological analysis in urban form.

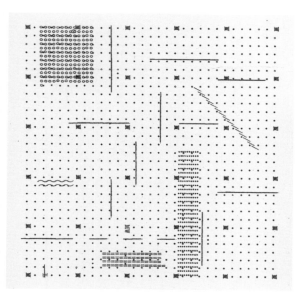

Figure 7.11 Archizoom Associati, Andrea Branzi, et al., No-Stop City, plan diagram, 1968–71.

Figure 7.12 Archizoom Associati, Andrea Branzi, et al., No-Stop City, model, 1968–71.

Figure 7.13 Andrea Branzi, Dante Donegani, Antonio Petrillo, Claudia Raimondo
with Tamar Ben David and Domus Academy, Agronica, model, 1993–94.

Figure 7.14 Andrea Branzi, Lapo Lani, and Ernesto Bartolini, Masterplan Strijp
Philips, Eindhoven, model, 1999–2000.

Figure 7.15 Pier Vittorio Aureli and Martino Tattara/Dogma, Stop City, aerial photomontage, 2007–8.

Figure 7.16 Pier Vittorio Aureli and Martino Tattara/Dogma, Stop City, typical plan, forest canopy, 2008.

In this regard, the fact that Aureli was a student of Bernardo Secchi and Paola Viganò is equally significant here. As Secchi and Viganò have articulated the concept of the *città diffusa*, they have reconciled a tradition of critical theory and architectural autonomy with the increasingly evident empirical facts of diffuse urban form. Secchi has referred to the "*città diffusa*" as the most important urban morphology for the twenty-first century. In this regard, Secchi and Viganò have articulated a theoretical framework, political position, and methodological approach using landscape as a medium of urbanism for the contemporary city.[21]

.....

From the perspective of contemporary understandings of landscape as urbanism, this genealogy offers a number of significant insights. The first of these is the notion of program or plan as a social agenda, as evidenced in quite distinct political points of view. While Futurama was clearly conceived as a corporate advertisement by way of popular amusement, Broadacre and the New Regional Pattern were conceived as critical responses, at least in part, to the social pathologies, economic injustices, and unhealthful conditions of the traditional industrial city. Both projects advocated limits on the physical scale of industry, agriculture, and housing, arguing in favor of meaningful proximate relationships between work, family, food, and civic life. Proposed remedies to the social inequities and ill health of pure capitalist development feature in both Broadacre and the New Regional Pattern as the projects imagine the spatial implications of social limits on private ownership, accumulation, and speculation.

Each of the three projects propose radical decentralization, not simply as a depiction of a mature Fordist industrial economy as in Futurama, but as the organic condition of North American settlement patterns. Both Wright and Hilberseimer refer in other contexts to the failings of the modern metropolis as a dangerous and unsupportable contradiction of the organic relationship evident in human occupation of the landscape over a longer historical trajectory in the West. In this regard, Wright's interest in an organic architecture tends much more fully toward a regional argument for the midsection of America, whereas Hilberseimer located an organic urbanism in the conditions of modern industrial economy itself, as distinct from Wright's interest in models of regional adaptation. In both instances, the relatively unexamined relationship of Wright's and Hilberseimer's organic models of urbanism on theories of natural selection recommend themselves for further study.

To manifest their decentralized visions, each project maintains a significant role for architects, especially as a public figure in political and planning decisions, yet each equally depend upon a greatly reduced role for architecture as the primary medium of the public or civic realm. Instead, Wright's Broadacres, Hilberseimer's New Regional Pattern, and Branzi's Agronica propose landscape as the medium structuring spatial relations between extant natural environments and engineered infrastructure systems. Each project proposes a renewed and redefined role for agrarian in the ordering of public and private space. This definition stretches the traditional bounds of the landscape medium understood as a decorative art or environmental science. No small part of that relevance is landscape's promise to work across scales, rendering meaningful relationships between the larger regional environment and local social conditions. This potential is evident in Hilberseimer's use of variously scaled courts, yards, and gardens to relate domestic life to the larger public parklands that connect them. Wright's project places greater importance on family farming as a staple element of every citizen-subject's daily duty. In Broadacre, kitchen gardens give way to small-scale cooperative farms and their markets in the formation of a public landscape primarily formed by agricultural uses at a variety of scales, whereas the Settlement Unit is based upon pedestrian public parkland forming the confluence of individual semiprivate courtyards. This subtle yet significant distinction between the three authors' various conceptions of public life is evident in the status of public landscape: productive agricultural land for Wright, extensive parkway viewshed for Bel Geddes, occupied and programmed parklands for Hilberseimer. The cumulative effect of these strategies for contemporary interest in landscape as urbanism is to inflect the local conditions of individual dwelling and the broader civic realm of public infrastructure toward a more mature and robustly realized set of relationships with their ecological contexts.

Each of the projects described here in relation to the agrarian impulse in midcentury planning equally portend the ascendance of an aerial subject as the appropriate inhabitant of a democratically decentralized North American urbanism. Each of the projects proposes a renewed role for civil engineering and public works projects in the making of a newly conceived public realm. This new public space is primarily experienced through the automobile and its accommodations, replacing the traditional role of the pedestrian promenade and public plaza as the basic integers of public space. As a necessary corollary to the age of aerial subjectivity, each equally portends a public life of mass spectatorship, broadcast media, and electronic communications. As we will see in the next chapter, this correlation of landscape as a medium of urbanism with particular forms of aerial subjectivity and representation has a long history. This affinity between the sites and subjects of the aerial with the landscape medium continues to inform contemporary readings of landscape as urbanism, as the airport has itself become both subject and object of the landscape urbanist agenda.

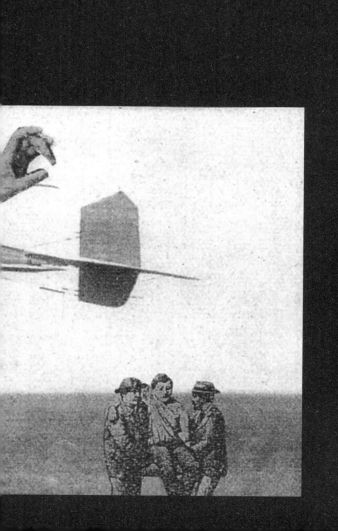

Eight: Aerial Representation and Airport Landscape

If the erasure of conventional boundaries is the most salient spatial feature of the late twentieth-century condition, the airport may be taken as its most perfect landscape expression.
—Denis Cosgrove, 1999

Contemporary interest in landscape as medium and model for the city was shaped by transformations in industrial economy. While much of the landscape urbanist agenda emerges in the wake of the formerly industrial and the formerly urban, the practice has much to do with sites of rapid urbanization and economic growth. This chapter examines one facet of that growth, the emergence of aerial representation and subsequent reading of the airport as a landscape. This topic shifts away from the role of landscape as an ameliorative medium for cleansing the toxic sites of industry and toward the potential for landscape urbanist strategies in the organization of the airport and its attendant urban field.

In landscape urbanism, the idea of landscape has shifted from scenic and pictorial imagery to that of a highly managed surface best viewed and arranged from above. If landscape architecture once represented a self-conscious act of placemaking set against an unknowable and untamable wilderness beyond, it has now become a practice of reworking an indexed terrestrial surface upon which all is known, or at least knowable, through the various lenses of remote aerial representation. Maps and plans are key here, but so too are aerial photographs.[1]

·····

Beginning with the development of the camera in the late eighteenth and nineteenth centuries, the making of a photograph from a height above the ground has been a minor genre within the larger project of photographing the landscape as well as a major obsession for a handful of individuals.[2] If, following Roland Barthes, one accepts Niepce's photograph of a dinner table bathed in natural light (circa 1823) as the first photograph, then one can also take that image as the first photograph of a landscape.[3] The first recorded photographic representation made from the air is credited to another Frenchman, Gaspard Félix Tournachon (Nadar). Nadar first succeeded in taking a photograph from the air in 1858 while stripped nearly naked behind a dark curtain in his Goddard balloon (figure 8.2). Nadar's photographs of the Champs de Mars in Paris were followed by a decade of technical improvements that culminated in his aerial documentation of Haussmann's renovations to the city in 1868. These balloon-photograph views of the Haussmannization of Paris are the first aerial views to reveal the urban order at work in the cutting of boulevards, sewers, parks, and other civil constructions through the fabric of the city.[4]

<Figure 8.1 Max Ernst, *Untitled* (*The Murderous Aeroplane*), photomontage, 1920.

Over the three decades between Nadar's first balloon photographs (1858) and the construction of the Eiffel Tower as a platform for mass aerial observation (1889), the spectator balloon served Parisian audiences as well as tourists, offering an early form of mass aerial spectatorship. In the United States, George Lawrence's kite photographs documented the devastation of San Francisco as early as the 1906 earthquake while the cities of the eastern seaboard, their civic parks, and natural features, had already been photographed from the air well before the Wright brothers flight.[5] Ultimately, Eiffel's Parisian viewing platform would be supplanted with the construction of vast public grandstands at Parisian airfields, first among them at Le Bourget (1918). Lindbergh's nighttime arrival at Le Bourget outside Paris upon the completion of his solo transatlantic flight (1927) was typical of the mass spectacle attendant to aerial events. This culture of mass aerial spectatorship informed Le Corbusier's enthusiasms in this regard, and his publication *Aircraft* (1935) documented his experience as part of the aerial audiences outside Paris. Ultimately Le Corbusier and other modern urbanists invoked the aerial view as a technique of analysis and intervention (figure 8.3).

Densely illustrated with images proclaiming the new eroticism of aeronautical objects, this book speculates on the utility of aerial observation in revealing the failure of cities as well as the potential of new, synoptic planning practices. The unsentimental image of the city as photographed from above offered Le Corbusier the most telling evidence of the moribund failure that traditional cities had become. On the utility of aerial representation for revealing

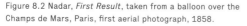

Figure 8.2 Nadar, *First Result*, taken from a balloon over the Champs de Mars, Paris, first aerial photograph, 1858.

Figure 8.3 Le Corbusier, *Aircraft*, aerial photograph, 1935.

the conditions of twentieth-century urbanism he would write: "the airplane indicts!"[6] Interestingly, as Le Corbusier would imply elsewhere, it was precisely the lack of a picturesque sentimentality to the aerial image of the city that recommended it as a unique tool for understanding its potential instrumentality in urban planning.[7]

. . . . .

While most early examples of aerial photography to survive tended to focus—albeit poorly and dimly—on the city as a an object, technical advances in photography taken from airplanes moved early experiments in aerial representation toward the collective potential of looking down upon a landscape. Ultimately, this new form of spectatorship would come to be experienced by future populations of air travelers and occasion new audiences for the reception of landscape. Together with aerial photography, the mass availability of air travel has today produced a distinctly modern perceptual mode for the airborne subject. This is very distinct from previous modes of perception based on a sequence of ground-level views. This form of subjectivity has influenced a number of cultural practices, each founded on the notion of an aerial viewing subject as spectator-consumer.

As a technique perfected during the First World War for representing the continually changing face of battle, aerial photography became a metaphor for the surveillance, control, and projection of military power across the landscape. The capacity for landscape viewed from the air to produce a particular kind of human subjectivity for the terrestrial spectator is especially evidenced in the writing of the Futurists as well as by its use in Soviet and Fascist propaganda.[8] This perception-representation-projection mechanism manifested itself in the use of aerial photographs of mass rallies as a primary tool of Fascist propaganda for representing the power of the state. This power was evidenced in the reproduction and dissemination of aerial views of mass

Figure 8.4 NASA, Apollo 8 Earthrise, photograph, December 24, 1968.

audiences assembled to simultaneously project and perceive a new form of collective subjectivity.

The development of aerial photography during the twentieth century has been largely dependent upon the funding, practical experience, and theoretical principles developed as a result of military applications of the technology. Among these, military techniques of surveillance, countersurveillance, and camouflage offer some of the most directly applied research as to the impact of aerial representation on the built and natural environments.[9] As developed by the military, with generous funding, technical expertise, and popular political support, the practice of renovating the landscape so as to avoid aerial observation can be seen to mirror developments in aerial imaging itself. While most military camoufleurs in the first half of the century came from the ranks of visual artists, set designers, and architects, postwar techniques of countersurveillance have increasingly become the purview of technicians and specialists in military surveillance. With the development of supersonic spy planes, intercontinental missiles, and aerial reconnaissance satellites, the Cold War became a pretext for truly global surveillance of the earth's surface.[10] This conception of the earth's surface as continually surveyed by overhead orbits continues to this day as a general cultural condition (figure 8.4).

.....

Beginning in the 1950s and '60s a very small number of institutions were beginning to look at digital media vis-à-vis landscape architecture. One of the first was the Laboratory for Computer Graphics founded in the mid-1960s at Harvard (figures 8.5, 8.6).[11] The Lab, as it came to be known, was founded at Harvard with funding from the Ford Foundation to explore the role of digital

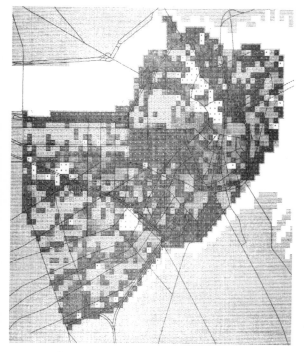

Figure 8.5 Harvard Laboratory for Computer Graphics, digital mapping, 1967–68.

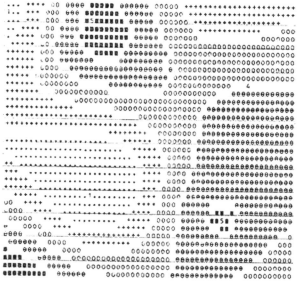

Figure 8.6 Harvard Laboratory for Computer Graphics, digital mapping, 1967–68.

applications and computer graphics for the social, spatial, and urban problems of the American city. Harvard had one supercomputer in 1965; one assembled punch cards and got in line to queue up to have them processed. While this work was still quite crude by contemporary standards, the Lab developed software and hardware to represent the challenges of the American city. Beginning in 1967, video was used at the Lab as a means to record and disseminate animations generated from the SYMAP program that the Harvard laboratory ran in the late 1960s.[12] In one of its first applications, a video was made illustrating the growth of Lansing, Michigan. Those early attempts to use video to develop digital modeling techniques tended to focus on social, environmental, and urban challenges.

One of the goals of the Lab was to aggregate ecological, sociological, and demographic data and to spatialize that data. In this regard the laboratory was a peer institution with a range of other institutions across North America and Europe trying to harness the capacity of computation to visualize data in service of better social policy and planning decisions. Carl Steinitz was among the Graduate School of Design faculty in landscape architecture working in the Lab and engaged in digital media in relation to landscape planning. Steinitz came to the Lab from the completion of his PhD at MIT where he worked with Kevin Lynch. Steinitz took from his work with Lynch an interest in the structure of the city and its experience by human subjects. Steinitz offered design studios focusing on the potential of computation to inform ecological and social planning projects at the so-called large scale.[13] At more or less the same moment Ian McHarg working at the University of Pennsylvania was developing

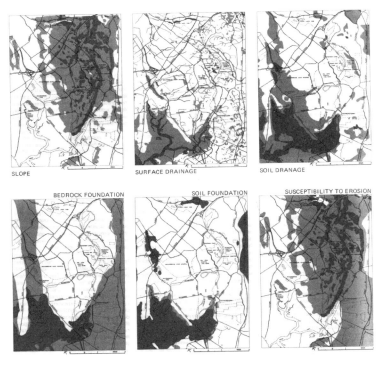

Figure 8.7 Ian McHarg, Staten Island, New York, overlay mapping, reprinted from *Design with Nature*, 1969.

analogue techniques of composite overlay analysis from ecological and sociological data (figures 8.7, 8.8).[14]

Much of the intellectual energy of the Lab went into mapping and modeling
that ultimately produced platforms such as geographic information systems
(GIS). One goal of the Lab's digital mapping work was to model social, demographic, and population data. Another goal was to model environmental and
ecological data. By the mid-1970s, the Lab, which at its peak had been about
forty researchers and staff, had shrunk to a core group of about a dozen
people. The Lab was generating revenue through licensing proprietary software for profit, and it was focusing more of its energies on GIS. A number of the
members of the laboratory went on to form private spin-off companies, and
that technology transfer produced a demand for GIS and associated services
within the public sector at federal, state, and regional scales.[15]

The Lab persisted with its interests in abstraction and demographics
through the 1970s. Much of the intellectual curiosity and practical energy of
that work was focused on building more robust mimetic models of natural
environments. The Lab worked on studies for the US Forest Service in the late
1970s in which they sought to model complex natural environments through
the spatialization of empirical knowledge. This work had as a goal the construction of a mimetic model, the idea being that one could build a digital model
that was sufficiently detailed and robust enough to stand in for the complexity,
indeterminacy, and autonomous agency of the natural world. More contemporary
versions of this mimetic modeling are available today with ubiquitously available off-the-shelf software and conventional commercial hardware replacing the

Figure 8.8 Ian McHarg, Staten Island, New York, overlay
mapping, reprinted from *Design with Nature*, 1969.

Lab's proprietary custom software yet sharing the Lab's focus on the mimesis of nature through digital environments.

·····

Whether for purposes of military surveillance, property description, or environmental analysis, aerial imaging has become one of the scientific tools of first resort for a variety of purposes. While these representations may sometimes be quite beautiful to look at, their primary use value is to visually collate quantifiable data in a global economy of information. Such data allows for the analysis of weather patterns, land use, military maneuvers, natural disasters, population estimates, and limitless other forms of social self-objectification.[16] While certain of these instrumental aerial representations are useful as analytical tools in revealing a given condition, the use of aerial imaging in this century has increasingly conflated the analysis of the given with its renovation toward possible futures. The projective potential in the seemingly neutral and objective information of quantification is evident in the speed with which census becomes population control, military surveillance becomes intervention, land use analysis becomes planning, and weather prediction becomes emergency management.[17]

Over the past two decades, the trajectory of ecological planning through aerial imaging reached a point of epistemological exhaustion. First, in spite of the rapid growth of computing speed and capacity, the complexity of the natural world continues to elude modeling. Second, over the past decades design culture has emerged as the framework for much urban decision making. Much of the impetus behind these models was based on the assumption that more accurate models of the natural world and greater ecological knowledge could improve social and environmental policy. This was based on the reasonable sense

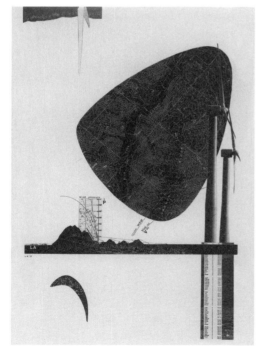

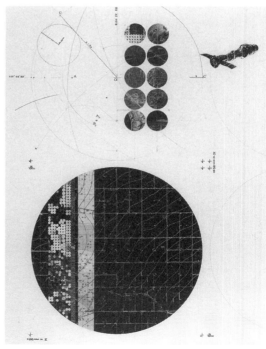

Figure 8.9 James Corner, Windmill Topography, photomontage, 1994.

Figure 8.10 James Corner, Pivot Irrigators, photomontage, 1994.

that if policy makers had access to environmental and demographic information, they might be led to make more socially just and environmentally healthful decisions about the built environment. Unfortunately, at the moment that digital media was allowing greater empirical data to be spatialized and visualized in service of planning practice, the political economy in the United States began to favor laissez-faire modes of deregulated urbanization. Over the past decades, North American urbanization has continued apace, largely driven by speculative capital and absent the most robust forms of digitally informed planning practice the research of the Lab at Harvard and its peers internationally provided.

Over that time, various alternatives to the paradigm of digital modeling of empirical knowledge in service of planning practice have emerged in the context of postmodernism and landscape architecture. Among those critical of positivistic models for planning, James Corner has argued for the centrality of landscape representation to the eidetic operations and imaginative capacity of landscape as a medium of design. Corner was a student of McHarg at Penn, and was trained in McHarg's overlay analysis as well as GIS in service of landscape planning. In his groundbreaking 1996 publication *Taking Measures Across the American Landscape* (coauthored with Alex MacLean) Corner advocated for the conflation of aerial photography, scientific knowledge, and cultural reference that would come to inform a postmodern sensibility of landscape representation commensurate with the aspirations of landscape as a medium of urbanism (figures 8.9, 8.10).[18]

Corner's *Taking Measures* suggests the aerial photograph's complicity with the map as a modern tool of instrumentality, surveillance, and control, useful for exposing hidden relationships between cultural and environmental processes while also establishing new frames for future projects.[19] Aerial imaging over the course of the twentieth century has effectively shifted the definition of landscape from a premodern view that can be measured to a modern measure that can be viewed. This shift is from a purely visual representation toward an indexical trace.[20] In this sense, the aerial photograph functions as a kind of map of the horizontal field condition.

·····

One compelling intersection of the imaginary and instrumental in Corner's formulation of *field operations* is found in the notion of the "flatbed" as a simultaneous representation and projection mechanism. In the aerial representation of the landscape, a working definition of the flatbed is found in the fortuitous coincidence of Leo Steinberg's notion of "flatbed" painting as well as the "flatbed" light table on which aerial reconnaissance photos are analyzed. Steinberg coined the term "flatbed" to describe the painter Robert Rauschenberg's transformation of the picture plane from a vertical surface replicating bodily perception to a horizontal surface of cultural signification (figure 8.11).[21] Steinberg likens the flatbed to a printing press as a horizontal surface capable of accumulating diverse cultural contents. As the daily newspaper accumulates an absolutely irreconcilable collection of diverse contents, Steinberg's flatbed is a surface of visual representation that rejects the humanistic assumptions of upright posture and visual verisimilitude in favor of a problematic heterogeneity of semiological signification.[22] Also significant is the shift from the hand crafting of a picture's surface as an original artifact to the mechanical reproduction of a plate (either photographic or textual) with the attendant loss of aura and problems of authorship.[23] This reading of visual representations as signifying semiologically rather than optically shifts the site of reception from the retinal field to that of culturally accrued language. It also infers that indexical traces of light on an emulsion become imbued with meaning through a system of reading and writing cultural contents.

In contemporary practice, the interpretation of remote satellite imagery for purposes of military surveillance operates under similar assumptions. Across "flatbed" light tables, specially trained analysts pore daily over endless reels of footage of the earth's surface.[24] Rather than reproducing some fictive picture plane of an aerial viewing subject, these filmic swaths of landscape are read semiologically for the indexical clues they hold with regard to movement patterns, human construction, and changes in environmental processes. As horizontal surfaces for the collection of diverse cultural contents, these swaths allow the incongruous juxtaposition of missile launch site with soybean field, nuclear plant accident with seasonal crop burn, or secret airfield with regional farm road. The flatly banal and the politically charged, the mundane and the mistaken, accumulate on the daily strip sampling of the planet from unseen aerial eyes. The flatbed light table of aerial interpretation (now replaced by vertical computer monitors) recommends itself as a point of fortuitous conflation of the recording of the earth's surface and its reading as cultural content.

·····

Evidence of the importance of airborne spectatorship to the cultural construction of landscape can be found in the increasing attention paid to the

Figure 8.11 Robert Rauschenberg, *Third Time Painting*, 1961.

landscape of the airport itself as a site of aerial observation. This is an expansion of the practice of landscape onto sites that have historically not been considered landscapes.[25] This shift in the understanding of what a landscape is and where it should be says as much about contemporary landscape practice as it does about contemporary cultural conditions. Among these cultural conditions is the predominance of the purely visual dimension of landscape, as the airport landscape is among the least bodily accessible. In lieu of its bodily occupation, phenomenal experience, or material quality, the visual is brought to the fore.

While many may be struck by the seeming incongruity of reading an airport as landscape, further study reveals the impossibility of adequately conceiving the contemporary airport site as alternatively either a building or simply urban infrastructure. What is a modern jet-age airport if not a contiguous, highly choreographed, scrupulously maintained, and regularly manicured landscape? The work of Robert Smithson offers a case study in landscape informed by airborne spectatorship. In 1966, Smithson was retained by Tippetts, Abbett, McCarthy & Stratton Engineers and Architects to serve as an "artist-consultant" for the design of the new Dallas/Fort Worth International Airport (figure 8.12). In this role, Smithson consulted on the design of an aerial gallery/landscape that was intended to be experienced from the air as well as from the ground. The introduction of a gallery or museum as part of the terminal complex was intended to serve as a kind of curatorial or representational lens through which the aerial experience of the landscape could be read. Two articles by Smithson, "Towards the Development of an Air Terminal Site" and "Aerial Art," explored the theoretical potential of these new forms of cultural production and reception.

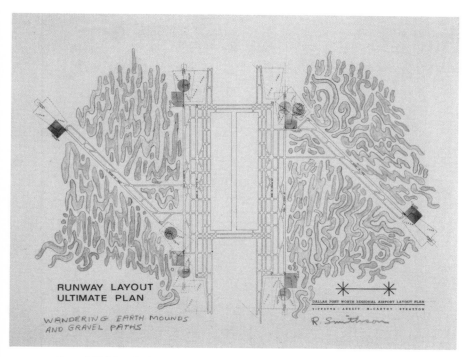

Figure 8.12 Robert Smithson, Dallas Airport, plan with earth mounds, 1967. Art © Holt Smithson Foundation/Licensed by VAGA, New York, NY.

Smithson's interest in the dialectical relationship between the representation of a site within the gallery and the subsequent aerial experience of that site culminated in his development of the "non-site" as a representational and projective practice. Smithson's conception of aerial art and his formulation of the non-site as representational mechanisms warrant further investigation as they postulate an aerial viewing subject for contemporary landscape practice.[26]

In the wake of Smithson's unrealized proposal for "aerial art" at Dallas/ Fort Worth International Airport, landscape architect Daniel Kiley was retained to execute a landscape plan for the site. Kiley produced a range of landscape projects specifically implicating an aerial subject. Among these, Kiley's landscape projects for Dallas/Fort Worth International Airport (1969) and Dulles International Airport (1955–58) are especially significant in the evolution of the jet-age airport typology (figure 8.13). Beyond his landscape projects for Dallas and Dulles, Kiley developed at least two specifically aerial gardens, intended to be experienced from the air, as much as on the ground. These aerial gardens each deployed large pools connected by pathways and structured allées of trees. These two aerial gardens were also connected by the fact that the collaborators on the first, the Air Force Academy campus, provided the recommendation for the second, an obscure public park and waterworks infrastructure on Chicago's lakefront. Kiley's Air Force Academy campus landscape plan (1954–62), in collaboration with Walter Netsch and Skidmore, Owings & Merrill, features a large central "Aerial Garden" as the centerpiece of the cadet campus (figure 8.14).[27]

Based on his experience working with Kiley on the Air Force Academy project, Chicago architect Stan Gladych recommended Kiley to C. F. Murphy for the Jardine Water Filtration Plant project after a previous scheme by Hideo Sasaki had been rejected as unfeasible. Based on the success of the Kiley landscape and public reception of the Water Filtration Plant, Murphy was subsequently awarded the largest public works commission in the city's history, the design of O'Hare International Airport. Regrettably, Murphy didn't include Kiley, or any

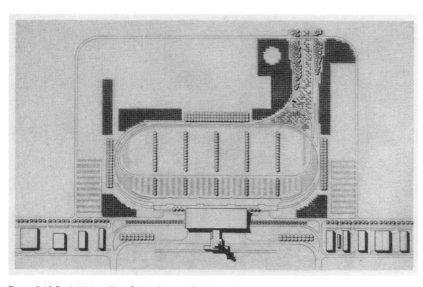

Figure 8.13 Daniel Urban Kiley, Dulles Airport, Washington, DC, site plan, 1955–58.

landscape architect, in the O'Hare team. As a result, the most important airport in the jet-age world failed miserably to produce a public landscape equal to its architectural innovation.

Kiley's subsequent collaboration with C. F. Murphy Associates on the Jardine Water Filtration Plant on Chicago's lakefront features another aerial garden. In this instance, the garden was to provide an aerial view for the "cliff-dwelling" residents of the gold coast's hi-rise apartment buildings. The project included the landscape for the Jardine Plant itself, as well as an adjacent public park. The park features a classical Kiley allée of locust trees extending toward the horizon and culminating in a cantilevered plane. The main structuring device of the park is a set of five large fountains recalling the Great Lakes. These vast pools invoke the rhetorical dimension of the largely prosaic function of the water treatment facility. Kiley's design unites the public works facility with the public park through the representation of water as seen by an aerial viewing subject.[28]

·····

The subject of the airport as a landscape has been reanimated in recent years as a central venue in the discourse around landscape as a medium of urbanism. The past decade has seen a number of high-profile projects for converting redundant airfields into parks, including international design competitions for public parks around the world. The shift of the international airport serving Athens from the coastal airport site at Hellenikon to Mesogeia in 2001 opened a 530-hectare site to the Athenian public for use as a public park. An international design competition invited proposals for the design of

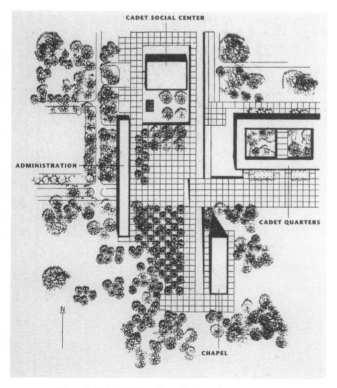

Figure 8.14 Daniel Urban Kiley, Air Force Academy, site plan, 1968.

the public park over its redundant runways as well as the organization of future urban development around the edges of the site. This ambitious program proposed housing, commercial buildings, and cultural venues in the context of a vast horizontal stretch of land overlooking the sea. The winning scheme by Philippe Coignet / Office of Landscape Morphology with DZO Architecture, Elena Fernandez, David Serero, Arnaud Descombes, and Antoine Regnault, featured complex waveform landscape berms traversing the formerly flat airfield and reconnecting the higher elevation neighborhoods above with the coast below (figure 8.15). This strategy of cut and fill, while reconciling the enormously scaled airfield with the spatial requirements of a distinctly designed landscape, also assists in delivering flows of fast-moving surface water and slow-moving strollers across the park. Throughout this topographic construction, a complex counterdiagram of succession planting is set in motion to register the shift of the park from an initially ordered arrangement that slowly gives way to a self-regulating arboreal ecosystem. While the ambitious scheme remains unrealized, it offers a compelling case study in the potentials of landscape urbanism and the abandoned airport as public park.[29]

Downsview Park, located on the site of an abandoned military airbase in Toronto, was among the most ambitious of these initiatives for reclaiming abandoned airport sites with a two-stage international design competition for a public park to be built on a former military airbase in the rapidly aging and no-longer-peripheral suburbs of Canada's most populous city. The Downsview project represented a portion of Canada's peace dividend from the end of the Cold War. The airbase was used for a variety of military aviation purposes during its half century of use between the 1940s and its decommissioning in the 1990s when its future came up for public discussion. While the site was quite peripheral to Toronto's pre–World War II population, postwar

Figure 8.15 Philippe Coignet/Office of Landscape Morphology,
Hellenikon Athens Airport Park competition, plan, 2001.

suburbanization engulfed the area and Downsview now sits near the heart of metropolitan Toronto. Almost inevitably, airfields tend to be sited on topographically and ecologically undistinguished terrain. Downsview is no exception. The airfield was designed to occupy the higher and drier, yet still relatively flat, open ground between two of the region's important watersheds: the Don River to the east and the Humber River to the west.

The finalist project for Downsview by James Corner and Stan Allen is exemplary of the potentials of the airport site as landscape park and is viewed as a canonical example of landscape urbanism. Typical of this project, and by now standard fare for projects of this type, are detailed diagrams of phasing, animal habitats, succession planting, and hydrological systems, as well as programmatic and planning regimes. Particularly compelling is the complex interweaving of natural ecologies with the social, cultural, and infrastructural layers of the contemporary city.[30]

Both Koolhaas/OMA (with Bruce Mau) and Bernard Tschumi submitted entries as finalists in the Downsview Park competition. In this project, they found their historical fortunes reversed, more or less precisely from their roles as first and second place authors of the Parc de la Villette competition of two decades prior. The imageable and media-friendly Koolhaas/OMA and Mau scheme for Downsview, "Tree City," was awarded first prize and the commission, while the more sublime, layered, and intellectually challenging scheme of the office of Bernard Tschumi will doubtless enjoy greater influence within architectural culture, particularly as the information age transforms our understandings and limits of the "natural." Tschumi's "The Digital and the Coyote" project for Downsview presented an electronic analogue to his interest in urban event, with richly detailed diagrams of succession planting and the seeding of ambient urbanity in the midst of seemingly desolate prairies (figures 8.16, 8.17). Tschumi's position at Downsview is symmetrical with his original thesis for la Villette. Both projects were based on a fundamental indictment of the nineteenth-century Olmstedian model, offering in its place an understanding of landscape as implicated in an effectively "planetary urbanization." As Tschumi put it in his project statement, "neither theme park or wildlife preserve, Downsview does not seek to renew using the conventions of traditional park compositions such as those

Figure 8.16 Bernard Tschumi, Downsview Park, Toronto, view, 2000.

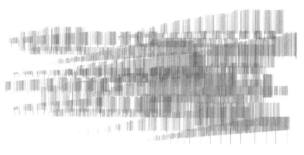

Figure 8.17 Bernard Tschumi, Downsview Park, Toronto, succession diagrams, 2000.

of Vaux or Olmsted. ... Airstrips, information centers, public performance spaces, internet and worldwide web access all point to a redefinition of received ideas about parks, nature, and recreation, in a 21st century setting where everything is 'urban,' even in the middle of the wilderness."[31]

Since the canonical case of Downsview, international design competitions have invited landscape and urbanism proposals for a host of redundant airport sites in cities around the world. Recent projects for airport conversions in Berlin, Germany (2012); Reykjavik, Iceland (2013); Quito, Ecuador (2011); Caracas, Venezuela (2012); Casablanca, Morocco (2007); and Taichung, Taiwan (2011) are indicative of this tendency. In each of these cases, the finalist projects collectively embodied the aspirations of landscape urbanist practice. Eelco Hooftman/Gross.Max.'s competition-winning project for the conversion of Berlin's Tempelhoff Airport; Henri Bava/Agence Ter's proposal for Casablanca; Luis Callejas's proposals for Quito and Caracas; and Chris Reed/Stoss Landscape Urbanism's proposal for Taichung Gateway Park are notable evidence of the fecundity of landscape urbanist practices for the abandoned airfield.

·····

While the redevelopment of abandoned airfields as large landscape projects is clearly relevant to the projective potentials of landscape urbanism, the much more challenging project is for the conception of the operational airfield as a landscape in its own right. The most comprehensive and conceptually challenging project to explore the operational airfield as a constructed landscape is the master plan project for Schiphol International Airport outside Amsterdam by Adriaan Geuze/West 8.[32]

West 8's ambitious scheme for the Schiphol Amsterdam Airport landscape abandons the professional tradition of specifically detailed planting plans, deploying instead a general botanical strategy of sunflowers, clover, and beehives. This work, by avoiding intricate compositional designs and precise planting arrangements, allows the project to respond to future programmatic and political changes in Schiphol's planning, positioning landscape as a strategic partner in the complex process of airport planning rather than (as is more often the case) simply an unfortunate victim of it. This positioning of the landscape medium as an open-ended and flexible matrix for future indeterminacy echoes Tschumi's arguments for both la Villette and Downsview, while reiterating one of the most often staked claims for landscape urbanism. In spite of the fact that runway alignments tend to be among the most durable of urban constructions, rarely if ever being removed once constructed, the operational airfield, the airport itself, and the surrounding urban field face a virtually continual program of construction, demolition, and ongoing renovation. In the context of such urban malleability and flux, particularly one characterized by enormous horizontal fields of urbanization, landscape offers a medium and model for urban order.

One urbanist grappling with the airport as a site for landscape is the Colombian architect Luis Callejas. In a provocative range of projects Callejas proposes a new era of aerial affect. Beginning with his 2010 "Airplot" project for the guerilla decommissioning of London's Heathrow Airport sponsored by Greenpeace (figure 8.18), Callejas has proposed a range of projects for operating abandoned airports. Callejas's proposal for the Parque del Lago in Quito,

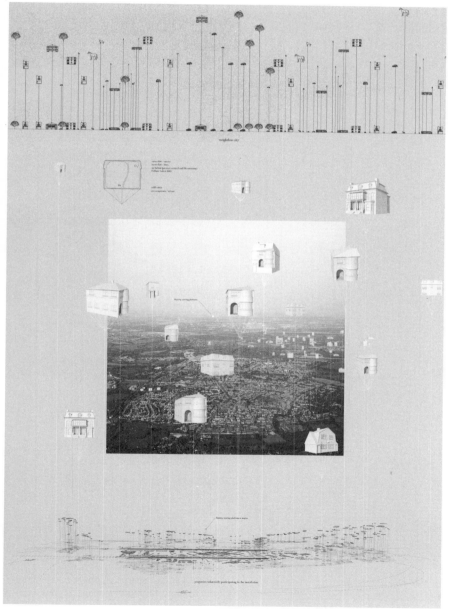

Figure 8.18 Luis Callejas, Airplot, Heathrow Airport,
London, England, aerial photomontage, 2010.

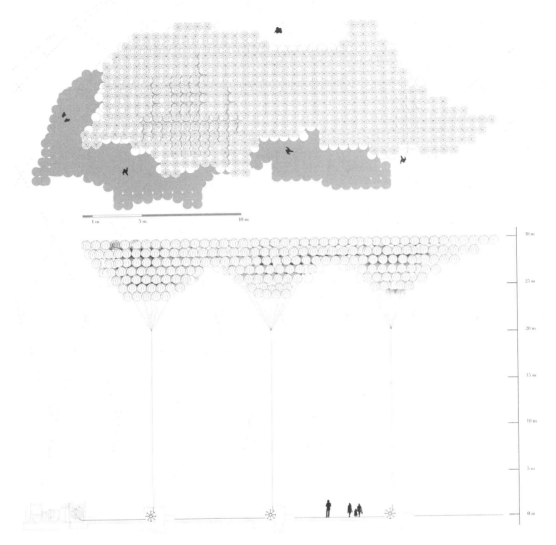

Figure 8.19 Luis Callejas/Paisajes Emergentes, Clouds,
Ituango, Colombia, plan and elevation, 2009.

Figure 8.20 Luis Callejas/Paisajes Emergentes, Clouds,
Ituango, Colombia, view, 2009.

Ecuador, juxtaposes the reflectivity and endlessness of pools stretching to the horizon of an abandoned airfield with the reflective metallic surfaces of the airplanes that once occupied the site.[33] In a provocative range of projects Callejas has proposed the use of large arrays of aerial inflatables. These include his proposal for the installation of inflatable replicas of terrestrial objects outside Heathrow. They also include monumental totemic structures commemorating communities impacted by the Ituango hydroelectric plant in Colombia (figures 8.19, 8.20). In pushing his architecture to the limits of the object, Callejas has developed a pneumatic architecture evident through the public spectacle of aerial suspension.

Callejas's appropriation of landscape as a frame for a diverse body of work illustrates an appetite for addressing the ecological imperatives of contemporary design culture as well as the diverse array of international environments in which his work is projected. Callejas's interest in the aerial might also be read in relation to contemporary debates regarding the critical and the performative in architecture. The architectonic language and design sensibility evident in this work reveal a deep literacy with contemporary architectural culture, particularly the work of those architects committed to problematizing buildings and their grounds. In this regard Callejas's projects share affinities with the work of Miralles/Pinós and Zaera-Polo/Moussavi that we revisited earlier. Of course these projects share an interest in the conflation of buildings with their grounds, and in the more extreme examples give way to the construction of complex horizontal surfaces. It would be equally productive to consider Callejas's work in relation to the Ungers/Koolhaas axis and the contemporary potentials for a "green archipelago."[34] The work of Callejas shares with Ungers's project a particular interest in a radically decentered notion of site, one that is often conceived as an island, whether inland or literally at sea. In contrast with work that eschews or denies context, Callejas's projects often radically delimit their sitedness, thereby revealing some latent, local conditions isolated from larger territorial conditions.

Callejas's projects often transcend their precedents by pushing the limits of the architectural object up to and well beyond their limits, into environments, experiences, and atmospheres. These projects often invoke the aerial as both subject and object of architectural projection. While these affects can occasionally manifest themselves through architectural artifice or edification, they are best described as landscapes. Since the original claims of landscape as urbanism, a variety of urban practices have developed lines of work that are best captured, if imperfectly, with the term *landscape*. However, the status of these practices and the projects they propose often remain ambivalent relative to the more specific professional identity of landscape architecture. On one hand, these practices suggest the co-option of the medium of landscape by architects and urbanists. On the other, these practices can be read as simply engaging in modes of practice that have already been circumscribed in the professional role of the landscape architect. In the final chapter, we will turn full circle and reconsider the impact of the emergence of landscape as a form of urbanism for the discipline and profession of landscape architecture, by revisiting the original claims for the "new art" in the nineteenth century.

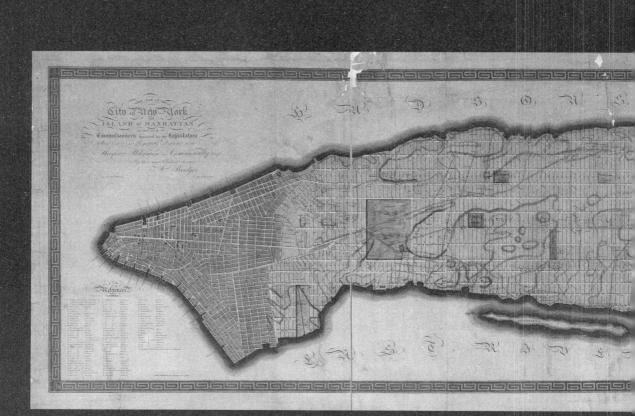

Scale of One Mile.

Nine: Claiming Landscape as Architecture

The landscape architect ... is still surely wrongly named.
—Sir Geoffrey Jellicoe, 1960

The emergence of landscape urbanism over the past two decades raises fundamental questions of disciplinary and professional identity for the field of landscape architecture. Although the various etymologies of the term "landscape" have rightly preoccupied scholars and practitioners for decades, the origins of "landscape architecture" as a professional identity have received less critical attention.[1]

Questions of professional nomenclature have troubled proponents of the so-called new art since its inception in the nineteenth century. Long-standing debates over the term reveal a tension between disciplinary identity and scope of work. Founders of the new field advanced an array of positions—from those embodying a tradition of landscape gardening and rural improvement to those advocating for landscape as an architectural and urban art. Many American proponents of the field held a strong cultural affinity for English practices of landscape gardening. In contrast, continental practices of urban improvement allied with landscape promised a different scope of work. Complicating matters further was the desire by many for a singular identity, not easily confused with existing professional and artistic categories.

In its American formation, this new field was imagined as a progressive response to the social and environmental challenges of rapid urbanization in the second half of the nineteenth century. Although there was great enthusiasm for the articulation of those concerns, it was much less clear what to call the new profession and its related field of study. By the end of the nineteenth century, available professional identities (architect, engineer, gardener) were perceived by many as inadequate to new (urban, industrial) conditions, which demanded a new identity explicitly associated with landscape. What did it mean for the founders of the new field to claim landscape as architecture? And how do those choices resonate with the contemporary understanding of landscape as urbanism?

By the end of the nineteenth century, American boosters of the new art of landscape committed the nascent profession to an identity associated with the old art of architecture. This decision to identify architecture (as opposed to art, engineering, or gardening) as the proximate professional peer group is significant for contemporary understandings of landscape architecture. This history sheds compelling light on the subsequent development of city planning as a distinct professional identity spun out of landscape architecture in the first decades of the twentieth century, as well as on debates regarding landscape as a form of urbanism at the close of the century.

.....

The English poet and gardener William Shenstone coined the term "landscape gardener" in the middle of the eighteenth century. Humphry Repton adopted the term "landscape gardening" for his professional identity (figure 9.2) as well as the titles of his three major texts around the turn of the following century: *Sketches and Hints on Landscape Gardening* (1794), *Observations on the Theory and Practice of Landscape Gardening* (1803), and *An Enquiry into the Changes of Taste in Landscape Gardening* (1806).

The French architect, engineer, and garden designer Jean-Marie Morel is credited with coining the formulation *architecte-paysagiste*. Morel was, at the time of his death in 1810, among France's most notable designers advocating the English style in gardening. His obituary was widely circulated in France with the professional appellation *architecte-paysagiste*. Morel had previously described himself as *architecte et paysagiste*, a description of his multiple professional identities. Sometime around the turn of the nineteenth century, he elided the "et" in favor of a hyphenated compound. Two decades later, Morel would be referred to posthumously, sans hyphen, as simply *architecte paysagiste*. Morel's neologism predates the usage of the English term "landscape architect" and is generally considered the origin of the modern professional identity.[2]

The first usage of the English-language compound "landscape architecture" is found in Gilbert Meason's *On the Landscape Architecture of the Great Painters of Italy* (1828). Meason used the neologism to refer specifically to architecture set in the context of Italian landscape painting. Twelve years later John Claudius Loudon employed the same terminology on the title page of his publication of the collected works of Repton, *The Landscape Gardening and Landscape Architecture of the Late Humphry Repton, Esq.* (1840). Although

Figure 9.2 Humphry Repton, Landscape Gardener, business card, ca. 1790.

some debate persists regarding the precise meaning of landscape architecture in the title, it is reasonable to infer from the available evidence that Loudon, following Meason, was using the term to designate architecture set within the landscape, rather than to describe Repton's practice, which is consistently referred to as landscape gardening in both the title and the text of the publication (figures 9.3, 9.4).[3]

Meason's and Loudon's publications and the term "landscape architecture" were certainly available to, and likely read by, American proponents of English taste in landscape gardening in the nineteenth century. Among the most prominent was Andrew Jackson Downing, who would play a central role in advocating for the new art in America. Considered by many to have prepared the ground for the development of landscape architecture as a profession, Downing would have been aware of the wording "landscape architecture" from Meason's book and Loudon's writing. Yet he persisted with his preference for the term "landscape gardening" throughout his career, from the publication of *A Treatise on*

Figure 9.3 Humphry Repton, *Red Book of Moseley Hall* [*sic*], Birmingham, before and after views, 1792.

Figure 9.4 Humphry Repton, *Red Book of Moseley Hall*
[*sic*], Birmingham, before and after views, 1792.

the Theory and Practice of Landscape Gardening (1841) to his untimely death in 1852. In section 9 of his *Treatise*, titled "Landscape or Rural Architecture," it is clear that Downing follows Meason in using the term to refer to architecture in landscape or rural contexts.[4] By the time of Downing's death, at least one English garden designer, William Andrews Nesfield, was referred to in print as a landscape architect, in John Weale's *London Exhibited* (1852). Yet this remained the exception in English practice throughout the nineteenth century.

In that same year, the French landscape gardener Louis-Sulpice Varé was appointed *jardiniere paysagiste* (landscape gardener) for the improvements at the Bois de Boulogne. By 1854, Varé stamped drawings of the Bois de Boulogne with an improvised seal reading "Service de l'architecte-paysagiste" (Office of the Landscape Architect).[5] Varé was soon replaced by Adolphe Alphand and Jean-Pierre Barillet-Deschamps, yet his identification as a landscape architect would prove to be particularly important as the Bois de Boulogne emerged as the most significant precedent for the Central Park in New York City.

·····

In 1857, Frederick Law Olmsted was appointed "Superintendent of the Central Park" in New York. Finding himself without prospects, as his forays into farming and publishing had left him in debt, Olmsted pursued the position at the recommendation of Charles Wyllys Elliott, a family friend and member of the newly

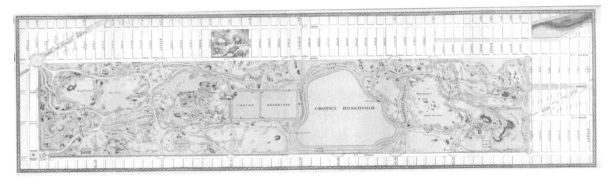

Figure 9.5 Frederick Law Olmsted & Calvert Vaux, Plan of Central Park, New York, 1868.

Figure 9.6 Martel's Panorama of New York's Central Park, aerial view, ca. 1864.

created Board of Commissioners of the Central Park. Elliott and the commissioners awarded Olmsted (and his collaborator, the English architect Calvert Vaux) first prize in the design competition for the new park the following year. The Olmsted Vaux scheme was premiated by the Republican majority jury split along a strictly political party-line vote. Following their victory, Olmsted's title was enhanced to "Architect-in-Chief and Superintendent," and Vaux was appointed "Consulting Architect" (figures 9.5, 9.6).[6]

Although the proposal of one member of the Central Park board to invite Adolphe Alphand himself to serve as a member of the competition jury was unsuccessful, there is ample evidence that boosters of the new park looked to Paris for their urban inspiration. One member of the advisory board, James Phalen, retired to Paris in 1856, funded, at least in part, by profits from the sale of land that formed part of the new Central Park. On his arrival in Paris, Phalen requested, on behalf of the Central Park board, a history of the improvements to the Bois de Boulogne presently underway as part of Alphand's larger urban project. Phalen introduced Olmsted to Alphand during Olmsted's 1859 tour of European park precedents. Alphand met with Olmsted multiple times at the Bois de Boulogne and provided background information and guided tours of his program of urban improvements (figures 9.7, 9.8).[7]

From the time of Olmsted's appointment as superintendent in 1857 and through his subsequent elevation to architect-in-chief in 1858, he made no reference to the professional title *landscape architect*. Olmsted may have been aware of the French usage of *architecte-paysagiste* and would have known of the English-language antecedents of Meason and Loudon, but there is no evidence that Olmsted conceived of the term as a professional identity before his November 1859 visit to Paris. The term emerged only subsequent to Olmsted's tour of European parks and meetings with Alphand. Olmsted would likely have seen drawings stamped "*Service de l'architecte-paysagiste*" associated with the improvements at the Bois de Boulogne, and, more significantly, witnessed the expanded scope of Parisian practice in which landscape gardening was set in relation to infrastructural improvements, urbanization, and the management of large public projects. Olmsted visited the Bois de Boulogne

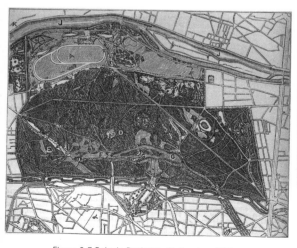

Figure 9.7 Bois de Boulogne, Paris, plan, 1852.

Figure 9.8. Bois de Boulogne, Paris, aerial view, 1852.

more than any other precedent project, making eight visits in two weeks.[8] Following his return to New York in late December 1859, every subsequent professional commission that Olmsted accepted for urban improvements included specific reference to his preferred professional identity as landscape architect.

The earliest recorded evidence of the professional title *landscape architect* in America is found in personal correspondence from Olmsted to his father, John Olmsted, in July 1860. This letter, and subsequent correspondence, refers to the April 1860 commissioning of Olmsted and Vaux as "Landscape Architects" by the "Commissioners for laying out the upper part of New York island." Among those commissioners charged with the planning of Manhattan above 155th Street was Henry Hill Elliott, the older brother of Central Park commissioner Charles Wyllys Elliott.[9] The first appointment of a landscape architect in America was not for the design of a park, pleasure ground, or public garden, but for the planning of northern Manhattan (figure 9.9). In this context the landscape architect was originally conceived as a professional responsible for divining the shape of the city itself, rather than pastoral exceptions to it (figure 9.10).

In April 1862, as evidence of their enthusiasm for the new collective identity, Olmsted and Vaux had their appointments clarified as "Landscape Architects to the Board" of Central Park. Following the interruption of the Civil War years, they were reappointed "Landscape Architects to the Board of Commissioners of Central Park" in July 1865. In May of the following year, Olmsted and Vaux were appointed "Landscape Architects" for Prospect Park in Brooklyn, and the

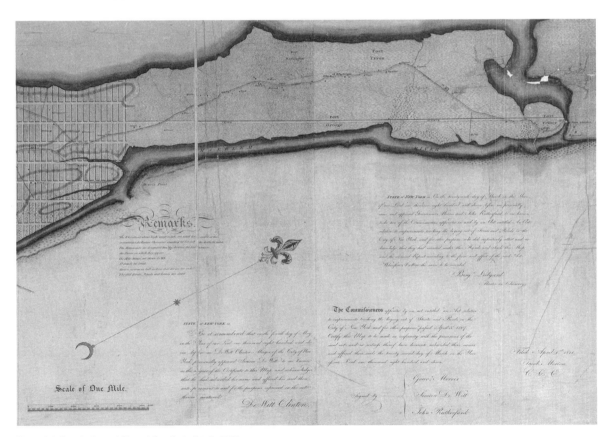

Figure 9.9 Commissioners' Plan of New York, detail, 1811.

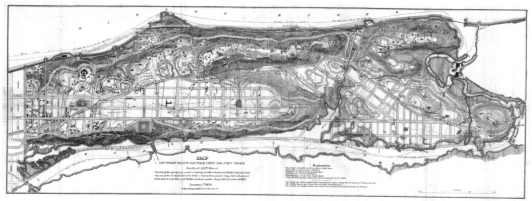

Figure 9.10 Knapp Plan for Washington Heights, New York, 1868.

Figure 9.11 Olmsted, Vaux & Co., Prospect Park, Brooklyn, plan, 1870.

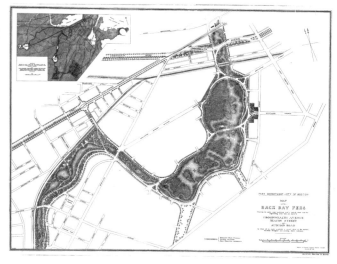

Figure 9.12 Olmsted & Partners, Back Bay Fens, Boston, plan, 1887.

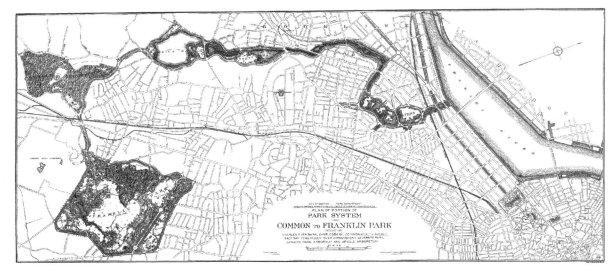

Figure 9.13 Olmsted, Olmsted & Eliot, Plan of Portion of
Park System from Common to Franklin Park, Boston, 1894.

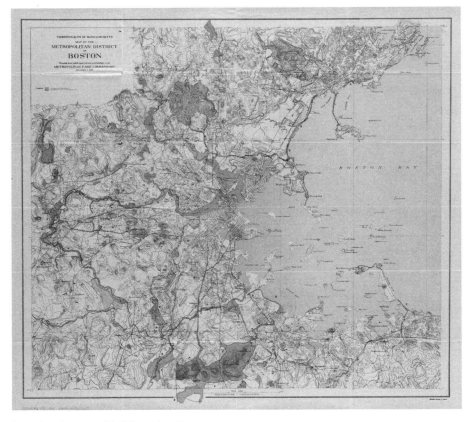

Figure 9.14 Commonwealth of Massachusetts,
Metropolitan Park Commission, Metropolitan Park System,
Boston, map, 1901.

term was well on its way to being consolidated as the definitive professional identity for American practitioners of the new art (figures 9.11, 9.12).[10]

Despite his conversion to the new identifier, Olmsted remained "all the time bothered with the miserable nomenclature" of landscape architecture and longed for a new term to stand for the "sylvan art." He groused that "*Landscape* is not a good word, *Architecture* is not; the combination is not. *Gardening* is worse." He longed for specific English translations for the French terms that more adequately captured the subtleties of the new art of urban order.[11] So the question persists, given the enduring anxiety of conflating landscape *with* architecture, why did proponents of the new profession ultimately choose to claim landscape *as* architecture? Olmsted was convinced that adopting the mantle of the architect would bolster the new field in the eyes of the public and militate against the tendency to mistake the work as being primarily concerned with plants and gardens. It would also, Olmsted argued, guard against the "greater danger" of landscape's potential future "disalliance" with architecture. Olmsted became convinced that the range of study required by the increasing demands for scientific knowledge would result in alienation of the new field from the fine arts and architecture.[12]

.....

By the final decade of the nineteenth century, enthusiasm had built for the claiming of a new profession. Although many antecedent practices on both sides of the Atlantic predated it, the first professional body for the field, the American Society of Landscape Architects (ASLA), was formed in 1899. Based on Olmsted's successful advocacy for the French terminology, American founders ultimately adopted the Francophone "landscape architect" over the Anglophone "landscape gardener" as the most suitable professional nomenclature for the new art. Based on this semantic distinction, and its implicit claim to practices of urban order and infrastructural arrangement, the profession was fully embodied in America (figures 9.13, 9.14).

Olmsted's stature and decades of precedent notwithstanding, many of the founders of the ASLA chafed at the title "landscape architect." Beatrix Farrand rejected the term outright and persisted in her preference for "landscape gardener." As evidence of this ambivalence, the original constitution of the ASLA invited fellowship from either landscape gardeners or landscape architects in good standing. The larger concern among the founders of the field was to establish the new art as a "liberal profession" rather than a commercial activity. Thus the constitution offered membership to those who earned their livelihood from the professional activity of design rather than commissions from the selling of labor, plants, or other commercial interests.[13] Following the creation of the ASLA, the new profession quickly set about establishing a new academic discipline and professional journal. The first academic program in landscape architecture was founded in 1900 at Harvard, where it was housed alongside architecture in the Lawrence Scientific School as a liberal art and profession. *Landscape Architecture* appeared as a quarterly journal in 1910, further consolidating the institutional foundation (figures 9.15, 9.16).[14]

The professional identity of landscape architect and the professional field of landscape architecture were solidified internationally through the foundation

Figure 9.15 Kongjian Yu/Turenscape, Qunli Stormwater
Park, Haerbin, China, aerial photograph, 2011.

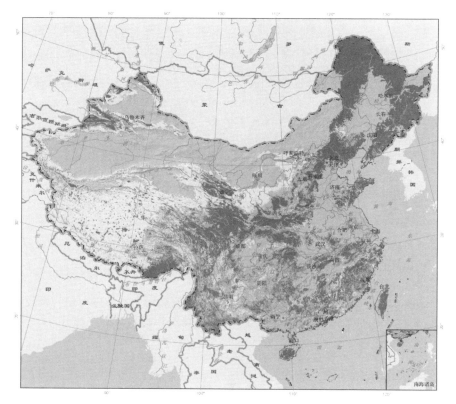

Figure 9.16 Kongjian Yu/Turenscape, Chinese National
Ecological Security Plan, map, 2007–8.

of the International Federation of Landscape Architects (IFLA) in 1948. Yet even founding IFLA president Sir Geoffrey Jellicoe expressed misgivings about "landscape architect," shortly after leaving office.[15] Jellicoe was not the last to lament the lack of a distinct singular international identity for the field. Many persist to this day in their frustration with the "miserable nomenclature" of landscape architecture. If Jellicoe's desire for a distinct single term were to be realized, it would likely direct us back to the Francophone origins of the English term. In contemporary Paris, landscape architects have reappropriated *paysagiste*. This originally referred to a painter of the landscape, though in contemporary usage it is the distilled modern edition of *architecte-paysagiste*, which now comes across as formal and even somewhat officious. Happily, the word "paysagiste" meets Jellicoe's requirements for a distinct, singular term for the profession, and one that shares linguistic affinities across French, Spanish, Italian, and Portuguese. The translation of the term into English offers itself readily as simply "landscapist." Only time will tell if this singular identity will prove more durable than the last, which has held up since the nineteenth century. Despite its ongoing anxiety over landscape architecture's nomenclature, the field has come to be known through the contradictions inherent in claiming *landscape as architecture*.

·····

The origins and aspirations of landscape as architecture emerge from very specific cultural, economic, and social conditions attendant to western European and North American industrialized modernity. The "miserable nomenclature" of landscape architecture has only recently been appropriated for use in the context of East Asian urbanization. Although there are many East Asian traditions of landscape gardening, including specific cultural formations in Japan, Korea, and China, none of those cultures have produced a precise equivalent of landscape architecture. Only recently, with the transfer of knowledge on urbanism and design from West to East, has the English language term "landscape architecture" been adopted for use in China. Not surprisingly, the first professional practice of landscape architecture in China has developed over the past decade in response to the demand for an ecologically informed practice of urban planning.

Kongjian Yu was the first landscape architect to open a private firm in China following the Western model of private consulting practices in design and planning. As such, Yu represents a historical singularity and is arguably the most important landscape architect practicing in China today. He has emerged as a leading figure for international audiences in the English language over the past decade. Based on the national awards and honors that have been bestowed upon Yu and his firm Turenscape, the Chinese have tended to reinforce this perception, particularly with respect to recognition by national political and cultural organizations.[16]

Yu / Turenscape have leveraged this unique historical position to lobby Chinese political elites, most notably national leadership and mayors, for the adoption of Western-style ecological planning practices at the metropolitan, provincial, and even national scales. The fullest articulation of this aspiration is embodied in Yu / Turenscape's 2007–8 project for a Chinese National

Ecological Security Plan. Taken together with a decade of lectures to the Chinese Ministry of Construction's Conference of Mayors (1997–2007) and the Chinese publication of his influential treatise *The Road to Urban Landscape: A Dialogue with Mayors* (with Dihua Li, 2003), Yu has effectively articulated a scientifically informed ecological planning agenda at a national scale to domestic and international audiences.[17]

Yu was born the second son and third child of peasant farmers in rural Zhejiang Province, southwest of Shanghai, in 1963.[18] Coincidentally, that year saw the first public pronouncement of the so-called Four Modernizations, when at the Conference on Scientific and Technological Work held in Shanghai, Premier Zhou Enlai proposed to modernize Chinese agriculture, industry, defense, and science and technology. This early gesture toward economic transformation would founder for the next decade and a half until after Mao Zedong's death and the subsequent consolidation of power by Zhou Enlai's protégé Deng Xiaoping. Following his ascension to the highest offices of the Chinese Communist Party in late 1978, Deng Xiaoping announced the adoption of Zhou Enlai's project of the "Four Modernizations," which many now read as the beginning of the reform era in modern China.

As Yu was preparing to enter university in 1979–80, he was of precisely the age to benefit from economic reforms, scientific modernization, and opening to the West. Yu underwent the Soviet-style national standardized testing system of university placement, through which he was placed at Beijing Forestry University. Among the early indicators of the "Four Modernizations" was the return to Beijing in 1979 of Beijing Forestry University's undergraduate program in landscape architecture. The program had been among those exiled to Yunnan Province in the remote southwestern corner of the country during the 1960s in the context of the "Great Proletarian Cultural Revolution." Upon Yu's arrival in the capital, he was allowed to enter the program in landscape architecture. Sixty undergraduates were divided in two tracks: "Landscape Gardening" and "Landscape Design." As Yu was untrained in drawing, he was assigned to the gardening track.[19]

Following Yu's completion of the bachelor of landscape architecture at Beijing Forestry, he was subsequently admitted into the Master of Landscape Architecture (MLA) program. Yu was the first of five of his classmates in that cohort to open private consulting firms in China and practice as landscape architects. During his graduate studies in the MLA at Beijing Forestry, from 1984 to 1987, Yu had access to and made regular use of an exceptional library (by Chinese standards) of English-language books in landscape architecture and planning. While at Beijing Forestry, Yu read seminal works on landscape architecture and planning by Kevin Lynch, Ian McHarg, and Richard Forman, among many others.[20] Given his reading of these texts, his growing facility with English, and his status as a top graduate student from his program, Yu was asked to translate a series of lectures by Professor Carl Steinitz of Harvard that were delivered at Beijing Forestry University in 1987. Prior to Steinitz's lectures, Yu had already been completing work on his MLA thesis on the subject of "Quantitative Methods of Landscape Assessment," inspired in part by Steinitz's mentor Kevin Lynch. By the time of his encounter with Steinitz and completion of his master's thesis, Yu already harbored aspirations of postgraduate work in the United States. Based on Steinitz's recommendation, Yu was persuaded to apply to the recently inaugurated doctor of design program at Harvard to pursue a doctorate in ecological planning.[21]

The doctor of design was organized as a research-based degree, culminating in a written dissertation, but candidates advised by Carl Steinitz regularly entered his landscape planning studios as a part of their coursework. In addition to mentoring from Steinitz, Yu integrated into his course of study the principles of landscape ecology from classes with Richard Forman. He was also immersed in the representational and computational questions associated with aggregating large datasets of ecological information through geographic information systems (GIS). Through his work with Forman, he was introduced to the concept of strategic points in landscape ecology. During this time, Yu was also reading about game theory and came to associate the language of spatial conflict associated with games with Forman's language of landscape analysis, particularly as it pertained to the identification and maintenance of particular strategic points in a landscape, or what Yu would come to refer to as "security points." This understanding ultimately informed his conception of planning for ecological "security patterns."[22]

It was at Harvard during his doctoral studies that Yu integrated Steinitz's rigorous planning methods, Forman's language for analyzing complex landscape matrices, the tools and techniques of digital geographic information systems associated with the Lab for Computer Graphics, and the concepts of game theory. Through this synthesis, Yu first conceived of a national-scaled ecological security plan as a project for China. He developed the concept, methodological questions, representational means, and analytical approach for such a project through his doctoral thesis "Security Patterns in Landscape Planning," advised by Steinitz, Forman, and Stephen Ervin. The thesis included a case study for the ecological security planning of Red Stone National Park in China, but aspired to articulate a methodological approach to planning for ecological security across regional, provincial, and national scales. The thesis embodies a methodological integration of Yu's various influences from Beijing Forestry and Harvard, including the so-called layer method of McHarg, the visual analysis methods of Lynch, the ecological analysis of Forman, and the geographic information systems methods of Ervin and the legacy of GIS embodied in the Lab through the work of Jack Dangermond and others. During his studies at Harvard, Yu worked as a research associate in GIS as well as a teaching fellow. Over the summer of 1994, he was a researcher at Dangermond's Environmental Systems Research Institute (ESRI) in Redlands, California.

Among Yu's innovations in the thesis was the identification of particular "security points" ("SPs") through the analysis of ecological function as it is affected at particular thresholds of change in the form of a step-function. Yu recognized that ecological functions can withstand fairly large impacts without proportionate change, but will suddenly change drastically across particular thresholds of impact. Yu's thesis proposes three distinct SPs: ecological, visual, and agricultural.[23] These categories map closely to topics associated with ecology, tourism, and food security that his national plan for China's ecological security would embody. Yu's conception of a national ecological security plan for China is, however, not without its precedents in the West. While at Harvard, Yu was exposed to various historical antecedents for regional- and national-scaled landscape planning through Steinitz's courses, including Warren Manning's 1912 national plan for the United States.[24]

Following the completion of his doctoral work, Yu spent two years as a landscape architect in the Laguna Beach, California, offices of SWA. During this time, Yu published a series of journal articles based on his doctoral dissertation.[25] In 1997, he returned to Beijing to open his consulting firm, Turenscape, and take a faculty position at Peking University. The firm has engaged in a range of large-scale ecological planning projects, in addition to the national ecological security plan.[26] Turenscape's planning practice—its articulation of a national ecological security plan as well as its various regional, metropolitan, and municipal proposals—represents a transfer of scientific and cultural knowledge of historic significance. Beyond their technical efficacy, predictive accuracy, or ease of implementation, the very fact of these plans represents the unique historical circumstances of Kongjian Yu's personal and professional arc. They embody a great experiment in conveying, across generations and cultures, an idea of scientifically informed spatial planning that emerged in the West. Ironically, the first generation of Chinese professionals trained in landscape ecology and planning in the United States now represent the greatest probability for the renewed relevance of a tradition of planning that has been all but eclipsed in the United States. Since the 1978–79 declaration of the "Four Modernizations" in China, the political, economic, and cultural conditions in the United States have trended increasingly away from the prospect of scientifically infused spatial planning practice in favor of a neoliberal, decentralized, and privatized economy of spatial decision making. During those decades, improbably, and through the export of higher education in design and planning, practices of ecologically informed spatial planning have found fertile grounds for influencing public and political opinion in China. Contemporary China's unique combination of top-down political structure, centralized decision making, openness to Western conceptions in science and technology, and rapid ongoing urbanization render it uniquely capable of receiving Yu's interpretation of ecological planning strategies. Regardless of its scientific probity or prospects for implementation, the simple fact of Kongjian Yu's proposal for an ecological security plan at the scale of China represents a paradoxical yet promising return to a long tradition of landscape planning.

The paradoxical promise of an ecological planning practice in China offers an ironic parallel to the emerging tendency in discussions of landscape as a form of urbanism. On both sides of the Atlantic, the topic of an "ecological urbanism" has been recently proposed, offering both continuation and critique of the landscape urbanist agenda. While academic programs, publications, and professional practices in both landscape urbanism and landscape architecture continue to grow globally, an ecological urbanist discourse is rapidly reproducing itself. As we will see in the book's conclusion, an ecological approach to urbanism promises to render a more precise and delimited focus on ecology as model and medium for design. This approach suggests a refinement of terms and a more narrowly focused intellectual engagement with ecology as an epistemological framework available across the design disciplines. This has the duel benefit of avoiding some of landscape's luggage, while rebooting the now two-decades-old intellectual agenda of landscape urbanism. In this formulation, ecology offers access to an operating system underpinning practices of landscape as urbanism, while promising greater performative precision and professional impact while holding the potential for broader public participation in the discourse.

3500 m

Conclusion: From Landscape to Ecology

Interdisciplinarity is not the calm of an easy security; it begins effectively ... when the solidarity of the old disciplines breaks down—perhaps even violently, via the jolts of fashion—in the interests of a new object and a new language.
—Roland Barthes, 1971

As we have argued, landscape urbanism emerged over the past two decades as a critique of the disciplinary and professional commitments of neotraditional urban design. This critique has much to do with urban design's perceived inability to come to terms with the rapid pace of urban change and the essentially horizontal character of contemporary automobile-based urbanization across North America and much of western Europe. It also concerns the inability of traditional urban design strategies to cope with the environmental conditions left in the wake of deindustrialization, increased calls for an ecologically informed urbanism, and the ascendancy of design culture as an aspect of urban development. The established discourse of landscape urbanism is seemingly maturing, no longer sufficiently youthful for the avant-gardist appetites of architectural culture yet growing in significance as its key texts and projects are translated and disseminated globally. One aspect of this maturity is that the discourse on landscape urbanism, while hardly new in architectural circles, is rapidly being absorbed into the global discourse on cities within urban design and planning.

The established discourse of landscape urbanism as chronicled in this volume sheds interesting light on the ultimately abandoned proposal that urban design might have originally been housed in landscape architecture at Harvard. One reading of Josep Lluís Sert's original formulation for urban design at Harvard's Graduate School of Design is that he wanted to provide a trans-disciplinary space within the academy. Contemporary interpretations of Sert's multiple motives remind us of the innumerable questions raised at the landmark 1956 Harvard conferences on the potential relationships within and between the various design disciplines with respect to the city. Among those questions was the contentious one about the appropriate role for landscape within urban design, a topic of no small import today and of central significance to the origins of urban design.[1]

Also in 1956, one of North America's most successful modernist planning projects was commissioned: Detroit's Lafayette Park urban renewal, the results of the "Detroit Plan." That plan, and the project it promulgated, offers an alternative history of city making at midcentury, one emerging from an understanding of urban form as shaped by landscape. Lafayette Park did not benefit from the emergent practices that would come to be known as urban design. Ludwig Hilberseimer's project for Detroit anticipated contemporary interest in landscape as a medium of urban order for decentralizing US cities.

These contrasting events afford a potential alternative history for what came to be urban design. This is true even if we do not recall that Ludwig Mies van der Rohe was approached about the leadership of the architecture department at Harvard prior to the appointment of Walter Gropius. The history of urban design would be a very different one had Mies and Hilberseimer chosen to spend their American exile in Cambridge instead of on the south side of Chicago. But urban design was to have a very different genealogy and has yet to fulfill its potential as an intersection of the design disciplines engaging with the built environment. In light of that unfulfilled potential, landscape urbanism proposed a critical and historically informed rereading of the environmental and social aspirations of modernist planning and its most successful models. In so doing, it suggests a potential recuperation of at least one strand of modernist planning in which landscape offered the medium of urban, economic, and social order.

·····

One particularly enduring aspect of urban design's formation over the past quarter century has been the investment in traditional definitions of well-defended disciplinary boundaries, which contrasts markedly with tendencies toward cross-disciplinarity within design education and professional practice in North America. Several design schools have recently dissolved departmental distinctions between architecture and landscape architecture, while others have launched combined degree offerings or mixed-enrollment course offerings. This shift toward shared knowledge and collaborative educational experience has come partly in response to the increasingly complex inter- and multidisciplinary context of professional practice. And those practices have undoubtedly been shaped by the challenges and opportunities presented by the contemporary metropolitan condition. From this perspective, the recent discourse around urban design's histories and futures reads as ambivalent toward the project of disciplinary de-specialization. Yet cities and the academic subjects they sponsor rarely respect traditional disciplinary boundaries. The design disciplines should not expect to be an exception, and many leading designers have called recently for a renewed transdisciplinarity. Unfortunately, far too much of urban design's relatively modest resources and attention have been directed toward arguably marginal concerns in contemporary urban culture. Among these, three areas stand out.

First, by far the most problematic aspect of urban design in recent years has been its tendency to be accommodating to the reactionary cultural politics and nostalgic sentiment of "New Urbanism." While leading design schools have tacked smartly to put some distance between themselves and the worst of this nineteenth-century pattern making, far too much of urban design practice apologizes for it by blessing its urban tenets at the expense of its architectonic aspirations. This most often comes in the form of overstating the environmental and social benefits of urban density while acknowledging the relative autonomy of architectural form. Second, far too much of the main body of mainstream urban design practice has been concerned with the crafting of the "look and feel" of environments for destination consumption by the wealthy. Many have called for urban design to move beyond its implicit bias in favor of Manhattanism and its predisposition toward density and elitist enclaves explicitly understood as furnishings for luxury lifestyles. Finally, urban design's historic role of interlocutor between the design disciplines and planning has been too invested in public policy and process as a surrogate for the social. While the recent recuperation of urban planning within schools of design has been an important and long-overdue correction, it has the potential to overcompensate. The danger is not that design will be swamped with literate and topical scholarship on cities, but that planning programs and their faculties run the risk of reconstructing themselves as insular enterprises concerned with public policy and urban jurisprudence to the exclusion of design and contemporary culture.

In urban design's unrealized potential, landscape urbanism has emerged in the past decade, coming to stand for an alternative practice within the broad base of urban design historically defined. Incorporating continuity with the aspirations of an ecologically informed planning practice, landscape urbanism has been equally influenced by high design culture, contemporary modes of urban development, and the complexity of public-private partnerships. While it may be true (as has been recently argued) that the urban form proposed by landscape urbanism has not yet fully arrived, it would be equally fair to say that landscape urbanism remains the most promising avenue available to urban design's formation for the coming decades. This is in no small part due to the fact that landscape urbanism offers a culturally leavened, ecologically literate, and economically viable model for contemporary urbanization as a counter to urban design's nostalgia for traditional urban forms.

·····

The emerging discourse of "ecological urbanism" has been proposed to more precisely describe the aspirations of an urban practice informed by environmental issues and imbued with the sensibilities associated with landscape. This most recent adjectival modifier of urbanism reveals the need for requalifying urban design as it attempts to describe the environmental, economic, and social conditions of the contemporary city. In his introduction to the 2009 "Ecological Urbanism" conference at Harvard, Mohsen Mostafavi described the topic as a critique of and a continuation by other terms of the discourse of landscape urbanism.[2] Ecological urbanism proposes (just as landscape urbanism proposed more than a decade prior) to multiply the available lines of thought on the contemporary city to include environmental and ecological concepts, while expanding traditional disciplinary and professional frameworks for describing those urban conditions. As a critique of the landscape urbanist agenda, ecological urbanism promises to render that dated discourse more specific to ecological, economic, and social conditions of the contemporary city.

Mostafavi's introduction to the topic suggested that ecological urbanism "implied the projective potential of the design disciplines to render alternative future scenarios." He further indicated that those alternative futures might create "spaces of disagreement" that span the range of disciplinary and professional borders comprising the study of the city.[3] Any contemporary examination of those disciplinary frameworks would acknowledge that the challenges of the contemporary city rarely respect traditional disciplinary boundaries. This rather quaint realization recalls Roland Barthes's formulation on the various roles of language and fashion in the production of interdisciplinary knowledge.[4]

In reading the new language proposed by the ecological urbanism initiative, the subtitle of the conference, "Alternative and Sustainable Cities of the Future," is equally telling. This construction indicates the linguistic cul-de-sac that confronts much of contemporary urbanism, constructed around a false choice between critical cultural relevance and environmental survival. The conference title and subtitle further signify disciplinary fault lines between the well-established discourse on sustainability and the long tradition of using urban projections as descriptions of contemporary conditions for urban culture. This reading suggests that ecological urbanism might reanimate discussions of sustainability with the political, social, cultural, and critical potentials that have been drained from them. This shift would be particularly apt as a corrective to the profound opposition between environmental health and design cultures, which has produced a condition in which ecological function, social justice, and cultural literacy are perceived by many as mutually exclusive. Design culture has been depoliticized, distanced from the empirical and objective realities of urban life. At the same moment, increased calls for environmental remediation, ecological health, and biodiversity suggest the potential for reimagining urban futures. Yet we are collectively coerced into choosing among alternate urban paradigms, each espousing exclusive access to environmental health, social justice, or cultural relevance.

Homi Bhabha used his keynote address at the "Ecological Urbanism" conference to frame the project in temporal terms, arguing that, "It is always at once both too early and too late to talk about the future of the city."[5] Bhabha located the ecological urbanism project in a complex intertwined dialectic between the ecologies of the informal and the relentless reach of modernization, emphasizing that, "We are in effect always working with the problems of the past, but that these problems appear differently in new emergent contemporary conditions." The project of ecological urbanism, he maintained, is a "work of projective imagination."[6]

It is no coincidence that an adjectivally modified form of urbanism (be it landscape, ecological, or other) has emerged as the most robust and fully formed critique of urban design. The structural conditions necessitating an environmentally modified urbanism emerged precisely at the moment when European models of urban density, centrality, and legibility of urban form appear increasingly remote and when most of us live and work in environments more suburban than urban, more vegetal than architectonic, more infrastructural than enclosed. I believe that these structural conditions for urban practice and the disciplinary realignments attendant to them will persist, as our language morphs and transforms in an ultimately incomplete yet necessary attempt to describe them.

·····

The formulation "projective ecologies" has recently been proposed as an extension and elaboration of the ecological urbanism initiative.[7] The project aspires to articulate the contemporary role and status of ecology across the design and planning disciplines. Following from and building on the discourse of ecological urbanism, *Projective Ecologies* asks timely questions regarding the status of ecology as an adjectival modifier to urbanism.[8] While these inquiries are relevant for the range of disciplines responsible for the city, they are particularly apt for the discipline of landscape architecture. In the discourse around landscape urbanism and ecological urbanism, critical concerns persist as to the status and role of ecology in relation to design. Which ecologies are invoked in those formulations, by whom, and toward what ends? *Projective Ecologies* articulates the plural and projective potentials of the biological model for contemporary design culture.

Christopher Hight has claimed that ecology is among the most important epistemological frameworks of our age.[9] Hight's assertion is based on the fact that ecology has transcended its origins as a natural science to encompass a range of meanings across the natural and social sciences, history and the humanities, design and the arts. From a proto-disciplinary branch of biology in the nineteenth century, ecology has developed into a modern science in the twentieth century, and increasingly toward a multidisciplinary intellectual framework in the first decades of the twenty-first century. This disciplinary promiscuity is not without its problems, intellectually and practically. The slippage of ecology from natural science to cultural lens remains the source of confusion and limits communication within and across landscape architecture, urban design, and planning. *Projective Ecologies* sheds significant light on those diverse disciplinary valences and mobilizes the production of knowledge and projection of space, in three ways. First, the essays and projects begin by unapologetically defining ecologies in the plural. Second, the publication advocates for the projective potentials of the ecological framework by illustrating fluency across a spectrum of disciplinary formulations. Finally, the projects, drawings, and diagrams articulate a robust representational paradigm for the ecological in contemporary design culture.

Following Henri Lefebvre, we can postulate that the effects of urbanization are effectively planetary in scope.[10] If so, what are the implications for thinking about the relation between ecology and urbanism? The theoretical frameworks, analytical tools, and projective practices of the urban arts have been developed on a presupposed distinction between the urban and the ecological. For much of their history, both terms have been conceived to occlude each other. The origins of urbanism in architectural culture and a preoccupation with the architectonic form of the city have contributed to this collective blind spot. Equally, the classical definition of ecology as the description of species in relation to their environments, absent human agency, is equally problematic. Taken together, the cumulative effect of describing ecology as outside the city, and the urban as external to ecology, continues to have a profound impact for our thinking across the urban arts. *Projective Ecologies* questions those old oppositions in favor of multiple readings of ecology understood simultaneously as model, metaphor, and medium.

In their introductory essay, Reed and Lister refer to the enduring understanding of ecology as offering a model of the natural world.[11] This most fundamental definition is evident in the work of Richard Forman, Eugene Odum, and others referenced in the volume. It continues to apply, as ecology offers models to predict and account for the natural world. Lister and Reed invoke a point of tangency here between the production of scientific models through testing and falsification and the symmetrical activity of design through model making and matching. While the historical chasm between the habits of mind and methods in the sciences and design persists, *Projective Ecologies* articulates a plausible relation between ecology as a model of the world and the agency of design in the shaping of that world. In addition to its status as model, ecology has come to be an equally effective metaphor for a range of intellectual and disciplinary pursuits. Ecology has been found relevant as an epistemological framework operating at the level of a metaphor in the social or human sciences, the humanities, history, philosophy, and the arts. The work of Gregory Bateson, Giorgio Agamben, and Félix Guattari, to name but a few, illustrates the fecundity of ecological thinking across a range of fields. This metaphorical understanding of ecology has been particularly significant for its subsequent absorption into the discourse around design. While landscape architecture and urban planning have historically tended to view ecology as a kind of applied natural science, architecture and the arts have received ecology as a metaphor imported from the social sciences, humanities, and philosophy. The *Projective Ecologies* project aspires to articulate and integrate those diverse disciplinary anteced-ents within the discourses of design by invoking a third reading of ecology as a medium of thought, exchange, and representation. Lister and Reed invite readers to embrace the breadth of that medium, and to project an equally broad range of better futures through design. The prospect of "projective" ecologies offers a much-needed third term in the architectural debates of the day, be-tween the poles of autonomy and instrumentality. This timely proposition, and the work included in Reed and Lister's volume in support of its claim, aims to reconcile the critical potential of autonomous practice with the increasingly pressing demands for social, political, and environmental engagement.

As we have argued here, at least since Peter Eisenman's "post-function-alism" argument of the mid-1970s, architecture has relied on the putatively critical denial of utility as a basis for its cultural value.[12] This suppression of commodity and use value has also expressed itself as a claim for the "au-tonomy" of architectural culture, articulated as a form of resistance to archi-tecture's engagements with the social, political, and economic. Over the past decade, as architecture's implication in questions of environment and climate have returned to the fore, many have argued for the maintenance of the crit-ical cultural project of autonomy, as opposed to instrumentality. This has often been articulated as a project of resistance to architecture's entanglement in the "externalities" of energy and environment, among others. From this point of view, questions of climate are viewed as a pure externality to architecture's cultural value, as defined through its self-imposed alienation from instrumental impact.[13] The critical project has been confronted on another flank, with the proposition of a so-called postcritical position that espouses mood, cultural commodity, and "design intelligence" over distanced authorship.[14] *Projective Ecologies* affords a third term in these debates, avoiding pure opposition in favor of an opening toward a projective, if not precisely redemptive, project for contemporary architecture. This suggests the potential for an architecture of radically distanced authorship arrived at through highly measured performative dimensions. In lieu of the centrality of function, structure, urban coherence, humanist continuity, and capital accumulation, *Projective Ecologies* offers unanticipated urban outcomes, through the most instrumental of means. This "alienation" or decentering of authorship, while not without its antecedents in contemporary architectural culture, is radically distinct in that it occludes simple visibility in favor of a more complex array of ecological orders.

In this regard, we might find in the landscape urbanist agenda a performative turn that has reenergized landscape architecture with the potential for a paradoxical autonomy of urban form, derived from the highly scripted metrics of ecological logics and emergent forms.[15] Often these metrics are the result of highly choreographed relations between species and their environments over time. Recent work in this vein has suggested the potential for a dual distancing, twinning performative models from the natural world with computational and fabricational logics. In the most interesting of this work, a putatively critical distance from instrumental engagement with questions of energy and climate might be found through the modeling of relations between humans, the non-human, and their environments. This line of work holds the potential to transcend simple oppositions of the socially engaged and the culturally significant. In so doing, it proposes to reanimate contemporary urbanism with relevance for both its internal debates and its external demands. It equally suggests an ongoing relevance for landscape as an adjectival modifier of the urban.

Notes

Introduction
Epigraph: Ludwig Mies van der Rohe, transcript of interview with John Peter, 1955, Library of Congress, 14–15.

One: Claiming Landscape as Urbanism
Aspects of this argument were developed in Charles Waldheim, "Landscape as Urbanism," in *The Landscape Urbanism Reader*, ed. Charles Waldheim (New York: Princeton Architectural Press, 2006), 35–53; and Charles Waldheim, "Hybrid, Invasive, Indeterminate: Reading the Work of Chris Reed / Stoss Landscape Urbanism," in *StossLU* (Seoul: C3 Publishing, 2007), 18–25.

......

Epigraph: Stan Allen, "Mat Urbanism: The Thick 2-D," in *CASE: Le Corbusier's Venice Hospital*, ed. Hashim Sarkis (Munich: Prestel, 2001), 124.

1. Stan Allen, "Mat Urbanism: The Thick 2-D," in *CASE: Le Corbusier's Venice Hospital*, ed. Hashim Sarkis (Munich: Prestel, 2001), 124.
2. See James Corner, "Terra Fluxus," in *The Landscape Urbanism Reader*, ed. Charles Waldheim (New York: Princeton Architectural Press, 2006), 23–33. See also James Corner, ed., *Recovering Landscape* (New York: Princeton Architectural Press, 1999).
3. See Corner, introduction to *Recovering Landscape*, 1–26.
4. One marker of a generational divide between advocacy and instrumentalization has been the recent emergence of complex and culturally derived understanding of natural systems. An example of this can be found in the shift from pictorial to operational in landscape discourse that has been the subject of much recent work. See for example James Corner, "Eidetic Operations and New Landscapes," in *Recovering Landscape*, 153–69. Also useful on this topic is Julia Czerniak, "Challenging the Pictorial: Recent Landscape Practice," *Assemblage*, no. 34 (December 1997): 110–20.
5. Ian McHarg, *Design with Nature* (Garden City, NY: Natural History Press, 1969). For an overview of Mumford's work, see Mark Luccarelli, *Lewis Mumford and the Ecological Region: The Politics of Planning* (New York: Guilford Press, 1997).
6. See Corner, "Terra Fluxus."
7. Early critiques of modernist architecture and urban planning ranged from the populist Jane Jacobs, *Death and Life of Great American Cities* (New York: Vintage Books, 1961), to the professional Robert Venturi, *Complexity and Contradiction in Architecture* (New York: Museum of Modern Art, 1966).

8. Kevin Lynch, *A Theory of Good City Form* (Cambridge, MA: MIT Press, 1981). Also see Lynch's earlier empirical research in *Image of the City* (Cambridge, MA: MIT Press, 1960).
The most significant of these critics was Aldo Rossi. See Rossi, *The Architecture of the City* (Cambridge, MA: MIT Press, 1982).
Robert Venturi and Denise Scott-Brown's work is indicative of these interests. See Venturi, Scott-Brown, and Steven Izenour, *Learning from Las Vegas: The Forgotten Symbolism of Architectural Form* (Cambridge, MA: MIT Press, 1977).
9. Charles Jencks, *The Language of Post-Modern Architecture* (New York: Rizzoli, 1977). On Fordism and its relation to postmodern architecture, see Patrik Schumacher and Christian Rogner, "After Ford," in *Stalking Detroit*, ed. Georgia Daskalakis, Charles Waldheim, and Jason Young (Barcelona: ACTAR, 2001), 48–56.
10. Harvard University's Urban Design Program began in 1960, and the discipline grew in popularity with increased enrollments, increased numbers of degrees conferred, and the addition of new degree programs during the 1970s and '80s.
11. Allen, "Mat Urbanism: The Thick 2-D," 125.
12. For contemporaneous critical commentary on la Villette, see Anthony Vidler, "Trick-Track," in *La Case Vide: La Villette*, by Bernard Tschumi (London: Architectural Association, 1985), and Jacques Derrida, "Point de folie—Maintenant l'architecture," *AA Files*, no. 12 (Summer 1986): 65–75.
13. Bernard Tschumi, La Villette Competition Entry, "The La Villette Competition," *Princeton Journal*, vol. 2, "On Landscape" (1985): 200–210.
14. Rem Koolhaas, *Delirious New York: A Retroactive Manifesto for New York* (New York: Oxford University Press, 1978).
15. Rem Koolhaas, "Congestion without Matter," *S,M,L,XL* (New York: Monacelli, 1999), 921.
16. Kenneth Frampton, "Towards a Critical Regionalism: Six Points for an Architecture of Resistance," in *The Anti-Aesthetic*, ed. Hal Foster (Seattle: Bay Press, 1983), 17.
17. Kenneth Frampton, "Toward an Urban Landscape," *Columbia Documents* (New York: Columbia University, 1995), 89, 92.
18. Rem Koolhaas, "IIT Student Center Competition Address," Illinois Institute of Technology, College of Architecture, Chicago, March 5, 1998.
19. Peter Rowe, *Making a Middle Landscape* (Cambridge, MA: MIT Press, 1991).
20. Frampton, "Toward an Urban Landscape," 83–93.
21. Among these see, for example, Lars Lerup, "Stim

and Dross: Rethinking the Metropolis," in *After the City* (Cambridge, MA: MIT Press, 2000), 47–61.

22. Rem Koolhaas, "Atlanta," *S, M, L, XL* (New York: Monacelli, 1999), 835.

23. Among the sources of this material of interest to architects and landscape architects is ecologist Richard T. T. Forman. See Wenche E. Dramstad, James D. Olson, and Richard T. T. Forman, *Landscape Ecology Principles in Landscape Architecture and Land-Use Planning* (Cambridge, MA: Harvard University Graduate School of Design; Washington, DC: Island Press, 1996).

24. Richard Weller, "Toward an Art of Infrastructure in the Theory and Practice of Contemporary Landscape Architecture," keynote address, "MESH" conference, Royal Melbourne Institute of Technology, Melbourne, Australia, July 9, 2001. See also Richard Weller, "Between Hermeneutics and Datascapes: A Critical Appreciation of Emergent Landscape Design Theory and Praxis through the Writings of James Corner, 1990–2000," *Landscape Review* 7, no. 1 (2001): 3–44; and Richard Weller, "An Art of Instrumentality: Thinking through Landscape Urbanism," in *The Landscape Urbanism Reader*, ed. Charles Waldheim (New York: Princeton Architectural Press, 2006), 69–85.

25. On the work of Adriaan Geuze / West 8, see "West 8 Landscape Architects," in *Het Landschap / The Landscape: Four International Landscape Designers* (Antwerpen: deSingel, 1995), 215–53, and Luca Molinari, ed., *West 8* (Milan: Skira, 2000).

26. Downsview and Fresh Kills have been the subject of extensive documentation, including essays in *Praxis*, no. 4, Landscapes (2002). For additional information see Julia Czerniak, ed., *CASE: Downsview Park Toronto* (Munich: Prestel; Cambridge, MA: Harvard Graduate School of Design, 2001); and Charles Waldheim, "Park = City? The Downsview Park Competition," *Landscape Architecture Magazine* 91, no. 3 (2001): 80–85, 98–99.

27. On the work of Chris Reed and Stoss Landscape Urbanism, see *StossLU* (Seoul: C3 Publishers, 2007); *Topos: The International Review of Landscape Architecture and Urban Design*, no. 71, "Landscape Urbanism" (June 2010); and Jason Kentner, ed., *Stoss Landscape Urbanism*, Sourcebooks in Landscape Architecture (Columbus: Ohio State University, 2013).

28. Following the initial academic conference on the subject hosted by the Graham Foundation in Chicago in April 1997, academic programs in landscape urbanism were launched at the University of Illinois at Chicago in 1997–98 and the Architectural Association School of Architecture in London in 1999–2000.

29. See Mohsen Mostafavi and Ciro Najle, eds. *Landscape Urbanism: A Manual for the Machinic Landscape* (London: AA School of Architecture, 2004); and Waldheim, *Landscape Urbanism Reader*.

Two: Autonomy, Indeterminacy, Self-Organization

Aspects of this argument were developed in Charles Waldheim, "Indeterminate Emergence: Problematized Authorship in Contemporary Landscape Practice," *Topos: The International Review of Landscape Architecture and Urban Design*, no. 57 (October 2006): 82–88.

......

Epigraph: Rem Koolhaas, "Whatever Happened to Urbanism," *S, M, L, XL* (New York: Monacelli, 1999), 959, 971.

1. See Rem Koolhaas, "Congestion without Matter: Parc de la Villette," *S, M, L, XL* (New York: Monacelli, 1999), 894–935; and Bernard Tschumi, *Cinegram folie: Le Parc de la Villette* (New York: Princeton Architectural Press, 1988). For the theoretical underpinnings of Tschumi's concept of event and the city as an open work, see Bernard Tschumi, *Architecture and Disjunction* (Cambridge, MA: MIT Press, 1996).

2. Rem Koolhaas, "Project for a 'Ville Nouvelle,' Melun-Sénart, 1987," *Rem Koolhaas, Projectes urbans (1985–1990) = Rem Koolhaas, Urban Projects (1985–1990)* (Barcelona: Gustavo Gili, 1991), 44–47; Rem Koolhaas, "Surrender: Ville Nouvelle Melun-Sénart," *S, M, L, XL* (New York: Monacelli, 1999), 972–89.

3. Alex Wall, "Programming the Urban Surface," in *Recovering Landscape*, ed. James Corner (New York: Princeton Architectural Press, 1999), 233–49; Stan Allen, "Infrastructural Urbanism," and "Field Conditions," in *Points and Lines: Diagrams and Projects for the City* (New York: Princeton Architectural Press, 1999), 46–89, 90–137.

4. Michael Speaks, "Design Intelligence: Or Thinking after the End of Metaphysics," *Architectural Design* 72, no. 5 (2002): 4–6; and "Design Intelligence: Part 1, Introduction," *A+U* (December 2002): 10–18; James Corner, "Not Unlike Life Itself: Landscape Strategy Now," *Harvard Design Magazine*, no. 21 (Fall 2004 / Winter 2005): 32–34.

5. Detlef Mertins, "Mies, Organic Architecture, and the Art of City Building," in *Mies in America*, ed. Phyllis Lambert (New York: Harry Abrams, 2001), 591–641; Sanford Kwinter, "Soft Systems," in *Culture Lab*, ed. Brian Boigon (New York: Princeton Architectural Press, 1996), 207–28; Sanford Kwinter and Umberto Boccioni, "Landscapes of Change: Boccioni's 'Stati d'animo' as a General Theory of Models," *Assemblage*, no. 19 (December 1992): 50–65.

6. Michel Foucault, *Death and the Labyrinth* (Berkeley: University of California Press, 1986), 177.

7. Raymond Roussel, *Comment j'ai écrit certains de mes livres* (Paris: Gallimard, 1935, reprinted 1995).

8. Gloria Moure, *Marcel Duchamp*, trans. Robert Marrast (Paris: Editions Albin Michel, 1988).

9. Peter Eisenman, "Post-Functionalism," *Oppositions*, no. 6 (Fall 1976): i–iii.

10. Stan Allen, "Infrastructural Urbanism," in *Points and Lines: Projects and Diagrams for the City* (New York: Princeton Architectural Press, 1999), 46–89; Stan Allen, "From Object to Field," *Architectural Design*, Profile no. 127, Architecture after Geometry (1997): 24–31.

11. See Anatxu Zabalbeascoa, *Igualada Cemetery: Enric Miralles and Carme Pinós*, Architecture in Detail (London: Phaidon, 1996); Enric Miralles / Carme Pinós, "Obra construita / Built works, 1983–1994," *El Croquis* 30, no. 49–50 (1994).

12. Alejandro Zaera-Polo and Farshid Moussavi, *The Yokohama Project* (Barcelona: Actar, 2002); Alejandro Zaera-Polo and Farshid Moussavi, *Phylogenesis: FOA's Ark* (Barcelona: Actar, 2003).

13. Rosalind Krauss, "Sculpture in the Expanded Field," *October* 8 (Spring 1979): 30–44; reprinted in *The*

Originality of the Avant-Garde and Other Modernist Myths (Cambridge, MA: MIT Press, 1986), 276–90.

14. See James Corner, introduction to *Recovering Landscape* (New York: Princeton Architectural Press, 1999), 17.

15. While Geuze's indebtedness to Koolhaas could be described in the context of Dutch design culture more broadly, and Geuze dismisses any direct influence, many have found much in common in the work of West 8 and OMA.

16. Adriaan Geuze, "Second Nature," *Topos*, no. 71, Landscape Urbanism (June 2010): 40–42; Luca Molinari, ed., *West 8 Landscape Architects* (Milan: Skira, 2000).

17. Patrik Schumacher, *The Autopoiesis of Architecture: A New Framework for Architecture*, vol. 1 (London: Wiley, 2011); Patrik Schumacher, *The Autopoiesis of Architecture: A New Framework for Architecture*, vol. 2 (London: Wiley, 2012); Mohsen Mostafavi and Ciro Najle, eds., *Landscape Urbanism: A Manual for the Machinic Landscape* (London: AA School of Architecture, 2004).

18. *Groundswell: Constructing the Contemporary Landscape*, Museum of Modern Art, February 25–May 16, 2005; Peter Reed, ed., *Groundswell: Constructing the Contemporary Landscape* (New York: Museum of Modern Art, 2005).

19. Peter Reed, "Beyond Before and After: Designing Contemporary Landscape," in *Groundswell: Constructing the Contemporary Landscape*, 14–32.

20. See William Howard Adams and Stuart Wrede, eds., *Denatured Visions: Landscape and Culture in the Twentieth Century* (New York: Museum of Modern Art, 1991).

21. David Harvey, "Where Is the Outrage?," keynote lecture, *Groundswell: Constructing the Contemporary Landscape*, Museum of Modern Art, April 15, 2005.

22. Reed, "Beyond Before and After," 16–17.

23. David Harvey, *The Condition of Postmodernity: An Enquiry into the Origins of Cultural Change* (Oxford: Blackwell, 1990). On the topic of social conditions and the limits of design, see David Harvey, "The New Urbanism and the Communitarian Trap," *Harvard Design Magazine*, no. 1 (Winter/Spring 1997): 68–69.

Three: Planning, Ecology, and the Emergence of Landscape

Aspects of this argument were developed in Charles Waldheim, "Design, Agency, Territory: Provisional Notes on Planning and the Emergence of Landscape," *New Geographies*, no. 0 (Fall 2008): 6–15.

......

Epigraph: Julia Czerniak, "Introduction, Appearance, Performance: Landscape at Downsview," in *CASE: Downsview Park Toronto*, ed. Julia Czerniak (New York: Prestel, 2001), 16.

1. This gloss of the current paradigms available to planning has been summarized in *Harvard Design Magazine*, no. 22, "Urban Planning Now: What Works, What Doesn't?" (Spring/Summer 2005); and in the corresponding *Harvard Design Magazine Reader*, no. 3, *Urban Planning Today*, ed. William S. Saunders (Minneapolis: University of Minnesota Press, 2006).

2. Sert's implicit critique of planning and his conception of urban design are described in *Harvard Design Magazine*,

no. 24, "The Origins and Evolution of Urban Design, 1956–2006" (Spring/Summer 2006). Also included in that volume is evidence of the ironic and short-lived proposal that urban design at Harvard be housed within the discipline of landscape architecture; see Richard Marshall, "The Elusiveness of Urban Design: The Perpetual Problems of Definition and Role," *Harvard Design Magazine*, no. 24 (Spring/Summer 2006): 21–32.

3. The description of urban design in a state of crisis is an oft-repeated claim, most recently summarized in *Harvard Design Magazine*, no. 25, "Urban Design Now" (Fall 2006/Winter 2007). The most specific instance of this can be found in Michael Sorkin's introductory essay, which sets the tone for that volume: Michael Sorkin, "The End(s) of Urban Design," *Harvard Design Magazine*, no. 25 (Fall 2006/Winter 2007): 5–18. Further evidence is found in the following roundtable discussion moderated by William Saunders, "Urban Design Now: A Discussion," *Harvard Design Magazine*, no. 25 (Fall 2006/Winter 2007): 19–42.

4. Among the authors recently engaged in rereading the perceived failures of modernist planning vis-à-vis the city are Hashim Sarkis, ed., *CASE: Le Corbusier's Venice Hospital and the Mat Building Revival* (Munich: Prestel; Cambridge, MA: Harvard University Graduate School of Design, 2001); Farès el-Dahdah, ed., *CASE Lucio Costa: Brasilia's Superquadra* (Munich: Prestel; Cambridge, MA: Harvard University Graduate School of Design, 2005); Sarah Whiting, "Superblockism: Chicago's Elastic Grid," in *Shaping the City: Studies in History, Theory, and Urban Design*, ed. Rodolphe el-Khoury and Edward Robbins (New York: Routledge, 2004), 57–76; Richard Sommer, "The Urban Design of Philadelphia: Taking the Town for the City," in *Shaping the City: Studies in History, Theory, and Urban Design*, ed. Rodolphe el-Khoury and Edward Robbins (New York: Routledge, 2004), 135–76; Keller Easterling, *Organization Space: Landscapes, Highways, and Houses in America* (Cambridge, MA: MIT Press, 1999); and Hilary Ballon, *Robert Moses and the Modern City: The Transformation of New York* (New York: Norton, 2007).

5. This critique is both ambient in the contemporary discourse of landscape architecture and an ongoing source of great debate within and between the various flanks of the landscape discipline. It recommends an area deserving of more serious historical inquiry. As the majority of the historical material on McHarg has been relatively uncritical and occasionally veers into the metaphysical, the critical evaluation and historical contextualization of McHarg's work remains to be completed, and would be of great value to this discussion.

6. See Corner, introduction to *Recovering Landscape*; and Weller, "An Art of Instrumentality," *Landscape Urbanism Reader*.

7. As we saw in chapter 2, James Corner studied ecological planning at the University of Pennsylvania, and Adriaan Geuze studied ecological planning at Wageningen University in the Netherlands. Both subsequently explored the relation between ecology as a model for design and contemporary design culture associated with postmodern theory.

8. On this question, and the historical reception of McHarg's theories of ecological planning, see Frederick Steiner, "The Ghost of Ian McHarg," *Log*, no. 13–14 (Fall

2008): 147–51.

9. For an overview of the state of planning in the context of major urban projects in North America, see Alexander Garvin, "Introduction: Planning Now for the Twenty-First Century," in *Urban Planning Today*, ed. William Saunders (Minneapolis: University of Minnesota Press, 2006), xi–xx; and *Harvard Design Magazine*, no. 22, "Urban Planning Now: What Works, What Doesn't?" (Spring/Summer 2005); and for particular case studies in community consultation, donor culture, and design competitions, see Joshua David and Robert Hammond, *High Line: The Inside Story of New York City's Park in the Sky* (New York: Farrar, Straus, and Giroux, 2011); Timothy J. Gilfoyle, *Millennium Park: Creating a Chicago Landmark* (Chicago: University of Chicago Press, 2006); and John Kaliski, "Democracy Takes Command: New Community Planning and the Challenge to Urban Design," in *Urban Planning Today*, ed. William Saunders (Minneapolis: University of Minnesota Press, 2006), 24–37.

10. As we saw in chapter 2, the emergent practices of indeterminacy and open-endedness benefited from English language theory articulated through French *grands projets* for postindustrial parks, public amenities, and new towns.

11. For an overview of recent public space and infrastructure projects in western Europe from a landscape urbanist perspective, see Kelly Shannon and Marcel Smets, *The Landscape of Contemporary Infrastructure* (Amsterdam: NAI Publishers, 2010).

12. See David and Hammond, *High Line*; Gilfoyle, *Millennium Park*; and Gene Desfor and Jennifer Laidley, *Reshaping Toronto's Waterfront* (Toronto: University of Toronto Press, 2011).

13. See http://www.nycgovparks.org/park-features/fresh-kills-park (accessed December 31, 2013).

14. See David and Hammond, *High Line*.

15. See http://www.shoparc.com/project/East-River-Waterfront (accessed December 21, 2014); http://www.mvvainc.com/project.php?id=7&c=parks (accessed December 21, 2014); http://www.mvvainc.com/project.php?id=3&c=parks (accessed December 21, 2014); and http://www.west8.nl/projects/all/governors_island/ (accessed December 21, 2014).

16. See Gilfoyle, *Millennium Park*.

17. See http://www.west8.nl/projects/toronto_central_waterfront/ (accessed December 31, 2013); and http://www.waterfrontoronto.ca/explore_projects2/central_waterfront/planning_the_community/central_waterfront_design_competition (accessed December 31, 2013).

18. See http://www.waterfrontoronto.ca/lowerdonlands (accessed December 31, 2013); and http://www.waterfrontoronto.ca/lower_don_lands/lower_don_lands_design_competition (accessed December 31, 2013).

19. See Alex Wall, "Green Metropolis," *New Geographies* 0, ed. Neyran Turan (September 2009): 87–97; Christopher Hight, "Re-Born on the Bayou: Envisioning the Hydrauli[CITY]," *Praxis*, no. 10, Urban Matters (October 2008); Christopher Hight, Natalia Beard, and Michael Robinson, "Hydrauli[CITY]: Urban Design, Infrastructure, Ecology," *ACADIA*, Proceedings of the Association for Computer Aided Design in Architecture (October 2008): 158–65; and http://www.hydraulicity.org/ (accessed December 31, 2013).

20. See http://landscapeurbanism.aaschool.ac.uk/programme/people/contacts/groundlab/ (accessed December 31, 2013); and http://groundlab.org/portfolio/groundlab-project-deep-ground-longgang-china/ (accessed December 31, 2013).

Four: Post-Fordist Economies and Logistics Landscape

Aspects of this argument were developed in Charles Waldheim and Alan Berger, "Logistics Landscape," *Landscape Journal* 27, no. 2 (2008): 219–46.

......

Epigraph: Kenneth Frampton, "Toward an Urban Landscape," *Columbia Documents* (New York: Columbia University, 1995), 89.

1. See, among others, Jane Jacobs, *The Economy of Cities* (New York: Vintage, 1970).

2. Georg Simmel, "The Metropolis and Mental Life," in *On Individuality and Social Forms*, ed. D. Levine (Chicago: University of Chicago Press, 1903), 324–39.

3. David Harvey, *The Condition of Postmodernity: An Enquiry into the Origins of Cultural Change* (Cambridge: Blackwell Publishers), 1990; and Edward Soja, *Postmodern Geographies* (New York: Verso), 1989.

4. See Harvey, *The Condition of Postmodernity*; David Harvey, "Flexible Accumulation through Urbanization: Reflections on 'Post-Modernism' in the American City," in *Post-Fordism: A Reader*, ed. Ash Amin (Cambridge: Blackwell, 1994), 361–86; Soja, *Postmodern Geographies*; and Edward Soja, *Postmetropolis: Critical Studies of Cities and Regions* (Cambridge: Blackwell, 2000).

5. James Corner, "Terra Fluxus," in *The Landscape Urbanism Reader*, ed. Charles Waldheim (New York: Princeton Architectural Press, 2006), 22–33; and Richard Weller, "An Art of Instrumentality: Thinking through Landscape Urbanism," in *The Landscape Urbanism Reader*, ed. Charles Waldheim (New York: Princeton Architectural Press, 2006), 71.

6. See Corner, "Terra Fluxus"; and Weller, "An Art of Instrumentality."

7. Neil Brenner and Roger Keil, "Introduction: Global City Theory in Retrospect and Prospect," in *The Global Cities Reader*, ed. N. Brenner and R. Keil (London: Routledge, 2005), 1–16; Robert Bruegmann, *Sprawl: A Compact History* (Chicago: University of Chicago Press, 2005); and Patrik Schumacher and Christian Rogner, "After Ford," in *Stalking Detroit*, ed. G. Daskalakis, C. Waldheim, and J. Young (Barcelona: Actar, 2001), 48–56.

8. See Brenner and Keil, "Introduction: Global City Theory in Retrospect and Prospect"; and Schumacher and Rogner, "After Ford."

9. See Harvey, *Condition of Postmodernity*.

10. Ibid., 147.

11. See Corner, "Terra Fluxus"; and Peter Reed, *Groundswell: Constructing the Contemporary Landscape* (New York: Museum of Modern Art, 2005).

12. See David Harvey, "Where Is the Outrage?" keynote lecture, *Groundswell: Constructing the Contemporary Landscape*, Museum of Modern Art, April 15, 2005; and Peter Reed, "Beyond Before and After," *Groundswell*.

13. Harvey, *Condition of Postmodernity*; and Harvey, "Flexible Accumulation through Urbanization."

14. Marc Levinson, *The Box: How the Shipping Container Made the World Smaller and the World Economy Bigger* (Princeton, NJ: Princeton University Press, 2006); and Brian J. Cudahy, *Box Boats: How Container Ships Changed the World* (New York: Fordham University Press, 2006).

15. Alejandro Zaera-Polo, "Order out of Chaos: The Material Organization of Advanced Capitalism," *Architectural Design Profile*, no. 108 (1994): 24–29.

16. Susan Nigra Snyder and Alex Wall, "Emerging Landscapes of Movement and Logistics," *Architectural Design Profile*, no. 134 (1998): 16–21.

17. Alex Wall, "Programming the Urban Surface," in *Recovering Landscape*, ed. James Corner (New York: Princeton Architectural Press, 1999), 233–49.

18. For more recent scholarship on logistics and urbanism, see Neil Brenner, ed., *Implosions/Explosions: Towards a Study of Planetary Urbanization* (Berlin: Jovis, 2014); Keller Easterling, *Extrastatecraft: The Power of Infrastructure Space* (Brooklyn: Verso, 2014); and Clare Lyster, "The Logistical Figure," *Cabinet* 47 (Fall 2012): 55–62.

19. See Levinson, *The Box*; and Cudahy, *Box Boats*.

20. See Levinson, *The Box*; and Cudahy, *Box Boats*.

21. See Levinson, *The Box*; and Cudahy, *Box Boats*.

22. See Adriaan Geuze, "Borneo/Sporenburg, Amsterdam," in *Adriaan Geuze / West 8 Landscape Architecture* (Rotterdam: 010 Publishers, 1995), 68–73; and Adriaan Geuze, "Borneo Sporenburg 2500 Voids," *West 8* (Milan: Skira, 2000), 24–33.

23. See Zaera-Polo, "Order out of Chaos"; Snyder and Wall, "Emerging Landscapes of Movement and Logistics"; and Wall, "Programming the Urban Surface."

24. Manuel Castells, *The Informational City* (Oxford: Blackwell, 1999); and Manuel Castells, *The Information Age: Economy, Society, and Culture*, vol. 1, *The Rise of the Network Society* (Oxford: Blackwell, 2000).

25. See Adriaan Geuze, "Schouwburgplein, Rotterdam," in *Adriaan Geuze / West 8 Landscape Architecture* (Rotterdam: 010 Publishers, 1995), 50–53; Stan Allen, "Infrastructural Urbanism," in *Points and Lines: Diagrams and Projects for the City* (New York: Princeton Architectural Press, 1999), 46; and Andrea Branzi, D. Donegani, A. Petrillo, and C. Raimondo, "Symbiotic Metropolis: Agronica," in *The Solid Side: The Search for Consistency in a Changing World*, ed. Ezio Manzini and Marco Susani (Netherlands: V+K Publishing / Philips, 1995), 101–20.

26. Richard Hanley, *Moving People, Goods, and Information in the 21st Century: The Cutting-Edge Infrastructures of Networked Cities* (London: Routledge, 2003); Stephen Graham and Simon Marvin, "More Than Ducts and Wires: Post-Fordism, Cities, and Utility Networks," in *Managing Cities: The New Urban Context*, ed. P. Healy et al. (New York: John Wiley and Sons, 1995), 169–90; Stephen Graham and Simon Marvin, *Telecommunications and the City* (London: Routledge, 1996); and Stephen Graham and Simon Marvin, *Splintering Urbanism: Networked Infrastructure, Technological Mobilities, and the Urban Condition* (London: Routledge, 2001).

27. "Finance and Economics: Sizzling, the Big Mac Index," *Economist* (July 7, 2007): 82.

28. Michael Pollan, *The Omnivore's Dilemma: A Natural History of Four Meals* (New York: Penguin, 2006).

Aspects of this argument were developed in Charles Waldheim, "Detroit, *Disabitato*, and the Origins of Landscape," in *Formerly Urban: Projecting Rustbelt Futures*, ed. Julia Czerniak (New York: Princeton Architectural Press, 2013), 166–83; and Charles Waldheim, "Motor City," in *Shaping the City: Case Studies in Urban History, Theory, and Design*, ed. Rodolphe el-Khoury and Edward Robbins (London: Routledge, 2003), 77–97.

⋯⋯

Epigraph: Christopher Wood, *Albrecht Altdorfer and the Origins of Landscape* (Chicago: University of Chicago Press, 1993), 25.

1. "Formerly Urban: Projecting Rust Belt Futures" conference, Syracuse University School of Architecture, October 13–14, 2010.

2. Michel de Certeau, *The Practice of Everyday Life*, trans. Steven Rendall (Berkeley: University of California Press, 1984), 190.

3. While the topic of "shrinkage" was manifest in the work of several American academics and theorists dealing with urban restructuring through the 1990s, the German Federal Cultural Ministry gave it greater visibility in 2002 with the funding of a multiyear research program under the English-language title "Shrinking Cities" and led by Philip Oswalt. See Oswalt et al., *Shrinking Cities: The Complete Works*, vols. 1–2 (Berlin: Hatje Cantz, 2006); and Oswalt et al., *Atlas of Shrinking Cities* (Berlin: Hatje Cantz, 2006).

4. On the topic of Detroit and the postindustrial American city, see Thomas Sugrue, "Crisis: Detroit and the Fate of Postindustrial America," in *The Origins of the Urban Crisis* (Princeton, NJ: Princeton University Press, 1996), 259–71.

5. Detroit Vacant Land Survey, City of Detroit City Planning Commission, August 24, 1990.

6. "Day of the Bulldozer," *Economist* (May 8, 1993): 33–34.

7. Paul Virilio, "The Overexposed City," *Zone*, no. 1–2, trans. Astrid Hustvedt (New York: Urzone, 1986). In 1998, Detroit's mayor Dennis Archer secured $60 million in loan guarantees from the US Department of Housing and Urban Development to finance the demolition of every abandoned residential building in the city. See "Dismantling the Motor City," *Metropolis* (June 1998): 33.

8. Dan Hoffman, "Erasing Detroit," in *Stalking Detroit*, ed. G. Daskalakis, C. Waldheim, and J. Young (Barcelona: ACTAR, 2001), 100–103.

9. Cultural geographer Denis Cosgrove argues that landscape "first emerged as a recognized genre in the most economically advanced, densest settled and most highly urbanized regions of fifteenth-century Europe: in Flanders and upper Italy." See Denis Cosgrove, *Social Formation and Symbolic Landscape* (Madison: University of Wisconsin Press, 1984), 20.

10. E. H. Gombrich, "The Renaissance Theory of Art and the Rise of Landscape," in *Gombrich on the Renaissance*, vol. 1, *Norm and Form* (New York and London: Phaidon Press, 1985), 107–21.

11. Denis Cosgrove, *Social Formation and Symbolic Landscape* (Madison: University of Wisconsin Press, 1984), 87–88.

12. J. B. Jackson, "The Word Itself," in *Discovering the Vernacular Landscape* (New Haven, CT: Yale University Press, 1984), 1–8.

13. "Landscape," *Oxford English Dictionary*, 2nd ed., vol. 8 (1989), 628–29.

14. Howard Hibbard, *Carlo Maderno and Roman Architecture, 1580–1630* (London: A. Zwimmer, 1971). For further characterization of Rome's recession in late antiquity, see Bertrand Lançon, *Rome in Late Antiquity: Everyday Life and Urban Change, 312–609*, trans. Antonia Nevill (Edinburgh: Edinburgh University Press, 2000).

15. The *Dizionario Etimologico Italiano* (p. 1321) describes "disabitato" as a transitive reflexive form of "abitare," the verb for dwell or inhabit. On the sequence and timing of "disabitato" as a generic term and a specific place name, see Richard Krautheimer, *Rome: Profile of a City, 312–1308* (Princeton, NJ: Princeton University Press, 1980); and Gerhart B. Ladner's book review of R. Krautheimer, *Rome: Profile of a City, 312–1308*, in the *Art Bulletin* 65, no. 2 (1983): 336–39.

16. Krautheimer, *Rome: Profile of a City, 312–1308*, 256.

17. Charles L. Stinger, *The Renaissance in Rome* (Bloomington: Indiana University Press, 1985).

18. Marten von Heenskerck, *Sketchbook*, 1534–36; Hieronymus Cock, *Sketchbook*, 1558; Du Pérac-Lafrérly, *View of Rome*, 1575; Du Pérac-Lafrérly, *Map of Rome*, 1577; Cartaro, *Map of Rome*, 1576; Brambilla, *Map of Rome*, 1590; Tempesta, *Map of Rome*, 1593.

19. John Dixon Hunt, *Garden and Grove: The Italian Renaissance Garden in the English Imagination, 1600–1750* (Philadelphia: University of Pennsylvania Press, 1996), 32, 21.

20. G. B. Falda, *Map of Rome*, 1676; G. B. Falda, *Li Giardini di Roma*, 1683.

21. G. B. Nolli, *La Nuova Topografia di Roma*, 1748.

22. Richard Deakin, *Flora of the Colosseum of Rome; or, Illustrations and Descriptions of Four Hundred and Twenty Plants Growing Spontaneously upon the Ruins of the Colosseum of Rome* (London: Groombridge and Sons, 1855). For further context on Deakin's depiction of spontaneous vegetation among the ruins, see Christopher Woodward, *In Ruins* (London: Vintage, 2001), 23–24.

23. Denis Cosgrove, *Social Formation and Symbolic Landscape* (Madison: University of Wisconsin Press, 1984), 158.

24. Richard Rand, *Claude Lorrain: The Painter as Draftsman, Drawings from the British Museum* (New Haven, CT: Yale University Press, 2006). Michael Kitson, *Claude Lorrain, Liber Veritatis* (London: British Museum, facsimile edition reprinted 1978). See also Marcel Rothlisberger, *Claude Lorrain: The Paintings*, vols. 1–2 (New Haven, CT: Yale University Press, 1961); and Marcel Rothlisberger, *Claude Lorrain: The Drawings*, vols. 1–2 (Berkeley: University of California Press, 1968).

25. Rand, *Claude Lorrain: The Painter as Draftsman*, 52–53.

26. Ibid., 58.

27. Ibid., 23.

28. Jeremy Black, *Italy and the Grand Tour* (New Haven, CT: Yale University Press, 2003), 51.

29. Ibid., 205.

30. John Dixon Hunt, *The Figure in the Landscape: Poetry, Painting, and Gardening during the Eighteenth Century* (Baltimore: Johns Hopkins University Press, 1989), 39–43.

31. John Dixon Hunt, *The Picturesque Garden in Europe* (London: Thames and Hudson, 2002), 34.

32. For example, see William Gilpin's *Remarks on Forest Scenery* (1791), as referenced in Hunt, *The Picturesque Garden in Europe*, 337–38; and Uvedale Price's *An Essay on the Picturesque* (1794), as referenced in Hunt, *Picturesque Garden in Europe*, 351.

33. E. H. Gombrich, "From Light into Paint," and "The Image in the Clouds," in *Art and Illusion: A Study in the Psychology of Pictorial Representation*, 6th ed. (New York and London: Phaidon Press, 2002), 29–54, 154–69.

34. Rand, *Claude Lorrain: The Painter as Draftsman*, 22.

Six: Urban Order and Structural Change

Aspects of this argument were developed in Charles Waldheim, "Introduction: Landscape, Urban Order, and Structural Change," in *CASE: Lafayette Park Detroit*, ed. Charles Waldheim (Munich: Prestel; Cambridge, MA: Harvard Graduate School of Design, 2004), 19–27.

......

Epigraph: Ludwig Hilberseimer, *The New Regional Pattern: Industries and Gardens, Workshops and Farms* (Chicago: Paul Theobald, 1949), 171, 174. Hilberseimer extended this argument specifically to the Gratiot (Lafayette) site in his preliminary project notes, declaring: "Our existing street system is going back to ancient times; however motor vehicles have rendered this once perfect system obsolete. Therefore we construct highways but usually forget the pedestrian for whom each street corner is a death-trap. To avoid this there should be no through traffic within a residential area but it should also be possible to reach each house or building by car." Ludwig Hilberseimer, unpublished notes on Gratiot Redevelopment Project, July 1955 (two pages), Hilberseimer Papers, Series VI (Projects), Ryerson and Burnham Libraries, Art Institute of Chicago.

1. The press release by developers Greenwald and Katzin announcing the Gratiot (Lafayette) Redevelopment promised that the project would "transform the cleared 50-acre slum area ... into a flowering residential community which will help rehabilitate the core of the City." Press release from Oscar Katov and Company, Public Relations, February 1, 1956 (five pages), Hilberseimer Papers, Series VI (Projects), Ryerson and Burnham Libraries, Art Institute of Chicago.

2. See recent scholarship on Lafayette Park including Detlef Mertins, "Collaboration in Order," in *CASE: Lafayette Park Detroit*, ed. Charles Waldheim (Munich: Prestel; Cambridge, MA: Harvard Graduate School of Design, 2004), 11–17; Caroline Constant, "Hilberseimer and Caldwell: Merging Ideologies in the Lafayette Park Landscape," in *CASE: Lafayette Park Detroit*, 95–111; and Danielle Aubert, Lana Cavar, and Natasha Chandani, *Thanks for the View, Mr. Mies: Lafayette Park Detroit* (New York: Metropolis Books, 2012).

3. For a detailed account of race relations in post–World War II Detroit, see Thomas Sugrue, *The Origins of the Urban Crisis* (Princeton, NJ: Princeton University Press, 1996), especially pertinent to the discussion of race and housing is the section "Urban Redevelopment" in the chapter "Detroit's Time Bomb: Race and Housing in the 1940s," 47–51. For a thorough accounting of the urban renewal process in Detroit, see Roger Montgomery,

"Improving the Design Process in Urban Renewal," *Journal of the American Institute of Planners* 31, no. 1 (1965): 7–20.

4. See Constant, "Hilberseimer and Caldwell." Hilberseimer explicitly referred often in his teaching to Lafayette Park as an alternative to Levittown, see Oral History of Peter Carter (Chicago: Art Institute of Chicago, 1996).

5. For a detailed analysis of this subject, see Janine Debanne, "Claiming Lafayette Park as Public Housing," in *CASE: Lafayette Park Detroit*, 67–79. Also see Aubert, Cavar, and Chandani, *Thanks for the View, Mr. Mies: Lafayette Park Detroit*. US Census Bureau figures for Detroit indicate that in 2000 the city of Detroit's population was nearly 80 percent African American while the surrounding suburban population was nearly 80 percent white. While much of the professional press on Lafayette Park was quite positive, accepting Greenwald's progressive politics at face value, certain critics found the project bourgeois at best, and racist at worst.

6. George Danforth, "Pavilion Apartments and Town Houses, 1955–1963" and "Lafayette Towers, 1960," in *Mies van der Rohe Archive*, ed. Arthur Drexler, vol. 16 (New York: Museum of Modern Art, 1992), 412–99, 612–22. For a more detailed account of the settlement unit, see Caroline Constant, "Hilberseimer and Caldwell: Merging Ideologies in the Lafayette Park Landscape," in *CASE: Lafayette Park Detroit*, 95–111. For an account of the origins and development of the settlement unit for Lafayette Park, see David Spaeth, "Ludwig Hilberseimer's Settlement Unit: Origins and Applications," in *In the Shadow of Mies: Ludwig Hilberseimer, Architect, Educator, and Urban Planner*, ed. Richard Pommer, David Spaeth, and Kevin Harrington (New York: Rizzoli; Chicago: Art Institute of Chicago, 1988), 54–68.

7. On the planning and spatial development of the IIT campus plan in the context of Chicago's urban renewal, see Sarah Whiting, "Bas-Relief Urbanism: Chicago's Figured Field," in *Mies in America*, ed. Phyllis Lambert (New York: Harry Abrams, 2001), 642–91.

8. Oral history of Joseph Fujikawa, Chicago, Art institute of Chicago, 1996, 133.

9. See Constant, "Hilberseimer and Caldwell"; and, Oral history of Alfred Caldwell, Chicago, Art Institute of Chicago, 1987.

10. Richard Pommer, "'More a Necropolis than a Metropolis,' Ludwig Hilberseimer's Highrise City and Modern City Planning," in *In the Shadow of Mies: Ludwig Hilberseimer. Architect, Educator, and Urban Planner*, 16–53.

11. See Spaeth, "Ludwig Hilberseimer's Settlement Unit," 54–68.

12. See ibid.

13. Ludwig Hilberseimer, *The New Regional Pattern: Industries and Gardens, Workshops and Farms* (Chicago: Paul Theobald, 1949), 171, 174. See also Detlef Mertins, "Mies, Organic Architecture, and the Art of City Building," in *Mies in America*, ed. Phyllis Lambert (New York: Harry Abrams, 2001), 591–641; and Detlef Mertins, "Collaboration in Order," in *CASE: Lafayette Park Detroit*, 11–17.

14. Phyllis Lambert, "In the Shadow of Mies," symposium, Art Institute of Chicago, September 14–17, 1988.

15. Hilberseimer's commitment to equity informed planning projects that embodied equal conditions for all, most notably through equitable access to healthful housing. For Hilberseimer this suggested the necessity of equitable distribution of land as well as access to sunlight throughout the year. By correlating social equity to arable land and access to sunlight Hilberseimer proposed a proto-ecological urbanism.

16. Lambert, "In the Shadow of Mies."

17. Hilberseimer and Caldwell advocated for decentralization as a civil defense strategy in the wake of Hiroshima. See Caldwell, "Atomic Bombs and City Planning," *Journal of the American Institute of Architects* 4 (1945): 289–99; and also Hilberseimer, "Cities and Defense" (ca. 1945) reprinted in *In the Shadow of Mies: Ludwig Hilberseimer, Architect, Educator, and Urban Planner*, 89–93.

18. Hilberseimer, "Cities and Defense."

19. Ludwig Mies van der Rohe, introduction to *The New City*, by L. Hilberseimer (Chicago: Paul Theobald, 1944), xv.

20. Ludwig Hilberseimer, unpublished notes on Gratiot Redevelopment Project, July 1955, Hilberseimer Papers, Series VI (Projects), Ryerson and Burnham Libraries, Art Institute of Chicago.

21. Press release from Oscar Katov and Company, Public Relations, February 1, 1956, Hilberseimer Papers, Series VI (Projects), Ryerson and Burnham Libraries, Art Institute of Chicago.

22. In his 1956 book on Mies's work, Hilberseimer credits himself as planner for the Gratiot Redevelopment Project. Ludwig Hilberseimer, *Mies van der Rohe* (Chicago: Paul Theobald, 1956), 104–8.

23. On Costa's landscape urbanism at Brasilia, see Farès el-Dahdah, ed., *CASE: Lucio Costa: Brasilia's Superquadra* (Munich: Prestel; Cambridge, MA: Harvard University Graduate School of Design, 2005).

24. Oral history of Peter Carter, interviewed by Betty Blum, Chicago, Art Institute of Chicago, 1996, 346.

25. George Danforth, "Hilberseimer Remembered," in *In the Shadow of Mies: Ludwig Hilberseimer, Architect, Educator, and Urban Planner*, 13.

26. "A Tower Plus Row Houses in Detroit," *Architectural Forum* 112, no. 5 (1960): 104–13, 222.

27. Alison Smithson and Peter Smithson, *Without Rhetoric: An Architectural Aesthetic, 1955–1972* (Cambridge, MA: MIT Press, 1974); reviewed by Kenneth Frampton, *Journal of the Society of Architectural Historians* 35, no. 3 (1976): 228.

28. Sybil Moholy-Nagy, "Villas in the Slums," *Canadian Architect* (September 1960): 39–46.

29. Manfredo Tafuri and Francesco Dal Co, *Modern Architecture*, vol. 2 (Milan: Electa, 1980), 312.

30. Charles Jencks, "The Problem of Mies," *Architectural Association Journal*, no. 81 (May 1966): 301–4.

31. Charles Jencks, *The Language of Post-Modern Architecture* (New York: Rizzoli, 1977). The televised event on April 22, 1972, was actually the second in a series of demolitions that began in March and ended in June of that year. For a historically informed rebuttal of Jencks, see Katharine G. Bristol, "The Pruitt-Igoe Myth," *Journal of Architectural Education* 44, no. 3 (1991): 163–71.

32. George Baird, "Les extremes qui se touchant?" *Architectural Design* 47, no. 5 (1977): 326–27.

33. Joseph Rykwert, "Die Stadt unter dem Stricht: Ein bilzanz," Berlin, 1984.

34. Peter Blundell Jones, "City Father, book review of *In the Shadow of Mies: Ludwig Hilberseimer, Architect, Educator, and Urban Planner* by Richard Pommer, David Spaeth, and Kevin Harrington," *Architect's Journal* 190, no. 7 (1989): 75.

35. K. Michael Hays, *Modernism and the Posthumanist Subject: The Architecture of Hannes Meyer and Ludwig Hilberseimer* (Cambridge, MA: MIT Press, 1992).

Seven: Agrarian Urbanism and the Aerial Subject

Aspects of this argument were developed in Charles Waldheim, "Notes Toward a History of Agrarian Urbanism," *Bracket*, vol. 1, On Farming (2010): 18–24; Charles Waldheim, "Agrarian Urbanism and the Aerial Subject," *Making the Metropolitan Landscape* (London: Routledge, 2009), 29–46; and Charles Waldheim, "Urbanism, Landscape, and the Emergent Aerial Subject," in *Landscape Architecture in Mutation*, ed. Institute for Landscape Architecture (Zurich: ETH Zurich, gta Verlag, 2005), 117–35.

......

Epigraph: Ford's precise formulation was: "Industry will decentralize. There is no city that would be rebuilt as it is, were it destroyed—which fact is in itself a confession of our real estimate of our cities." Henry Ford and Samuel Crowther, *My Life and Work* (New York: Doubleday, 1922), 192. Hilberseimer published his slightly amended version in "Cities and Defense" (1945), which is reprinted in *In the Shadow of Mies: Ludwig Hilberseimer, Architect, Educator, and Urban Planner*, ed. Richard Plommer, David Spaeth, and Kevin Harrington (New York: Rizzoli; Chicago: Art Institute of Chicago, 1988), 89–93.

1. The subtitle to Hilberseimer's *The New Regional Pattern: Industries and Gardens, Workshops and Farms*, makes explicit reference to Petr Kropotkin's 1898 *disurbanist* manifesto, *Fields, Factories, and Workshops*.

2. Ford and Crowther, *My Life and Work*.

3. See Frank Lloyd Wright, *The Living City* (New York: Horizon Press, 1958); Ludwig Hilberseimer, *The New Regional Pattern: Industries and Gardens, Workshops and Farms* (Chicago: Paul Theobald, 1949); Andrea Branzi, D. Donegani, A. Petrillo, and C. Raimondo, "Symbiotic Metropolis: Agronica," in *The Solid Side*, ed. Ezio Manzini and Marco Susani (Netherlands: V+K Publishing / Philips, 1995), 101–20; and Andrea Branzi, "Preliminary Notes for a Master Plan," and "Master Plan Strijp Philips, Eindhoven 1999," *Lotus*, no. 107 (2000): 110–23.

4. The principles underpinning Wright's Broadacre project were published in 1932 in Frank Lloyd Wright, *Disappearing City* (New York: W. F. Payson, 1932); subsequently reformulated as *When Democracy Builds* (Chicago: University of Chicago Press, 1945); and referenced again in Frank Lloyd Wright, *The Living City* (New York: Horizon Press, 1958). For a historical overview of Broadacre's influences and contemporary reception, see Peter Hall, *Cities of Tomorrow: An Intellectual History of Urban Planning and Design in the Twentieth Century* (Oxford: Blackwell, 1996), 285–90.

5. For an overview of the Tennessee Valley Authority, see Walter Creese, *TVA's Public Planning* (Knoxville: University of Tennessee Press, 1990); Timothy Culvahouse, ed., *The Tennessee Valley Authority: Design and Persuasion* (New York: Princeton Architectural Press, 2007); and Hall, *Cities of Tomorrow*, 161–63.

6. On Wright's pacifist and isolationist politics and FBI file, see Meryle Secrest, *Frank Lloyd Wright: A Biography* (Chicago: University of Chicago Press, 1998), 264; and Robert McCarter, *Frank Lloyd Wright* (New York: Phaidon, 1999), 100–101.

7. On the work and life of Bel Geddes, see Norman Bel Geddes, *Miracle in the Evening: An Autobiography*, ed. William Kelley (New York: Doubleday, 1960).

8. On the role of the aerial subject in Futurama, see Adnan Morshed, "The Aesthetics of Ascension in Norman Bel Geddes's Futurama," *Journal of the Society of Architectural Historians* 63, no. 1 (2004): 74–99.

9. Norman Bel Geddes, *Magic Motorways* (New York: Stratford Press, 1940).

10. On the aerial view in urbanism, see chapters 8 and 9 in this publication.

11. David Spaeth, "Ludwig Hilberseimer's Settlement Unit: Origins and Applications," in *In the Shadow of Mies: Ludwig Hilberseimer, Architect, Educator, and Urban Planner*, ed. Richard Pommer, David Spaeth, and Kevin Harrington (New York: Rizzoli; Chicago: Art Institute of Chicago, 1988), 54–68.

12. For a detailed account of Caldwell's work, see Dennis Domer, *Alfred Caldwell: The Life and Work of a Prairie School Landscape Architect* (Baltimore: Johns Hopkins University Press, 1997).

13. George Baird, "Organicist Yearnings and Their Consequences," in *The Space of Appearance* (Cambridge, MA: MIT Press, 1995), 193–238.

14. See Pier Vittorio Aureli, *The Project of Autonomy: Politics and Architecture within and against Architecture* (New York: Princeton Architectural Press, 2008).

15. Archizoom Associates, "No-Stop City. Residential Parkings. Climatic Universal System," *Domus* 496 (March 1971): 49–55. For Branzi's reflections on the project, see Andrea Branzi, "Notes on No-Stop City: Archizoom Associates, 1969–1972," in *Exit Utopia: Architectural Provocations, 1956–1976*, ed. Martin van Schaik and Otakar Macel (Munich: Prestel, 2005), 177–82. For more recent scholarship on the project and its relations to contemporary architectural culture and urban theory, see Kazys Varnelis, "Programming after Program: Archizoom's No-Stop City," *Praxis*, no. 8 (May 2006): 82–91.

16. On field conditions and contemporary urbanism, see James Corner, "The Agency of Mapping: Speculation, Critique and Invention," in *Mappings*, ed. Denis Cosgrove (London: Reaktion Books, 1999), 213–300; and Stan Allen, "Mat Urbanism: The Thick 2-D," in *CASE: Le Corbusier's Venice Hospital and the Mat Building Revival*, ed. Hashim Sarkis (Munich: Prestel, 2001), 118–26. On logistics and contemporary urbanism, see Susan Nigra Snyder and Alex Wall, "Emerging Landscape of Movement and Logistics," *Architectural Design Profile*, no. 134 (1998): 16–21; and Alejandro Zaera-Polo, "Order out of Chaos: The Material Organization of Advanced Capitalism," *Architectural Design Profile*, no. 108 (1994): 24–29.

17. Andrea Branzi, D. Donegani, A. Petrillo, and C. Raimondo, "Symbiotic Metropolis: Agronica," in *The Solid*

Side, ed. Ezio Manzini and Marco Susani (Netherlands: V+K Publishing / Philips, 1995), 101–20.

18. Andrea Branzi, "Preliminary Notes for a Master Plan," and "Master Plan Strijp Philips, Eindhoven 1999," *Lotus*, no. 107 (2000): 110–23.

19. Andrea Branzi, "The Weak Metropolis," "Ecological Urbanism" conference, Harvard Graduate School of Design, April 4, 2009; and Andrea Branzi, "For a Post-Environmentalism: Seven Suggestions for a New Athens Charter and the Weak Metropolis," in *Ecological Urbanism*, ed. Mohsen Mostafavi with Gareth Doherty (Zurich: Lars Müller; Cambridge, MA: Harvard Graduate School of Design, 2009), 110–13.

20. See Pier Vittorio Aureli and Martino Tattara, "Architecture as Framework: The Project of the City and the Crisis of Neoliberalism," *New Geographies*, no. 1 (September 2008): 38–51.

21. See Paola Viganò, *La città elementare* (Milan: Skira, 1999); Paola Viganò, ed., *Territori della nuova modernita / Territories of a New Modernity* (Napoli: Electa, 2001).

Eight: Aerial Representation and Airport Landscape

The formulation "airport landscape" was the subject of an eponymous essay by geographer Denis Cosgrove. See Cosgrove, with paintings by Adrian Hemmings, "Airport/Landscape," in *Recovering Landscape*, ed. James Corner (New York: Princeton Architectural Press, 1999), 221–32. More recently the topic was the subject of an international conference and exhibition. See "Airport Landscape: Urban Ecologies in the Aerial Age," curated and convened by Charles Waldheim and Sonja Duempelmann, Harvard University Graduate School of Design, conference, November 14–15, 2013, and exhibition, October 30–December 19, 2013. Aspects of this argument were developed in Charles Waldheim, "Aerial Representation and the Recovery of Landscape," in *Recovering Landscape: Essays in Contemporary Landscape Architecture*, ed. James Corner (New York: Princeton Architectural Press, 1999), 120–39; and Charles Waldheim, "Airport Landscape," *Log*, no. 8 (September 2006): 120–30.

......

Epigraph: Denis Cosgrove, "Airport/Landscape," 227.

1. For an account of the development of landscape photography, see Joel Snyder, "Territorial Photography," in *Landscape and Power*, ed. W.J.T. Mitchell (Chicago: University of Chicago Press, 1994), 175–201.

2. Naomi Rosenblum, "Photography from the Air," in *A World History of Photography* (New York: Abbeville Press, 1984), 245–47.

3. Roland Barthes, "Authentication," in *Camera Lucida* (New York: Hill and Wang, 1981), 85–89.

4. Shelley Rice, "Souvenirs: Nadar's Photographs of Paris Document the Haussmannization of the City," *Art in America* 76 (September 1988): 156–71.

5. See Simon Baker, "San Francisco in Ruins: The 1906 Aerial Photographs of George R. Lawrence," *Landscape* 30, no. 2 (1989): 9–14. Also see Alan Fielding, "A Kodak in the Clouds," *History of Photography* 14, no. 3 (1990): 217–30.

6. Le Corbusier, *Aircraft: The New Vision* (London: The Studio, 1935), 5.

7. For a description of Le Corbusier's relation to the picturesque, see Sylvia Lavin, "Sacrifice and the Garden: Watelet's Essai sur les jardins and the Space of the Picturesque," *Assemblage*, no. 28 (1996): 16–33.

8. Karen Frome, "A Forced Perspective: Aerial Photography and Fascist Propaganda," *Aperture*, no. 132 (Summer 1993): 76–77.

9. Roy Behrens, *Art and Camouflage: Concealment and Deception in Nature, Art, and War* (Cedar Falls, IA: North American Review, 1981).

10. Jeffrey Richelson, *America's Secret Eyes in Space* (New York: Harper and Row, 1990).

11. Nick Chrisman, *Charting the Unknown: How Computer Mapping at Harvard Became GIS* (Redlands, CA: ESRI Press, 2006).

12. See ibid.

13. Carl Steinitz, *A Framework for Geodesign: Changing Geography by Design* (Redlands, CA: ESRI Press, 2012).

14. Ian McHarg, *Design with Nature* (Garden City, NJ: Natural History Press, 1969).

15. See Chrisman, *Charting the Unknown*.

16. Priscilla Strain and Frederick Engle, *Looking at Earth* (Atlanta: Turner Publishing, 1992).

17. The sentiment that representation already implies a renovation is evident in Foucault's histories of the social sciences. See Michel Foucault, "The Human Sciences," in *The Order of Things*, ed. R. D. Laing (New York: Vintage Books, 1970), 344–87. A more direct political critique of this effect can be found in James Scott, "State Projects of Legibility and Simplification," in *Seeing Like a State* (New Haven, CT: Yale University Press, 1998), 9–84.

18. James Corner and Alex MacLean, *Taking Measures Across the American Landscape* (New Haven, CT: Yale University Press, 1996).

19. James Corner, "The Agency of Mapping: Speculation, Critique, and Invention," in *Mappings*, ed. Denis Cosgrove (London: Reaktion, 1999), 213–52.

20. See Rosalind Krauss, "Sculpture in the Expanded Field," in *The Anti-Aesthetic*, ed. Hal Foster (Seattle: Bay Press, 1983), 31–42.

21. Leo Steinberg, "Other Criteria," in *Other Criteria: Confrontations with Twentieth-Century Art* (New York: Oxford University Press, 1972), 55–91.

22. Douglas Crimp, "On the Museum's Ruins," in *The Anti-Aesthetic: Essays on Postmodern Culture*, ed. Hal Foster (Seattle: Bay Press, 1983), 43–56.

23. Walter Benjamin, "The Work of Art in the Age of Mechanical Reproduction," in *Illuminations*, trans. Harry Zohn (New York: Schocken Books, 1969), 217–51.

24. See Richelson, *America's Secret Eyes in Space*.

25. See Cosgrove, "Airport/Landscape."

26. Robert Smithson, "Towards the Development of an Air Terminal Site," *Artforum*, no. 6 (June 1967): 36–40; and Robert Smithson, "Aerial Art," *Studio International*, no. 177 (April 1969): 180–81. This understanding of Smithson's interest in aerial representation has been illuminated by the research of Mark Linder. See Linder, "Sitely Windows: Robert Smithson and Architectural Criticism," *Assemblage*, no. 39 (1999): 6–35; which clarifies the relation between Smithson's work as an "artist-consultant" to the Dallas/Fort Worth International Airport and his subsequent development of the "non-site."

27. Dan Kiley and Jane Amidon, *Dan Kiley: The Complete Works of America's Master Landscape Architect* (Boston: Little, Brown, 1999); also see Sonja Dümpelmann, *Flights of Imagination: Aviation, Landscape, Design* (Charlottesville: University of Virginia Press, 2014).

28. Kiley and Amidon, *Dan Kiley*.

29. See http://www.o-l-m.net/zoom-projet.php?id=40 (accessed December 21, 2014).

30. Julia Czerniak, ed., *CASE: Downsview Park Toronto* (Cambridge, MA: Harvard University Graduate School of Design; Munich: Prestel, 2001).

31. Bernard Tschumi, "Downsview Park: The Digital and the Coyote," in Czerniak, *CASE: Downsview Park Toronto*, 82–89.

32. See Adriaan Geuze / West 8, "West 8 Landscape Architects," in *Het Landschap / The Landscape: Four International Landscape Designers* (Antwerpen: deSingel, 1995), 215–53; and Luca Molinari, ed., *West 8* (Milan: Skira, 2000).

33. Luis Callejas, *Pamphlet Architecture*, no. 33 (2013).

34. Florian Hertweck and Sebastien Marot, eds., *The City in the City / Berlin: A Green Archipelago* (Zurich: Lars Müller, 2013).

Nine: Claiming Landscape as Architecture

Aspects of this argument were developed in Charles Waldheim, "Landscape as Architecture," *Harvard Design Magazine*, no. 36 (Spring 2013): 17–20; 177–78; and Charles Waldheim, "Afterword: The Persistent Promise of Ecological Planning," in *Designed Ecologies: The Landscape Architecture of Kongjian Yu*, ed. William S. Saunders (Basel: Birkhauser, 2012), 250–53.

......

Epigraph: The quote is from a paper Jellicoe delivered to the International Federation of Landscape Architects in 1960. In his address, Jellicoe argues that the profession is still searching for its identity, which should be "a single word, distinct from other fields, for all cultures." Geoffrey Jellicoe, "A Table for Eight," in *Space for Living: Landscape Architecture and the Allied Arts and Professions*, ed. Sylvia Crowe (Amsterdam: Djambatan, 1961), 18. Thanks to Gareth Doherty for bringing this to my attention.

1. Joseph Disponzio's work on this topic has been a rare exception in tracing the origins of the professional identity. His doctoral dissertation and subsequent publications offer the definitive account of the emergence of the French formulation *architecte-paysagiste* as the origin of professional identity of the landscape architect. See Disponzio, "The Garden Theory and Landscape Practice of Jean-Marie Morel" (PhD diss., Columbia University, 2000). See also Disponzio, "Jean-Marie Morel and the Invention of Landscape Architecture," in *Tradition and Innovation in French Garden Art: Chapters of a New History*, ed. John Dixon Hunt and Michel Conan (Philadelphia: University of Pennsylvania Press, 2002), 135–59; and Disponzio, "History of the Profession," in *Landscape Architectural Graphic Standards*, ed. Leonard J. Hopper (Hoboken, NJ: Wiley and Sons, 2007), 5–9.

2. Disponzio, "Jean-Marie Morel and the Invention of Landscape Architecture," 151–52.

3. Ibid., 153.

4. Disponzio, "History of the Profession," 6–7.

5. Ibid., 5.

6. Charles E. Beveridge and David Schuyler, eds., *The Papers of Frederick Law Olmsted*, vol. 3, *Creating Central Park, 1857–1861* (Baltimore: Johns Hopkins University Press, 1983), 26–28, 45, n73.

7. Ibid., 241, n11. See also Frederick Law Olmsted Sr., *Forty Years of Landscape Architecture: Central Park*, vol. 2, edited by Frederick Law Olmsted Jr. and Theodora Kimball (Cambridge, MA: MIT Press, 1973), 31; as well as Board of Commissioners of the Central Park, Minutes, October 21, 1858, 140; November 16, 1858, 148.

8. Beveridge and Schuyler, *Olmsted Papers*, vol. 3, *Creating Central Park*, 234–35.

9. Ibid., 256–57; 257, n4; 267, n1.

10. Olmsted, *Forty Years of Landscape Architecture*, 11, biographical notes; David Schuyler and Jane Turner Censer, eds., *The Papers of Frederick Law Olmsted*, vol. 6, *The Years of Olmsted, Vaux & Co., 1865–1874* (Baltimore: Johns Hopkins University Press, 1992), 5; 46, n8.

11. Victoria Post Ranney, ed., *The Papers of Frederick Law Olmsted*, vol. 5, *The California Frontier, 1863–1865* (Baltimore: Johns Hopkins University Press, 1990), 422.

12. Charles E. Beveridge, Carolyn F. Hoffman, and Kenneth Hawkins, eds., *The Papers of Frederick Law Olmsted*, vol. 7, *Parks, Politics, and Patronage, 1874–1882* (Baltimore: Johns Hopkins University Press, 2007), 225–26.

13. Constitution of the American Society of Landscape Architects, adopted March 6, 1899. See also Melanie Simo, *100 Years of Landscape Architecture: Some Patterns of a Century* (Washington, DC: ASLA Press, 1999).

14. See Disponzio, "History of the Profession," 6. See also Melanie L. Simo, *The Coalescing of Different Forces and Ideas: A History of Landscape Architecture at Harvard, 1900–1999* (Cambridge, MA: Harvard University Graduate School of Design, 2000).

15. See Jellicoe, "A Table for Eight," 21.

16. Yu has received multiple national awards in China based in some measure on the reception of his work outside of China, including the Overseas Chinese Pioneer Achievement Medal (2003), the Overseas Chinese Professional Excellence Top Award (2004), and the National Gold Medal of Fine Arts (2004).

17. See Kongjian Yu, "Lectures to the Mayors Forum," Chinese Ministry of Construction, Ministry of Central Communist Party Organization, two to three lectures annually, 1997–2007; and Kongjian Yu and Dihua Li, *The Road to Urban Landscape: A Dialogue with Mayors* (Beijing: China Architecture and Building Press), 2003.

18. China's population in 1963 was approximately 80 percent rural, so it is not surprising that Yu's origins were agrarian. See Peter Rowe, "China's Water Resources and Houtan Park," in *Designed Ecologies: The Landscape Architecture of Kongjian Yu*, ed. William Saunders (Basel: Birkhauser, 2012), 184–90.

19. Kongjian Yu, interview with the author, January 20, 2011.

20. Beijing Forestry's library in landscape architecture and planning held English-language first-edition copies of Kevin Lynch's *The Image of the City* (1960), Ian McHarg's *Design with Nature* (1969), and Richard Forman's *Landscape Ecology* (with Michel Godron, 1986).

21. Carl Steinitz, interview with the author, January

20, 2011. See also Anthony Alofsin, *The Struggle for Modernism: Architecture, Landscape Architecture, and City Planning at Harvard* (New York: Norton, 2002), 299, n60.

22. Kongjian Yu, interview with the author, January 20, 2011.

23. Kongjian Yu, "Security Patterns in Landscape Planning: With a Case in South China" (doctoral thesis, Harvard University Graduate School of Design, May 1995). Yu makes a distinction between the recorded title of his doctoral thesis and that of his doctoral dissertation, "Security Patterns and Surface Model in Landscape Planning," advised by Professors Carl Steinitz, Richard Forman, and Stephen Ervin, and dated June 1, 1995.

24. Carl Steinitz, interview with the author, January 20, 2011. For more on the genealogy of Western conceptions of landscape planning that Steinitz made available to Yu, from Loudon and Lenné through Olmsted and Eliot, see Carl Steinitz, "Landscape Planning: A Brief History of Influential Ideas," *Journal of Landscape Architecture* (Spring 2008): 68–74.

25. Kongjian Yu, "Security Patterns and Surface Model in Landscape Planning," *Landscape and Urban Planning* 36, no. 5 (1996): 1–17; and Kongjian Yu, "Ecological Security Patterns in Landscape and GIS Application," *Geographic Information Sciences* 1, no. 2 (1996): 88–102.

26. For more on Yu/Turenscape's regional planning projects, see Kelly Shannon, "(R)evolutionary Ecological Infrastructures," in Saunders, *Designed Ecologies: The Landscape Architecture of Kongjian Yu*, 200–210.

Conclusion: From Landscape to Ecology

Aspects of this argument were developed in Charles Waldheim, "Weak Work: Andrea Branzi's 'Weak Metropolis' and the Projective Potential of an 'Ecological Urbanism,'" in *Ecological Urbanism*, ed. Mohsen Mostafavi with Gareth Doherty (Zurich: Lars Müller; Cambridge, MA: Harvard Graduate School of Design, 2010), 114–21; Charles Waldheim, "Landscape, Ecology, and Other Modifiers to Urbanism" *Topos: The International Review of Landscape Architecture and Urban Design*, no. 71 (June 2010): 21–24; and Charles Waldheim, "The Other '56," in *Urban Design*, ed. Alex Krieger and William Saunders (Minneapolis: University of Minnesota Press, 2009), 227–36.

......

Epigraph: Roland Barthes, "From Work to Text," in *Image Music Text*, trans. Stephen Heath (New York: Hill and Wang, 1977), 155.

1. On the origins of urban design at Harvard, see Eric Mumford, "The Emergence of Urban Design in the Breakup of CIAM," in *Urban Design*, ed. Alex Kreiger and William Saunders (Minneapolis: University of Minnesota Press, 2009).

2. Mohsen Mostafavi, "Introduction," "Ecological Urbanism" conference, Harvard University Graduate School of Design, April 3, 2009.

3. Ibid.

4. Barthes, "From Work to Text," 155.

5. Homi Bhabha, "Keynote Lecture," "Ecological Urbanism" conference, Harvard University Graduate School of Design, April 3, 2009.

6. Ibid.

7. Chris Reed and Nina-Marie Lister, eds., *Projective Ecologies* (Barcelona: Actar; Cambridge, MA: Harvard University Graduate School of Design, 2014).

8. See Mostafavi and Doherty, *Ecological Urbanism*.

9. Christopher Hight, "Designing Ecologies," in Reed and Lister, *Projective Ecologies*, 84–105.

10. Henri Lefebvre, *The Urban Revolution*, trans. Robert Bononno (Minneapolis: University of Minnesota Press, 2003).

11. Reed and Lister, "Parallel Genealogies," in Reed and Lister, *Projective Ecologies*, 22–39.

12. Peter Eisenman, "Post-Functionalism," *Oppositions* 6 (Fall 1976): 236–39.

13. Scott Cohen has been among the voices articulating such a position in recent years. See, for example, Cohen's recent Return of Nature project: Preston Scott Cohen and Erika Naginski, eds., *The Return of Nature: Sustaining Architecture in the Face of Sustainability* (New York: Routledge, 2014).

14. The debates around "criticality" and the "postcritical" have been well documented. See Michael Speaks, "Design Intelligence Part 1: Introduction," *A+U Architecture and Urbanism* (December 2002): 10–18; Robert Somol and Sarah Whiting, "Notes around the Doppler Effect and Other Moods of Modernism," *Perspecta*, no. 33 (2002): 72–77; George Baird, "Criticality and Its Discontents," *Harvard Design Magazine*, no. 21 (Fall 2004): 16–21.

15. An early account of landscape's shift "from appearance to performance" can be found in Julia Czerniak, "Challenging the Pictorial: Recent Landscape Practice," *Assemblage*, no. 34 (December 1997): 110–20.

Credits